Classroom Management

Creating Positive Outcomes
for All Students

LISA A. BLOOM
Western Carolina University

Merrill
is an imprint of

PEARSON

Upper Saddle River, New Jersey
Columbus, Ohio

Library of Congress Cataloging-in-Publication Data
Bloom, Lisa A.
  Classroom management : creating positive outcomes for all students/Lisa A. Bloom.
     p. cm.
  ISBN-13: 978-0-13-088838-9
  ISBN-10: 0-13-088838-9
  1. Classroom management. I. Title.
  LB3013.B544 2009
  371.102'4--dc22

                              2008019679

Vice President and Executive Publisher: Jeffery W. Johnston
Executive Editor: Ann Castel Davis
Editorial Assistant: Penny Burleson
Senior Managing Editor: Pamela D. Bennett
Production Editor: Sheryl Glicker Langner
Production Coordination: Vishal Harshvardhan, Aptara, Inc.
Design Coordinator: Diane C. Lorenzo
Cover Designer: Kristina Holmes
Cover Art: Fotosearch
Production Manager: Laura Messerly
Director of Marketing: Quinn Perkson
Marketing Manager: Erica DeLuca
Marketing Coordinator: Brian Mounts

This book was set in Clearface Regular by Aptara, Inc. It was printed and bound by R. R. Donnelley & Sons
Company. The cover was printed by R. R. Donnelley & Sons Company.

Pearson® is a registered trademark of Pearson plc
Merrill® is a registered trademark of Pearson Education, Inc.

Pearson Education Ltd., London
Pearson Education Singapore, Pte. Ltd.
Pearson Education Canada, Inc.
Pearson Education—Japan

Pearson Education Australia PTY, Limited
Pearson Education North Asia, Ltd., Hong Kong
Pearson Educación de Mexico, S.A. de C.V.
Pearson Education Malaysia, Pte. Ltd.
Pearson Education Upper Saddle River, New Jersey

Merrill
is an imprint of

10 9 8 7 6 5 4 3 2 1
ISBN 13: 978-0-13-088838-9
ISBN 10:   0-13-088838-9

PREFACE

*I*n a discussion of what courses our future teachers need at our institution, a colleague mentioned that classroom management was not an appropriate course because classroom management was not a discipline. He maintained that topics related to classroom management belonged within a psychology course. In one sense, I had to agree: Classroom management in itself does not benefit from having a status as a discipline; rather, classroom management practices are informed by disciplines such as education, psychology, and sociology. Even so, classroom management is what many teachers struggle with the most. Classroom management has been my passion my entire professional career. From research, to time in the classroom as a teacher and observer, to time spent talking with children and youth, I have always been concerned with how we care for children in classrooms and schools and how we can create classrooms that promote caring, responsibility, and learning.

With the complexities and diversity of today's classrooms and the pressure on teachers in this age of high-stakes accountability, teachers who haven't studied classroom management often look for quick fixes for issues that arise in the classroom. They spend time putting out fires and trying to control students. This text takes an approach to classroom management quite different from those which attempt to supply teachers with recipes, technical solutions (if you just do it this way, then . . .), and/or quick fixes. I try to emphasize a more comprehensive look at the myriad factors that affect school and classroom climate and student well-being, behavior, motivation, and learning. To that end, I encourage teachers to be proactive and to fashion goals for creating safe, peaceful, engaging classrooms and schools, and nurturing responsible and caring learners.

One emphasis of this text is the teacher as a professional rather than technician. As a professional, the role of a teacher is to use the research and wisdom of the profession and the knowledge of the unique context of the community, school, classroom, and learners to craft solutions to unique circumstances. In contrast, as a technician, the role of a teacher is to apply known solutions to known problems. No one approach to classroom management, no one approach to motivating students or handling disruptive behavior, works in all classrooms or schools or for all learners. Hence, a professional view of teaching affords teachers the status and expertise to be both good consumers of, and contributors to, the knowledge of the profession.

As professionals, teachers become learners in their classrooms. Classroom management practices continually evolve out of teacher goals, evaluations, reflection, and action in the classroom.

As professionals, teachers are members of a large community of practice. Reflection and collaboration with other professionals create opportunities for examining systemic issues and addressing school and classroom climate, behavior, and motivation within the context of broader school, community, and culture.

Another emphasis of this text is the examination of multiple perspectives. Each learner is unique, each family is unique, and each culture is unique. Classroom practices that fail to take account of these perspectives are likely to fail. With regard to learners and families, our attempt, even with the best of intentions, to improve the school and classroom climate and learning experiences will not yield the best results if our consumers do not perceive those attempts as helpful. Gaining and using student and family perspectives enhances the student's and family's sense of belonging, efficacy, autonomy, and commitment to what teachers want to accomplish. With regard to culture, understanding cultural perspectives and developing culturally responsive classroom management practices allows us not only to meet the needs of culturally diverse learners, but also to appreciate and celebrate the richness of a diverse classroom.

A third emphasis of the text is relationships. Caring, positive, productive student–teacher relationships and student–student relationships don't just happen. This text seeks to help teachers create a community atmosphere in which teachers and learners enjoy each other's company, take delight in each other's accomplishments, and help and care for each other.

Finally, research does yield strategies and structures that help us predict and respond to predicaments in the classroom; motivate learners; enhance learning; deal with difficult issues, such as bullying, violence, and aggression; and support students who are reluctant or unable to behave the way we would like. I present research-based strategies, drawing from research from several disciplines and emphasizing practices that create classrooms that promote responsibility, community, and learning.

ACKNOWLEDGMENTS

This project has been a long and joyful, though sometimes arduous, journey. Thankfully, I haven't taken it alone. I've benefited from, and appreciated the support of, many people. I want to thank Tim Martin, my husband, and Lane and Todd Martin, my boys, who have put up with messes of papers, long nights, and weekends of my head in the computer and have been patient and supportive the entire way.

Thank you to my colleagues and coworkers: Marissa, Sharon, Jane, Dale, and Denise, who all laughed with me, pondered with me, and encouraged me. To my running coach, Jim Hamilton, thanks for keeping me fit.

Thank you to Anne Davis and Penny Burrelson from Pearson, who never gave up on me despite the delays and gaps in my writing.

Thank you to the reviewers, whose comments and critiques were invaluable: Jim Allen, The College of Saint Rose; Alice Anderson, Radford University; Gerlinde G. Beckers, Southeastern Louisiana University; Robin Brewer, University of Northern Colorado; Jane Cranston, University of Iowa; Robert Gates, Bloomsburg University; Edwin Helmstetter, Washington State University; Jean E. Horton, Portland State University; Meredith

Jamieson, Ashland University; Jodi Katsafanas, La Roche College; Dan Kelly, State University of New York at Geneseo; J. Cynthia McDermott, Emeritus, California State University at Dominguez Hills; Grace A. Meier, Ed.D., Martin Methodist College; Eun-Ja Kim Park, California State University at Bakersfield; Jo Anne W. Putnam, University of Maine; Carl Schavio, Farleigh Dickinson University; Kevin Scott Sherman, Auburn University; Bruce Smith, Henderson State University; Stanley W. Wollock, William Patterson University; and Wendy M. Wood, University of North Carolina at Charlotte.

I want to acknowledge the many teachers who have welcomed me into their classrooms and shared their ideas. I especially want to thank Jonnie Walkingstick and Ron Watson, inspiring classroom teachers who care about children and make good teaching look easy. They let me into their classrooms, talked with me, and let me use their stories.

Finally, I want to thank and dedicate this book to my mother, "the good dame in the cottage"—the most remarkable woman I know, my teacher, my rock, and my inspiration.

Brief Contents

CONTENTS

Note: Every effort has been made to provide accurate and current information in this book. However, the Internet and information posted on it are constantly changing; it is inevitable that some of the Internet addresses listed in this textbook will change.

PHILOSOPHICAL ORIENTATION

I

INTRODUCTION: HISTORICAL PERSPECTIVE, TRADITIONAL APPROACHES

1

The classroom should be an entrance into the world, not an escape from it.
John Ciardi

When I walk into Jonnie Walkingstick's classroom, I am always amazed at the comfort level in her room—the quiet happy buzz of students working together; the materials, learning centers, and books that reflect the Native American heritage of her students; and the displays of student work. I'm also amazed at the engagement, enthusiasm, and competence that she creates with her students. I hear her saying things to her students like "Do you think this is your best work?" You worked really hard to figure this out, can you show some of the others how you did it?" What are we learning from this activity?" and "Is this a good choice for you today?" Each day starts with a recitation of the classroom pledge: "We the peacekeepers promise to be truthful, respectful, caring, and responsible." All learners in her room, even those who had been unsuccessful the year before are successful, responsible, and caring.

When teachers begin their careers in the classroom, they often start with idealistic visions of their classrooms and their relationships with students. They envision inspiring learners and sharing their passion for their content area. Most teachers report entering teaching because of a desire to help young people learn and develop (Feistritzer & Haar, 2005).

Classroom management and discipline are among the most compelling demands of teachers' work. Some teachers tend to be "naturals" with regard to classroom management. Their classrooms are characterized by warm and caring relationships; inviting, positive classroom environments; and motivated students. For other teachers, the perceived apathy and irresponsibility of their students is a source of frustration and stress. Often new teachers are caught off guard by students who aren't motivated, who can't sit still, or who challenge their authority.

Never before has the role of the teacher been so complex. Today's teachers are driven by accountability and high stakes assessment. In most states, schools and teachers are held accountable for test scores of students through a system of rewards and sanctions. At the same time, schools and classrooms are becoming increasingly diverse, as are the needs of learners. Teachers identify dealing with issues of diversity, juggling multiple ability levels of learners, motivating students, and handling disruptions and distractions as challenges they face in classrooms (National Center for Education Statistics [NCES], 2005). Student discipline problems, lack of support from the school administration, poor student motivation, and lack of teacher influence over schoolwide and classroom decision making are reasons many teachers report for leaving the profession (Ingersoll & Smith, 2003; NCES, 2005). Many teachers identify student discipline as a source of stress (Lewis, 1999) and many teachers, especially new teachers, feel inadequately prepared for dealing with discipline in the classroom (Feistritzer & Haar, 2005). Bullying is one of the most frequently identified discipline problems identified by teachers, students, and administrators (U.S. Department of Justice, 2007). Teachers often leave their jobs in the first 5 years of teaching because of issues related to behavior problems in the classroom (NCES, 2005) and school violence (Smith & Smith, 2006).

In response to the increasing demands on teachers, in the last three decades, many systematic approaches to classroom management with the mission of bringing order to the classroom and creating safe schools have surfaced. While myriad approaches to classroom management offer teachers good strategies, the focus often centers on order and obedience. A comprehensive approach to classroom management considers multiple perspectives, intentionally sets goals for the development of caring classroom communities, utilizes relationships and strategies to achieve those goals, and engages teachers in critical evaluation and reflection.

CLASSROOM MANAGEMENT AND TEACHING VARIATIONS

Current classroom management practices and teaching styles can be characterized by several traits, including whether the classroom is teacher centered or student centered, whether management is proactive or reactive, whether the predominant teaching style is authoritarian and unresponsive or authoritative and nurturing, and whether teacher knowledge is based on a linear model of research or a model where teachers are participants in research. Each of these characteristics is described below.

Teacher-Centered Versus Student-Centered Classrooms

Classrooms can be characterized with regard to the level of control, direction, and input from teachers and learners. In classrooms that are teacher centered, teachers set the curriculum, solve the discipline issues, and make decisions about how content will be delivered (Brown, 2003). In learner-centered classrooms, teachers take time to know students with regard to their culture, their areas of strength and weakness, their preferred approaches to learning, and their interests. The teacher engages learners in developing a learning community and solving problems that arise in the classroom. Their input regarding classroom practices, as well as the curriculum and how it is delivered, is sought and considered. Learner-centered classrooms foster student motivation and investment in learning (McCombs & Whisler, 1997). Jonnie Walkingstick's classroom can be described as learner centered. Decisions about instructional and management practices are informed by the characteristics of the individual learner's interests, talents, and culture, as well as academic, social, and emotional needs. Figure 1.1 summarizes the characteristics of teacher- and learner-centered classrooms.

Figure 1.1   Teacher Centered Versus Learner Centered

TEACHER CENTERED	LEARNER CENTERED
Control for learning and behavior is in the hands of the teacher.	Students are active participants in creating rules and solving problems.
For the most part, instruction and management processes are the same for everyone.	Accommodate and modify for varying needs and abilities of students.
The teacher uses his or her expertise in content knowledge to impart knowledge.	Teachers provide a variety of instructional methods and techniques for helping learners construct their learning and develop a system for applying what they learn. Teachers create an environment where learners can make learning connections and learn from each other.
The effort to get to know learners and how they learn and what their strengths, talents, and interests are is secondary.	The student perspective is important. Teachers know individual learner cultures, preferred ways of learning, capabilities, strength, talents, and interests.
Classroom management processes and practices, for the most part, are static.	Classroom management processes and practices are dynamic and responsive to students' changing skills, interests, and needs.

Proactive Versus Reactive Discipline

Classroom management practices can differ with regard to their emphasis on proactive or reactive strategies. Proactive classroom management strategies are practices that are designed to prevent discipline problems. At the heart of proactive discipline is instruction that engages the hearts and minds of learners. When learners are actively engaged in learning, there is little time for mischievous behavior. Behavior is viewed as integrally connected to instruction and the climate of the classroom and school (Carpenter & McKee-Higgins, 1996). In addition, proactive discipline involves establishing classroom norms and expectations so that learners are aware of the behavior that is acceptable and unacceptable in the classroom. On the other hand, reactive strategies involve waiting for misbehavior to occur and then applying consequences or sanctions in reaction to the behavior. Teachers who employ reactive strategies often rely on threats and punishment to control their classrooms. Undesirable behavior is viewed as the problem rather than school or classroom instructional variables or climate (Carpenter & McKee-Higgins, 1996). Research indicates that the less teachers use dominance, threats, and punishments to control their classrooms, the more students demonstrate positive attitudes toward school and a commitment to learning (Lunenburg & Schmidt, 1989). Figure 1.2 summarizes proactive and reactive characteristics. Jonnie's style is proactive. By incorporating

Figure 1.2 Reactive Versus Proactive

REACTIVE	PROACTIVE
Discipline is reactive in that consequences are applied on a misbehaving child.	Discipline is preventive in that the teacher uses engaging instruction and promotes a positive climate to motivate students.
Academic planning occurs without consideration of child factors such as interest and ability and waits until problems arise before responding.	Teachers plan well, and develop instruction to ensure maximum student engagement and motivation. Teachers predict how students will respond to certain activities or assignments to avoid problems.
The teacher decides what are good behaviors and bad behaviors and reacts accordingly.	Teachers act rather than react act—think through actions when problems occur instead of knee-jerk reactions that may lead to power struggles.
Classroom management processes and practices, for the most part, are static.	Classroom management processes and practices are dynamic and responsive to students' changing skills, interests, and needs.

knowledge of learners in her instruction, communicating expectations, and teaching students to respect and care for each other, classroom disruptions are minimal.

Teaching Styles

Teaching style also comes into play in classroom management. As with the work of Baumrind (1971), who studied parenting styles along dimensions of responsiveness, level of demand, and authoritarian versus authoritative discipline, teaching styles have also been the subject of inquiry. Teaching dimensions that have been found to affect student performance and behavior include authoritarian versus authoritative discipline, control, level of demand, fairness, communication, support for autonomy, and responsiveness (Birch & Ladd, 1996; Rydell & Henricsson, 2004; Soenens & Vansteenkiste, 2005; Wentzel, 2002). In short, teachers who have high but reasonable expectations, are firm but fair and flexible, are warm and nurturing, use democratic communication, support student autonomy, and are responsive to student needs will have a positive classroom climate, little student conflict, and high student motivation. Jonnie's teaching style is evident in her warm and caring interactions with students. She promotes autonomy by allowing choices and decisions within limits. "You can choose to sit on the floor for this assignment as long as it helps you learn." In addition, she involves students in solving classroom dilemmas and predicaments. Students in her room know that *fair* means that everyone is not treated the same, rather, everyone gets what they need. Dimensions of teaching styles are summarized in Figure 1.3.

Figure 1.3 Teaching Dimensions

AUTHORITATIVE, DEMANDING, RESPONSIVE	AUTHORITARIAN, DEMANDING, UNRESPONSIVE
Warmth and approval	Highly critical, negative feedback
Democratic communication—seeks and listens to learners' perspective	One-way communication, teacher's perspective is the only one that matters
Demands self-reliance and self-control	Demands obedience
Expectations to perform up to one's potential	High demands irrespective of student characteristics
Provides consistency and structure and firm limits, but flexible and considers learner's point of view	Inconsistent, inflexible, enforces rules through punitive measures
Autonomy supportive	Overly controlling

Figure 1.4   Linear View of Research Versus Teacher as Researcher

LINEAR	TEACHER RESEARCHER
Classroom management and instructional practices are handed down from district mandates and published research. Classroom context and learner characteristics are secondary.	Information from published research and district agendae are reviewed within the context of classrooms and characteristics of learners in mind.
Professional development involves in-service training on best practices for teachers.	Professional development involves teachers' engagement in critical reflection and action research to address predicaments in the classroom.
Evaluation of classroom practices is completed by administrators.	Teachers assess classroom practices from multiple perspectives and with multiple sources of data. Evaluation is a collaborative process, including teachers and administrator.
Classroom management processes and practices, for the most part, are static.	Classroom management processes and practices are dynamic and responsive to students' changing skills, interests, and needs.

Research-Based Practices

According to Brown (2003), teacher-centered practices lend themselves to a linear view of research and a technical view of teaching. That is, research regarding best practices is handed down by school administrators and university research. Teachers are required or coaxed to implement those practices. On the other hand, in learner-centered classrooms, teachers act as professionals. They are researchers applying and investigating the effects of research-based practices and innovative ideas with regard to their unique classrooms and learners. Figure 1.4 summarizes two views of the teacher's role in research.

Popular Classroom and School Management Practices

There are many approaches to classroom management. The underlying premises of each approach reflect the teacher's philosophy, goals, and values. Two popular examples include positive behavioral support and assertive discipline.

Positive behavioral support represents a systematic approach for preventing inappropriate behavior and dealing with challenging behavior. It is widely used in many school systems in the United States. Positive behavioral support involves a three-tiered system for managing behavior. On the primary level, systems are put in place to increase the structure and support needed to promote prosocial behavior. School staff work collaboratively to determine schoolwide expectations that are then taught to all students, rewards for the performance of expected behaviors and consequences for rule infractions are put in place, and data are collected to evaluate the system (Sugai & Horner, 2002; Taylor-Greene et al., 1997). Office discipline referrals are typically used to determine the success of schoolwide positive behavioral support (Irvin et al., 2006). Studies regarding schoolwide positive behavioral support practices report reductions in office referrals, as well as improvements in school climate and academic gains (Horner et al., 2004; Luiselli, Putnam, & Sunderland, 2002; Terrance, 2001).

Because not all students respond to schoolwide positive behavioral support, a second level of support—group support—is a means for addressing groups with a need for more intensity (Turnbull et al., 2002). Examples of group support might include group reinforcers and classroom-wide self-monitoring or self-management systems.

At the third level of positive behavioral support are supports put in place for students with more chronic and severe behavioral issues (Irvin et al., 2006). For these students, functional assessment and individualized support plans are recommended (Sugai et al., 2000).

Another popular classroom and school management system is Canters' Assertive Discipline. Components of this discipline model include posting positively stated classroom rules, teaching classroom rules, and informing students of consequences for infractions and rewards for compliance; delivering consequences and rewards consistently; teaching behavioral expectations; and providing frequent positive interactions with students (Canter & Canter, 2002). Typically, this system involves some way of keeping track of rule infractions, such as names and subsequent checks on the board, so that repeated infractions earn higher levels of consequences. It shares some points in common with schoolwide positive behavioral support, including an emphasis on clear expectations, consequences, and rewards. Lane and Menzies (2003) report on a school that used Assertive Discipline as the schoolwide component of their positive behavioral support program.

Practices such as Assertive Discipline and schoolwide positive behavioral support offer step-by-step approaches to handling disruptive behavior and encouraging positive behavior. These structures can be a comfort to teachers experiencing distractions in the classroom. However, these approaches tend to be designed and directed by teachers and administrators with little input from students. Teacher- and administrator-centered approaches, such as Assertive Discipline and schoolwide positive behavioral support, have met with criticism. One criticism is that these approaches emphasize means and strategies rather than the goals that many teachers and parents desire for learners (Butchart, 1998). They are criticized for their narrow focus on such short-term goals as classroom order (Butchart, 1998; Kohn, 1995; Marshall, 2001). Although they may be helpful in achieving classroom order in the short term, approaches that focus solely on classroom order may not consider other social and emotional needs of learners, such as the need for autonomy, belonging, competence, and an ethos of caring, as well as the need to develop the skills for democratic citizenship (Butchart, 1998; Emmer & Stough, 2001; Kohn, 1995; Marshall, 2001). Furthermore, these programs have met with criticism because of their overreliance on rewards and sanctions, which may interfere with intrinsic motivation (Kohn, 1995; Marshall, 2001). With limited opportunity for input, choice, feedback, and participation in classroom government, attempts to help students become self-regulated learners, wise decision makers, and good citizens are defeated.

In addition to their short-term focus, teacher-centered programs take a technical view of the teacher's role (Brown, 2003). They are based on the premise that good classroom management is a matter of applying known solutions to known problems. In contrast, this text takes a more professional view of teaching based on the premise that the work of a professional requires finding solutions to problems that change from day to day and using professional judgment and multiple sources of information to gain insight and make careful decisions regarding those problems. Teaching brings many predicaments, circumstances, and decisions that vary according to the unique circumstances of the learners, the school, and the community.

Despite the criticisms, a routinized management approach like positive behavioral support can be beneficial if considered as one part of a comprehensive approach. Comprehensive approaches also seek to address the social and emotional needs of learners, foster positive dispositions toward learning, and teach responsibility.

TOWARD A COMPREHENSIVE, CONSTRUCTIVE APPROACH

Teachers can create the classrooms that inspired their decision to teach. Many professionals agree that good classroom management is more than a recipe for encouraging good behavior. The goals of classroom management and discipline practices warrant consideration of what teachers want for their learners and what kind of classroom they want to create. The challenges that classroom teachers face on a daily basis warrant consideration of multiple child, family, cultural, and community factors, as well as the perspectives of all stakeholders, including families, students, and other teachers. In addition, teachers must create classrooms where opportunities for learning are optimal and equitable for all learners.

This text presents a comprehensive look at classroom management and schoolwide discipline. The text is divided into four sections of consideration for classroom management: Philosophical Orientation, Multiple Perspectives, Relationships and Structures, and Goals and Outcomes. These areas are depicted in Figure 1.5 and discussed briefly below. They are presented in a circular model as it is the premise of this text that each area informs the others. Rather than promoting one fixed approach, this text is also based on the premise that classroom management is a dynamic process that requires engaging in critical reflection and thoughtful refinement of classroom practices as student populations change, new problems arise, new perspectives are gained, and new goals are developed. It is the premise of this text that positive productive classrooms and healthy school climates are created through continual reflection and inquiry.

Figure 1.5   Essential Aspects of Classroom Management

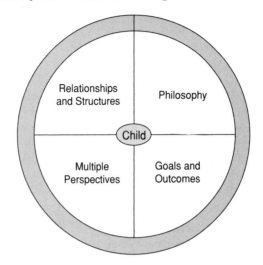

PHILOSOPHICAL ORIENTATION

Many philosophical orientations inform classroom management practices. Two common orientations are behavioral theory and constructivist theory. In Chapters 2 and 3, I explore the contributions of those orientations to classroom management practices. I also consider theories of motivation and engagement as relevant and informative for classroom management practices.

Behavioral theory and practice have provided many tools for systematically examining and changing the behavior of students. Practices based on behavioral theory include token economies and reward systems, as well as systems such as Canters' Assertive Discipline and schoolwide positive behavioral support. Although these practices can be helpful if used carefully, they often rely on external control of students. At the same time, behavioral principles can be unintentionally at work in the classroom with undesirable results.

The constructivist orientation allows teachers to consider the inherent social nature of the classroom and students, consider the students' perspective, and address the social and emotional needs of learners. The views of social constructivist theorists go beyond the behaviorists' perspective and acknowledge the contributions of the school curriculum, the classroom and school environments, families, and the broader culture and community in shaping school experiences and student learning. The behavioral theorist focuses on the prediction and control of events in the immediate environment; a social constructivist explores the entire sociocultural context of a student's life to gain insight into a student's school experience.

Careful examination of one's philosophical orientation can assist the teacher in developing classroom practices. Teachers have varying perspectives and ideas as to their role as a teacher. Teachers can develop their own metaphor for teaching as a basis for examining their role and understanding their current philosophical practices. Metaphors can help teachers make sense of who and what they are as teachers and be reflective about their practice. A teacher's metaphor may indicate whether his or her philosophical orientation lends itself toward a behavioral model or a constructivist model, reveal whether the classroom is student centered or teacher centered, and define what the teacher values. For example, constructivist teachers may see themselves as coaches or guides, while behaviorist teachers may see themselves as technologists or diagnosticians. The metaphor that a teacher adopts can reveal his or her perceptions of students and classroom life. For example, in a qualitative study, Hyland (2005) examined the metaphors of white teachers of African American learners. In this study, metaphors revealed how well-intentioned teachers may perpetuate racial bias in the classroom. For example, one teacher saw herself as a helper. Interviews with her revealed that she saw her children and their families as incapable of helping themselves. Other metaphors include the following:

Teacher as a leader
Teacher as a partner (Tabak, Gurion, & Baumgartner, 2004)
Teacher as a facilitator
Teacher as a nurturer
Teacher as a caregiver

The Circle of Courage (Brendtro, Brokenleg, & Van Bockern, 1990) provides a useful framework for considering desirable outcomes for learners. The Circle of Courage incorporates four universal human needs: the needs for belonging, mastery, independence, and generosity. This framework is discussed in detail in Chapter 2. Subsequent chapters use the framework to summarize and illustrate essential concepts for classroom management practices that are responsive to learners.

MULTIPLE PERSPECTIVES

Unlike more homogenous classrooms of the past, classrooms today represent diverse populations. Many classroom populations represent a wide range of cultures, ethnicity, family structures, and income levels. Often the teacher's culture is different from that of many of his or her students and their families. Empowering learners and families by seeking their perspective, input, and feedback in developing classroom practices can generate goodwill, greater commitment and investment in learning, and support for school and classroom activities. In addition, careful examination of assumptions, beliefs, and biases can assist teachers in developing classrooms that are culturally responsive. Often the perspectives of families and learners are ignored, but research tells us that gaining multiple perspectives can increase motivation and academic achievement. Family, student, and cultural perspectives are discussed in Chapters 4, 5, and 7.

As with family and student perspectives, teachers' perspectives are also key to developing positive and productive classroom and school environments. Teachers can engage in communities of practice and collaborative reflection and inquiry as a professional practice. Doing so allows teachers to take a systems view of predicaments that interfere with optimal learner engagement and achievement. For example, if bullying is a problem identified by students, families, and teachers, one approach is to target the bullies for intervention. Alternatively, a systems approach would involve looking at the school climate and classroom conditions that potentially nurture bullying. Addressing bullying at the systems level may lead to lasting improvements that will benefit all children. Teacher perspectives are discussed in Chapter 6.

RELATIONSHIPS AND STRUCTURES

At the heart of classroom management and positive school climate are the relationships and structures that teachers create and nurture. Taking advantage of the social nature of school can assist teachers in developing strong relationships based on respect, responsibility, and learning. Relationships come into play in classroom management and school climate both with regard to teachers' relationships with students and students' relationships with each other. Developing positive relationships at both levels requires intentional action. With regard to student relationships, teachers can take action to develop relationships with even the most reluctant children and youth. Research indicates that positive productive relationships with students increase academic achievement and a sense of belonging to the school. In addition, learners who establish positive connections with their teachers are more open to adult guidance and are more likely to follow school and classroom norms.

Developing a sense of community among learners has many known benefits as well. Community allows learners to feel a sense of belonging and attachment to school. It provides a foundation for engaging learners in solving problems and behaving in socially responsible ways. It also assists teachers in keeping the focus on learning—the work of the community—as opposed to obedience and control. Relationships are discussed in Chapters 8 and 9.

Most teachers desire for learners to want to learn. Attitudes and dispositions for learning that children and youth bring to the classroom can vary greatly. Some learners bring a curious nature and an insatiable appetite for learning while others, because of their individual circumstances, may be reluctant to fully engage in learning. In addition, motivation for schoolwork tends to decline as children get older. Motivating learners and maintaining academic engagement are proactive classroom practices that can help keep behavioral issues in check. Fueling a positive disposition for learning can be accomplished with an understanding of motivation and careful work to help children adopt learning goals and develop confidence. Motivation is discussed in Chapter 10.

In even the best of classrooms, disruptions and distractions occur. Bullying and violence is another, growing concern in many schools. Minor disruptions and distractions can be handled in ways that preserve dignity and allow the student to learn from his or her mistakes. A systemic approach is recommended for dealing with more persistent challenging behavior, as well as school violence. These issues are addressed in Chapter 11.

GOALS AND OUTCOMES

As with considering the teacher's role, an examination of what the teacher values can also be helpful in developing responsive classroom management practices. The Interstate New Teacher Assessment and Support Consortium (INTASC) standards, as seen in Table 1.1, indicate expected dispositions of teachers. Teachers are wise to review those dispositions and reflect on their meaning and application in the classroom. In addition, some teachers value quiet orderly students, students who are prepared for class, and students who are self-directed and self-motivated. Examining values can lend itself to establishing goals and practices that incorporate those values. Professional practice involves articulating goals and outcomes and assessing classroom practices in relation to desired goals. Strategies for developing goals and outcomes and assessing classroom practices are discussed in Chapter 13.

Table 1.1   Interstate New Teacher Assessment and Support Consortium (INTASC) Standards

#1: The teacher understands the central concepts, tools of inquiry, and structures of the discipline(s) that he or she teaches and can create learning experiences that make these aspects of subject matter meaningful.

#2: The teacher understands how children learn and develop and can provide learning opportunities that support their intellectual, social, and personal development.

#3: The teacher understands how students differ in their approaches to learning and creates instructional opportunities that are adapted for diverse learners.

#4: The teacher understands and uses a variety of instructional strategies to encourage students' development of critical thinking, problem solving, and performance skills.

#5: The teacher uses an understanding of individual and group motivation and behavior to create a learning environment that encourages positive social interactions, active encouragement in learning, and self-motivation.

#6: The teacher uses knowledge of effective verbal, nonverbal, and media communication techniques to foster active inquiry, collaboration, and supportive interaction in the classroom.

#7: The teacher plans instruction based on knowledge of subject matter, students, the community, and curriculum goals.

#8: The teacher understands and uses formal and informal assessment strategies to ensure the continuous intellectual, social, and physical development of the learners.

#9: The teacher is a reflective practitioner who continually evaluates the effects of his or her choices and actions on others (students, parents, and other professionals in the learning community) and who actively seeks opportunity to grow professionally.

#10: The teacher fosters relationships with school colleagues, parents, and agencies in the larger community to support students' learning and well-being.

RESEARCH AND PRACTICE

The research and professional literature that informs classroom management comes from many disciplines, including psychology, sociology, and education. This text draws from each of those disciplines to synthesize what we know about learners, classrooms, motivation, behavior, and so forth. I use examples of classroom-based research from these disciplines. In addition, I have spent time in many classrooms as a teacher, as a participant observer, and as a parent. I use many examples from several wonderful teachers that I have spent time with and observed putting research into practice, including Jonnie Walkingstick, Ron Watson, Louise Burrell, and others. At times, I also compare these classrooms with classrooms in which management practices and resulting outcomes are less than desirable. I also include the voices of students who give firsthand accounts of life in the classroom. These experiences and accounts help to describe what great classroom management looks like, sounds like, and feels like.

SUMMARY

Classroom management practices are of concern to many students, families, and teachers. For optimal learning and development, children and youth need environments that nurture relatedness, autonomy, competence, and caring. Creating optimal classrooms requires consideration of philosophical perspectives, as well as the perspectives of all stakeholders. In addition, it involves creating and nurturing positive productive relationships and establishing structures that facilitate learning. While prescriptive approaches may be useful in some respects, they may ignore other desired goals and outcomes for learners, such as positive dispositions toward learning, self-responsibility, and appreciation of diversity. Drawing on research and accounts of real classrooms, this text presents a comprehensive learning approach to classroom management. It provides teachers with strategies for developing relationships and structures. And it provides teachers with the benefit of multiple perspectives and engages teachers' professional development through critical reflection, goal setting, and evaluating progress toward goals.

REFERENCES

Baumrind, D. (1971). Current patterns of parental authority. *Developmental Psychology Monograph, 4*(1, Part 2).

Birch, S. H., & Ladd, G. W. (1996). Interpersonal relationships in the school environment and children's early school adjustment: The role of teachers and peers. In J. Juvonen & K. Wentzel

(Eds.), *Social motivation: Understanding children's school adjustment* (pp. 199–225). New York: Cambridge University Press.

Brendtro, L. K., Brokenleg, M., & Van Bockern, S. (1990). *Reclaiming youth at risk: Our hope for the future.* Bloomington, In: National Education service.

Brown, K. L. (2003). From teacher-centered to learner-centered curriculum: Improving learning in diverse classrooms. *Education, 124*(1), 49–54.

Butchart, R. (1998). Punishments, penalties, prizes, and procedures: A history of discipline in U.S. schools. In *Classroom discipline in American schools: Problems and possibilities for democratic education* (pp. 19–49). Albany: State University of New York Press.

Canter, L., & Canter, M. (2002). *Assertive discipline: Positive behavior management for today's classroom* (3rd ed.). Santa Monica, CA: Canter & Associates.

Carpenter, S. L., & McKee-Higgins, E. (1996). Behavior managment in inclusive classrooms. *Remedial and Special Education, 17*(4), 195–204.

Emmer, E. T., and Stough, L. M. (2001). *Classroom management: Acritical part of educational psychology, with implications for teacher education, 36*(2), 103–112.

Feistritzer, E., & Haar, C. (2005). *Profile of teachers in the U.S.* Washington, DC: National Center for Education Information.

Horner, R. H., Todd, A. W., Lewis-Palmer, T., Irvin, L. K., Sugai, G., & Boland, J. B. (2004). The School-Wide Evaluation Tool (SET): A research instrument for assessing school-wide positive behavior support. *Journal of Positive Behavior Interventions, 6*(1), 3–12.

Hyland, N. E. (2005). Being a good teacher of black students? White teachers and unintentional racism. *Curriculum Inquiry, 35*(4), 429–459.

Ingersoll, R. M., & Smith, T. M. (2003, May). Keeping good teachers. *Educational Leadership, 60*(8), 30–33.

The Council of Chief State School Officers. Interstate New Teachers Assessment and Support Consortium (INTASC) standards (2008). Retrieved March 1, 2008, from http://www.ccsso.org/projects/interstate_new_teachers_assessment_and_support_consortium.

Irvin, L. K., Horner, R. H., Ingram, K., Todd, A. W., Sugai, G., Sampson, N. K., et al. (2006). Using office discipline referral data for decision making about student behavior in elementary and middle schools: An empirical evaluation of validity. *Journal of Positive Behavior Interventions, 8*(1), 10–23.

Kohn, A. (1995). *Punished by rewards: The trouble with gold stars, incentive plans, A's, praise, and other bribes.* Boston: Houghton Mifflin.

Lane, K. L., & Menzies, H. M. (2003). A school-wide intervention with primary and secondary levels of support for elementary students: Outcomes and considerations. *Education & Treatment of Children, 26*(4), 431–451.

Lewis, R. (1999). Teachers coping with the stress of classroom discipline. *Social Psychology of Education, 3*(3), 155–171.

Luiselli, J. K., Putnam, R. F., & Sunderland, M. (2002). Longitudinal evaluation of behavior support intervention in a public middle-school. *Journal of Positive Behavior Intervention, 4*(3), 182–188.

Lunenburg, F. C., & Schmidt, L. J. (1989). Pupil control ideology, pupil control behavior, and the quality of school life. *Journal of Research and Development in Education, 22*(4), 36–44.

Marshall, M. (2001). *Discipline without stress, punishments, or rewards.* Los Alamitos, CA: Piper Press.

McCombs, B. L., & Whisler, J. S. (1997). Learner-centered classrooms and schools: Strategies for increasing student motivation and achievement. *National Association of Secondary School Principals (NASSP) Bulletin, 81,* 1–14.

National Center for Education Statistics. (2005). Teacher attrition and mobility: Results from the 2004-05 teacher follow-up survey. Retrieved September 21, 2007, from http://nces.ed.gov/pubsearch/pubsinfo.asp?pubid=2007307

Rydell, A.-M., & Henricsson, L. (2004). Elementary school teachers' strategies to handle externalizing classroom behavior: A study fof relations between perceived control, teacher orientation, and strategy preferences. *Scandinavian Journal of Psychology, 45*(2), 93–102.

Smith, D. L., & Smith, B. J. (2006). Perceptions of violence: The views of teachers who left urban schools. *High School Journal, 89*(3), 34–42.

Soenens, B., & Vansteenkiste, M. (2005). Antecedents and outcomes of self-determination in 3 life domains: The role of parents' and teachers' autonomy support. *Journal of Youth & Adolescence, 34*(6), 589–604.

Sugai, G., & Horner, R. H. (2002). Introduction to the special series on positive behavior support in schools. *Journal of Emotional and Behavioral Disorders, 10*(3), 130–135.

Sugai, G., Horner, R. H., Dunlap, G., Hieneman, M., Lewis, T. J., Nelson, C. M., et al. (2000). Applying positive behavior support and functional behavioral assessment in schools. *Journal of Positive Behavior Interventions, 2*(3), 131–143.

Tabak, I., Gurion, B., & Baumgartner, E. (2004). The teacher as partner: Exploring participant structures, symmetry, and identity work in scaffolding. *Cognition and Instruction, 22*(4), 393–429.

Taylor-Greene, S., Brown, D., Nelson, L., Longton, J., Gassman, T., Cohen, J., et al. (1997). School-wide behavioral support: Starting the year off right. *Journal of Behavioral Education, 7*(1), 99–112.

Terrance, S. A. (2001). Schoolwide example of positive behavioral support. *Journal of Positive Behavior Interventions, 3*(2), 88–95.

Turnbull, A., Edmonson, H., Griggs, P. Wickham, D., Sailor, W., Freeman, R., et al. (2002). A blueprint for schoolwide positive behavior support: Implementation of 3 components. *Exceptional Children, 68*(3), 377–404.

U.S. Department of Justice & National Center for Education Statistics. (2007). School survey on crime and safety (SSOCS), pp. 22–36. In *Indicators of school crime and safety*. Washington, DC: Author.

Wentzel, K. R. (2002). Are effective teachers like good parents? Teaching styles and student adjustment in early adolescence. *Child Development, 73*(1), 287–301.

CONSTRUCTIVISM

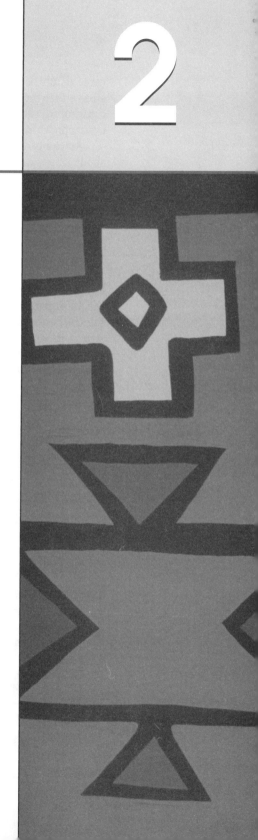

Through others, we become ourselves.
L. S. Vygotsky

Imagine the following classroom. The first week of school, Mrs. Philsinger engages learners in getting to know each other, participating in discussions about how the classroom should be, what behaviors are most conducive to learning, and ways to help each other learn. Students complete a WebQuest, which helps them explore rules and think about rules that are important to them and ones that will help everyone in the classroom community learn. Mrs. Philsinger contributes her own expectations throughout these discussions. From these discussions, learners create a classroom covenant. Each classroom member signs the covenant and a plan is developed for sharing the covenant with newcomers. Learners are asked to demonstrate examples of behavior that convey the classroom covenant and ones that do not. As issues come up, the teacher provides direct reminders of the covenant. Learners are engaged in finding solutions to classroom disruptions and in finding ways to ensure that everyone in the classroom learns. The covenant is discussed over the next several weeks to determine how it fits within the classroom community, whether it describes how they want their classroom to be, or whether it needs to be modified.

During these first weeks, Mrs. Philsinger also facilitates activities that allow students to get to know her and each other. She gives students a survey that asks about their interests, their talents, their learning preferences, and their concerns about school. She allows time for students to share something about themselves and guides them in finding things they have in common with each other. She engages learners in writing learning goals in journals and makes plans to conference with each student about their learning goals within the first 2 weeks. She communicates that she cares about the learning of each student and that she will do everything that she can to ensure that each student learns. She sets the stage for collaborative learning and peer tutoring by asking students to help each other learn and to look out for each other at every opportunity.

As you can see from the example, the learners are active participants in learning about rules and covenants and how they work; they are engaged in shaping how the classroom functions. Such activities at the beginning of the school year allow the learners and the teacher to get to know each other and the stage is set for caring and helping each other. Most important, the expectation is set that the classroom is a community whose primary mission is learning. Mrs. Philsinger is capitalizing on learners' experiences, perspectives, and interactions to assist in developing a positive classroom environment and helping students learn prosocial behaviors.

According to constructivist theory, learning is most meaningful when participants are engaged in constructing their own knowledge and understanding. Social constructivist theory recognizes that learners are influenced by their interactions with each other; with the teacher; and with the broader context of the school, community, and culture. Constructivist views also recognize that perceptions help to create individual understanding, meaning, and reality (Kukla, 2000). Informed by the perspectives of learners, constructivist teachers capitalize on, guide, and facilitate social interaction to enhance learning and develop a safe learning community in which all members are encouraged, valued, and respected. Attending to and capitalizing on interactions and relationships in the classroom can maximize student engagement and motivation, as well as provide a realistic context to develop the competencies learners need as citizens in a democratic society.

In this chapter, I describe constructivist theory as it relates to learning and classroom management. I describe a constructivist perspective with regard to classroom management that acknowledges the social nature of the classroom; the impact of relationships; the perspectives of learners; the classroom climate; and the broader school, community, and culture. I use the Circle of Courage as a framework for considering constructivist theory in enhancing academic engagement and social learning.

CONSTRUCTIVISM

Constructivist theory is based on the idea that individuals construct their own knowledge and understanding of the world through their interactions with problems, objects, and other individuals (Prawat & Floden, 1994; Reynolds, Sinatra, & Jetton, 1996). Prior learning and experience also play a critical role in the learning process. Learners create their own understanding based on past and present experiences and knowledge. According to the constructivist view, merely being present for the presentation of new information in a classroom does not necessarily constitute learning or understanding. Likewise, being told what to do and when to do it does not necessarily generate self-discipline, a sense of responsibility, or respect for community.

The many varieties of constructivism cover a wide terrain. One of these perspectives—social constructivism (Bruner, 1986, 1990; Vygotsky, 1962, 1978)—relates closely to issues related to classroom management.

Social Constructivism

For social constructivist theorists, learning is not only a creative process, but a social one as well. Learning occurs when a child develops inner speech or internalized thought processes through the social experience of interacting with peers and adults (Vygotsky, 1978). From this perspective, social interaction is a key means of learning in the classroom with regard to both academic and social behaviors. With regard to academic knowledge, critical thinking, reasoning, problem solving, and meaningful learning are enhanced when students have ample opportunity for dialogue and interaction with their peers (Palincsar, 1998). Knowledge and understanding of social skills, conflict resolution, problem solving, compromise, and so forth are enhanced by the same kind of social engagement and participation as academic learning (Carlsson-Paige & Lantieri, 2005; Dam & Volman, 2004). Hence, in the classroom, social activity and social interaction provide ripe opportunity for learning prosocial behaviors, effective communication, and democratic values. In the example at the beginning of this chapter, the teacher sets the stage for allowing learners these opportunities. She encourages discussion and participation in the development of classroom rules and she helps the students understand the purpose and the importance of participation in creating rules.

THE CIRCLE OF COURAGE

In the classroom described at the beginning of this chapter, Mrs. Philsinger understands the importance of students connecting with her and each other; she provides opportunities for students to help each other, she seeks student input, and she communicates that she cares about their learning. She is beginning to address the students' need to feel a sense of belonging, autonomy, generosity, and competence.

The Circle of Courage (see Figure 2.1) represents a holistic approach to childrearing and community building based on traditional Native American philosophy (Brendtro, Brokenleg, & Van Bockern, 1990). Although grounded in Native American tradition, the philosophy is not unique to this tradition. The basic tenet of the Circle of Courage—that to develop as healthy members of the community, children and youth require security, relationships with peers and adults that are characterized by affiliation and attachment, a sense of autonomy, and opportunities for caring and responsibility—corresponds to the principles of social constructivist frameworks for child development. Both social constructivist theory and the tradition represented by the Circle of Courage emphasize the role that peers and others play in the learning of young people (Reynolds, Sinatra, & Jetton, 1996).

Brendtro, Brokenleg, and Van Bockern (1990) first described the Circle of Courage, which is based on Native American philosophies of childrearing, the work of early pioneers in education, and contemporary resilience research. The four central values or "spirits" of the Circle of Courage include belonging, mastery, independence, and generosity. Many theories of motivation, including self-determination theory and the related developmental theories of motivation, agency, and initiative, suggest that student engagement in school is greater when the classroom and school climate meet individual needs of autonomy (independence), relatedness to others (belonging), and competence

Figure 2.1 The Circle of Courage

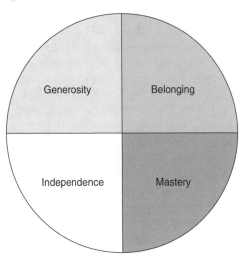

Circle of Courage	Practice	Description	Evidence	How it promotes belonging, independence, mastery, and generosity.
Belonging	Cooperative learning	Students work together to complete learning tasks	Hanze and Berger (2007)	Creates interdependence of group members and promotes working toward common goals.
	Democratic classroom practices	Students participate in activities such as making class and school rules, planning classroom events, finding solutions to problems, etc.	Vieno, Perkins, Smith, & Santinello (2005)	Students have a sense of ownership, investment in, and connection to the community when they have input.
Independence	Choice	Incoroporates students' interests and preferences and allows opportunities for students to make choices	Reeve, Jang, Carrell, Jeon, & Barch (2004)	Considers student perspective and empowers students to make decisions.

	Teaching Students To Be Peacemakers, a conflict resolution program	Teaches students conflict resolution skills	Johnson & Johnson (2004)	Students are empowered to regulate and control their own actions and find solutions to conflicts with peers.
	Class meetings	Engage students in learning to solve problems and conflicts, and use respectful language to communicate	Landau & McEwan (2000)	
Mastery	Learning orientation	Helps students to emphasize and adopt goals related to learning or mastery as opposed to demonstrating ability or measuring performance relative to others in the class (performance goal orientation)	Wolters (2004)	Learning goal orientations foster positive self-efficacy beliefs and encourage learners to seek challenges, as well as assistance, when needed.
Generosity	Cross-age peer tutoring Peer tutoring, peer-assisted learning	Older students are paired with younger students to assist with academic skills; each student takes a turn as coach and as learner	Patterson & Elliot (2006)	Students are given the opportunity to help others in the school community.

(mastery). While these theories do not specifically mention generosity, generosity contributes not only to belonging, mastery, and independence, but also to the development of respect for community. Our senses of belonging, mastery, independence, and generosity are created by our experiences, our perceptions, and our interactions with others.

Belonging

Mrs. Philsinger conducts activities from the very beginning of the school year to help learners gel as a community. Students develop ownership of the classroom by taking part in how it is arranged and in deciding on the rules. The activity of adjusting desks paves the way for students to understand and appreciate differences. Students are given the opportunity to learn about each other and the expectation for helping each other is set.

The acceptance, attention, and affection of others help individuals to gain a sense of attachment or belonging to their home, school, or community. A sense of belonging or relatedness is essential for emotional health and well-being. In school, connectedness is related to higher levels of many desirable behaviors and lower levels of negative behaviors. With a strong sense of belonging, youth become open to guidance from other members of the community. Some children and youth are more trusting of and open to positive relationships with adults than are others. However, research indicates that even children with difficulty forming positive relationships can benefit from practices that encourage belonging. School belonging tends to decline during adolescence, but practices geared toward enhancing belonging at this age can be particularly beneficial in protecting adolescents against the development of many undesirable behaviors and habits.

Belonging and Attachment

According to Brendtro, Brokenleg, and Van Bockern (1990), in traditional Native American society, all adults served as teachers for younger persons and children were taught to see themselves as related to everyone with whom they had regular contact. This notion of belonging is closely related to the concept of psychological attachment, which Flannery, Torquati, and Lindemeier (1994) defined as a "strong affectional bond between individuals which reflects an enduring relationship and a proclivity to seek proximity" (p. 16).

Although one's experience of attachment changes, with respect to both its objects and its emphasis, as one leaves childhood and progresses through adolescence and old age (Thornton, Orbuch, & Axim, 1995), Marrais (1996) suggests that attachment nevertheless "remains the single most compelling motive behind the construction of meanings in life" (p. 45). In their review of Western theoretical frameworks of individual behavior, Thornton, Orbuch, and Axim (1995) corroborated Marrais' claim about the fundamental importance of attachment. They pointed out that central to virtually all Western perspectives is the assertion that the quality of one's interpersonal relationships is strongly related to one's mental and physical well-being and, therefore, is vital to one's satisfaction and enjoyment in life.

Belonging in School

As with home and community, children flourish when they feel a sense of belonging or connectedness at school. Catalano et al. (2004) define school attachment as having close affective relationships with peers and adults at school, an investment in the school, and a commitment to doing well in school. Research indicates that students are more likely to experience increased academic engagement and consequently academic success and greater satisfaction with school when they feel connected to school (Blum, 2005; Blum, McNeely, & Nonnemaker, 2001, 2002; Furrer & Skinner, 2003; Klem & Connell, 2004). Researchers have also demonstrated that school attachment not only increases academic achievement but contributes to well-being and reduces the risk of behaviors such as drug and alcohol use, early sexual activity, delinquency, violence, and gang involvement (Catalano et al., 2004; McNeely & Falci, 2004). In their recent study, Hill and Werner (2006) demonstrated that strong school attachment can protect children and adolescents against aggression and delinquency.

For many children and youth, a sense of belonging and positive relationships with teachers are more tenuous. Some youth have insecure attachments (Bowlby, 1969), resulting in difficulty forming friendships with peers and trusting relationships with adults. In school, students who experience isolation, rejection, or alienation often are less likely to conform to group norms and classroom rules (Osterman, 2000).

Youth with insecure attachments may especially benefit from practices that generate belonging and positive relationships. While early attachment theorists asserted that young children who failed to attach to their mothers during infancy later in life become unable to establish and maintain friendships and to trust those with whom they have regular contact (Weitzman and Cook; 1986), recent research regarding attachment theory calls this assertion into question (Hill & Werner, 2006; Weitzman & Cook, 1986). Brendtro, Brokenleg, and Van Bockern (2002) posit that both belonging and attachment are powerful motives that can be satisfied, even for children and youth with insecure attachments. For many young persons, belonging and attachment to others and to school can be fostered by relationships with adults who recognize that belonging and attachment are central to the development of social competence and self-esteem.

In addition to positive relationships with adults, learners also benefit from positive relationships with their peers. Affording students the opportunity to collaborate and socialize with peers in positive classroom environments enhances belonging, as well as motivation and academic engagement (Hughes, Zhang, & Hill, 2006; Osterman, 2000). Unfortunately, many school practices can undermine these relationships. According to Osterman (2000), the current emphasis on standardized testing in schools often emphasizes individualism and competition over community and collaboration. This emphasis contributes to learners' experience of isolation and alienation, as well as the formation of cliques and clans.

School attachment and motivation tend to decline in the middle and high school years (Klem & Connell, 2004; Marks, 2000). However, it is increasingly recognized that positive relationships at school with peers and adults are beneficial to adolescent development. School friendships can help adolescents cope with the social and emotional challenges of high school and engender positive school affiliation (Hamm & Faircloth, 2005). Resilient adolescents who best overcome difficult life circumstances such as poverty and violence are often guided by strong and supportive adults (Rutter, 1987; Werner, 1995; Werner & Smith, 1982). Research suggests that intentional efforts to attend to attachment during the middle school years can negate the disenfranchisement that typically occurs during these years (Henry & Slater, 2007; Hill & Werner, 2006; King, Vidourek, Davis, & McClellan, 2002; McNeely, Nonnemaker, & Blum, 2002).

Fostering Belonging
What factors contribute to a sense of belonging? In his review of the literature, Blum (2005) notes that child-centered practices, positive classroom management, positive

peer relationships, and gaining student perspective all contribute to attachment. These practices are discussed throughout this text.

Mastery

In Mrs. Philsinger's classroom, students soon understand that the teacher and the class-room community care about and support each student's learning. By helping students set individual learning goals, each student will be able to see his or her own growth throughout the year. No comparisons of students will be made so that each student can feel confident that he or she can be successful.

Theorists agree that competence is an inherent psychological need of all human be-ings that serves the purpose of helping people develop and adapt to their environment. Children, as well as adults, strive for mastery of their environment. A sense of accom-plishment or achievement feeds motivation for further achievement. Success brings a sense of efficacy, whereas failure stifles motivation. In addition to its influence on moti-vation, competence can affect classroom behavior. According to Brendtro et al. (2002), children and youth with a low sense of competence can express their frustration through troubling behavior. While individuals with a strong sense of competence tend to be more highly motivated and engaged in learning, learners with a low sense of compe-tence avoid academic challenges and use inappropriate behavior to escape difficult work. Learners develop their perceived sense of competence through experiences and social interactions. While perceptions of competence tend to change over time and to be sub-ject specific, some learners develop an illusion of incompetence. Practices that encour-age high levels of competence can be implemented easily in the classroom.

Mastery and Motivation

The strong influence of perceptions of competence on motivation is a core component of most theories of motivation (Pajares, 1996; Valentine, Dubois, & Cooper, 2004). For example, self-efficacy theory, expectancy theory, and self-determination theory all in-clude competence as a significant factor that drives human behavior. These theories are discussed in greater detail in Chapter 10. Briefly, according to expectancy theory, the level of success that an individual perceives he or she can achieve is a strong fac-tor in the motivation equation. According to self-determination theory, intrinsic mo-tivation is the product of a sense of competence, relatedness, and autonomy. According to Bandura's self-efficacy theory, a person's perception of competence has a strong influence over their choices and behavior. While each theory has slight dif-ferences in the definition of competence, for learners in the classroom, the basic premise is the same: Learners thrive in classrooms when they believe that they can be successful.

Mastery, Achievement, and Behavior

Self-efficacy refers to "beliefs in one's capabilities to organize and execute the courses of action required to produce given attainments" (Bandura, 1995, p. 2). According to the research of Bandura and his colleagues, self-efficacy beliefs have influence over our course of action, our choices, our efforts, our perseverance in the face of obstacles, our resilience to adversity, whether our thoughts are self-hindering or self-aiding, stress levels, and accomplishments. Self-efficacy with regard to academics reduces vulnerability to depression; causes individuals to see setbacks, failures, and obstacles as surmountable, and encourages greater effort. In addition, students' levels of perceived competence are related to the value they place on academic tasks that may also lead to increased academic engagement (Jacobs et al., 2002).

According to researchers, the flip side, or low self-efficacy, affects motivation and achievement, as well as behavior. Bandura (1994) found that a low sense of self-efficacy creates despondency, diminishes motivation, and puts learners at risk for substance abuse, as well as transgressive acts. Other researchers have found that learners with low levels of competence exhibit less self-regulation, more negative attitudes, and less class participation (Bouffard, Boisvert, & Vezeau, 2003; Fleury-Roy & Bouffard, 2006).

In addition to lowered motivation, low self-efficacy can elicit escape and apathy. While the need for competence drives learners to direct their energy toward competence, depending on their perception of possible outcomes, they may be driven to either achieve competence or avoid incompetence. Learners can seek to avoid or escape academic work by engaging in inappropriate behavior. Inappropriate behavior may serve the purpose of avoiding an academic situation where failure appears imminent (Reid & Nelson, 2002). In addition, learners who have experienced failure and low grades may reduce effort and display an apathetic attitude toward grades and academic work to cover up for their perceived incompetency (Tollefson, 2004). Finally, learners with low self-efficacy may engage in self-handicapping behaviors. In order to escape appearing incompetent and deflect attention away from their ability, they engage in behaviors and/or excuses such as not putting forth effort (I didn't really try) or acting like grades are unimportant (I don't care how I do in this class) (Urdan & Midgley, 2001).

In addition to self-efficacy in the academic realm, students form perceptions of their competence with regard to social skills such as self-regulation, empathy (Bandura, 1994; Brendgen, Vitaro, Turgeon, Poulin, & Wanner, 2004), and the ability to make friends (Jacobs, Vernon, & Eccles, 2004). Children and youth with a low sense of social competence tend to engage in problem behavior, are more vulnerable to peer pressure and negative social influences, and have lower levels of self-regulation, while learners with high levels of social competence are able to maintain friendships, are less prone to depression and inappropriate behavior, and enjoy emotional well-being (Bandura, Barbaranelli, Caprara, & Pastorelli, 2001; Caprara, Barbaranelli, Pastorelli, & Cervane, 2004; Jacobs, Vernon, & Eccles, 2004).

Developing Competence

According to Bandura (1994), several factors influence one's perception of competence. These factors include mastery experiences, social persuasion, vicarious experiences, and emotional and physiological states. Others identify the threat of being stereotyped as a source of a deflated sense of competence and the goal structure of the classroom as relevant to student competence.

Mastery Experiences.   Probably the most compelling factor with regard to the development of perception of self-efficacy is mastery experience. Success fosters feelings of competence. With repeated failure, competence declines. In their study, Usher and Pajares (2006) demonstrate that a student's perception of mastery experiences is a strong predictor of that student's self-efficacy beliefs. These authors also explain that perception rather than actual performance is a key factor here. For example, a grade of B on an exam for a student accustomed to lower grades could be perceived as a successful experience, while an individual accustomed to A's could perceive the same grade of B as a failure. Not surprisingly, a decline in school grades tends to be accompanied by a decline in students' perceptions of competence (Bouffard et al., 2003).

Vicarious Experiences.   Vicarious experiences can also influence self-efficacy. If learners lack information or are uncertain about their ability with regard to certain activities, they may develop their self-efficacy perceptions based on observations of classmates. If classmates with perceived similar abilities experience success in certain activities, learners may assume that they will have the necessary competence as well.

Social Persuasion.   Social persuasion involves the verbal judgments of others. In the classroom, teachers, peers, or parents may convince learners to put forth greater effort by boosting their sense of competence. Bandura cautions, however, that instilling confidence through social persuasion is not always easy. A history of failure is difficult to overcome even with great encouragement. Furthermore, unrealistic boosts in self-confidence from a parent or teacher are quickly deflated if the learner experiences failure. In addition, social persuasion can more easily work to undermine confidence than to boost it. That is, learners can be easily persuaded that they lack ability and hence avoid challenges and give up easily. According to the research of Usher and Pajares (2006), social persuasion seems to influence girls and African Americans to a greater extent than white males.

Emotional and Physiological State.   Finally, emotional and physiological state can influence perceptions of competence. Persons who are experiencing stress, tension, despondent mood, fatigue, or sickness may feel less confident in their abilities. In the classroom, children and youth dealing with difficult circumstances in their homes, community, or school (e.g., children who are bullied at school or abused at home) may have lower self-efficacy due to these stressors, especially if these children are already beset with self-doubt. In addition, anxiety over exams or other academic tasks can undermine students' perceptions of academic competence.

Stereotype Threat.   Steele and Aronson (1995) identify stereotype threat as a source of diminished self-efficacy for certain groups. According to Aronson and Steele (2005), stereotype threat involves negative stereotypes, especially those that deal with intellectual inferiority. Stereotype threat plays an important role in the poor achievement of certain students—African Americans, Latinos, and girls in math-oriented domains. Social persuasion and emotional states may come into play with the notion of stereotype threat. Aronson (2004) explains that students who are aware of stereotypes may become anxious in certain academic situations, such as testing situations. They fear that the stereotype may be grounded in truth or that their performance will reinforce the stereotype. Aronson (2004) cites several experiments that document the powerful effect of stereotype threat on student performance. Students may be vulnerable to this threat as early as the sixth grade, when they begin to assess their own competence and they become aware of the negative expectations that others may have of certain groups.

Goal Structure of the Classroom. In addition to the factors described above, the goal structure of the classroom can influence learners' perceptions of competence (Urdan & Midgley, 2001). In classrooms where competition, grades, and achievement relative to peers are emphasized, students may adopt lower self-efficacy beliefs. Where practices emphasize mastery, effort, improvement, and intellectual development, students are more likely to feel confident that they can be successful.

Perceptions of Competence Over Time
Perceptions of competence can change over time and are subject specific. Young children are likely to have high levels of self-efficacy, which tend to become more realistic around third grade (Fleury-Roy & Bouffard, 2006). As with a sense of belonging, a student's sense of competence begins to decline in adolescence and this continues through high school (Jacobs, Lanza, Osgood, Eccles, & Wigfield, 2002; Summers, Schallert, & Ritter, 2003; Usher & Pajares, 2006). Researchers speculate that the decline in perceptions of competence may be due to the structure of middle school and students' changing perceptions of what it takes to be successful (Jacobs et al., 2002). With regard to school structure, in middle school, students are often grouped by ability, and become more aware of their performance in relation to their peers. In addition, in middle school, learners become more aware of their level of achievement and begin to perceive competence rather than effort as the reason for successes or failures. Finally, research indicates that perceptions of competence tend to be subject specific. For example, a student's perception of his or her level of competence in math tends to decline more rapidly over the school years than does self-efficacy for language arts (Jacobs et al., 2002).

Illusions of Incompetence
Children who have low self-efficacy with no apparent deficits in ability have an illusion of incompetence. Teachers may not be good judges regarding which students have illusions of incompetence (Fleury-Roy & Bouffard, 2006). Gaining student perspective with regard to self-efficacy can help teachers provide support for self-efficacy where needed. As with belonging, constructive teachers assist students in developing mastery, avoiding stereotype threat, and acquiring protection against an illusion of incompetence. The following strategies are suggested.

• Provide ample opportunities for students to master content and skills so that students can experience success.
• Assist students in making attributions of successes and failures in ways that enhance perceptions of mastery. Help students attribute success to effort and ability, and

failure to either lack of effort or other external factors rather than lack of ability. When her students are struggling with a skill or concept, Jonnie Walkingstick, an elementary school teacher, makes comments to her students like, "Oh, I must not have done my job today, let me try again."

- Avoid activities and grading practices that allow learners to compare themselves with each other.
- Use structures and activities that promote cooperation. Cooperative arrangements reduce competition, distrust, and stereotyping among students (Aronson, 2004).
- Teach learners that intelligence is fluid rather than fixed. Research indicates that stereotype threat is reduced when students are taught that intelligence is not a fixed trait, but rather that it is influenced by effort and practice (Aronson, 2004).
- Look for improvements rather than perfection. Help learners see their progress and growth and see mistakes as opportunities to learn rather than as failures.
- Teach students about stereotype threat. Aronson (2004) indicates that teaching students about stereotype threat can help improve test scores and study habits. He suggests that exposing students to models who have been successful through hard work and persistence despite academic struggles can be beneficial.

Independence

People need to have a sense of control over their own destiny. Independence or autonomy refers to one's sense of control and responsibility over their actions. Like belonging and mastery, independence plays a crucial role in growth and development (Osterman, 2000). And like mastery and belonging, it influences behavior, motivation, and achievement in the classroom. In Mrs. Philsinger's classroom, students participate in developing classroom rules, as well as finding solutions as problems arise. Constructivist teachers do classroom management *with,* not *to,* students and consequently build competence, ownership, and self-reliance instead of dependency. In addition, practices that foster autonomy prepare learners for responsible participation in citizenship. With a strong sense of autonomy, children can learn responsibility and self-discipline. Teachers can support or thwart autonomy in the classroom.

Benefits of Independence

Autonomy has great advantages for learners. Citing numerous studies, Vansteenkiste, Lens, and Deci (2006) report that these advantages include decreased drop out, deeper learning, greater creativity, less superficial information processing, higher achievement, and enhanced well-being. These findings have been replicated across cultures, genders, and age groups. Recent research also suggests that in classrooms where teachers support autonomy, students are more actively engaged (Reeve, Jang, Carrell, Jeon, & Barch, 2004; Reeve & Jang, 2006). In the self-determination theory of motivation, Deci and Ryan (2000) consider autonomy to be one of the keys to intrinsic motivation. In addition, many studies show the power of gaining student input in fostering belonging and engagement in school (Whitlock, 2006).

In addition to academic and social benefits, classroom practices that support student autonomy are also in line with democratic values and practices (Carlsson-Paige & Lantieri, 2005). Practices that engage learners in meaningful decision making and give students a voice in their classroom contribute to the preparation of students to participate independently in a meaningful and critical way in authentic social practices and activities.

With choice comes responsibility. Empowering children to make choices and decisions in ways that are socially responsible involves teaching perspective and encouraging reflection with regard to the impact of our decisions on the community. Practices that nurture these skills nurture greater self-discipline and self-responsibility rather than simple obedience to authority (Brendtro & Long, 1995).

People without a sense of autonomy often lack an internal locus of control and intrinsic motivation. Students who are empowered through opportunities for responsibility and decision making develop strong internal motivation, self-discipline, and a sense of autonomy (Brendtro, Brokenleg, & Van Bockern, 2002). Denied these opportunities, students develop an external locus of control and may be reliant on external motivation.

Practices that Support Independence

While teaching practices that support autonomy have many positive influences, many teachers more frequently use controlling motivational strategies that thwart autonomy, for example, rewards and punishment (Reeve & Jang, 2006). They may feel pressure to use more controlling procedures because of external influences such as high-stakes testing, or they may lack the know-how to implement practices that support autonomy. However, many such teaching practices can be easily implemented in the classroom.

Reeve and Jang (2006) identify two types of practices that support autonomy: those that attempt to gain student perspective and those that nurture independence. Those that gain student perspective include practices such as listening to students and asking students for input. Those that nurture autonomy include allowing students time to talk with each other, allowing students to have a choice in seating arrangements and the way they work, providing rationales for lessons, using praise as a way to give informational feedback, offering hints that allow students to generate answers and solutions on their own, letting students know that you recognize and accept their perceptions, and being responsive to student-generated questions.

Stefanou et al. (2004) also identify three ways that teachers can support autonomy. These include allowing students a decision-making role in terms of classroom management issues or organizational autonomy. Classroom meetings (discussed in Chapter 5) are an excellent example of a practice that allows students a voice in the classroom. Procedural autonomy allows students choices about how they use instructional resources. Giving choices of assignments, projects, and/or learning products is an example of procedural autonomy. The third way that teachers can support autonomy is allowing for cognitive autonomy or allowing students to think for themselves. An example of cognitive autonomy would include engaging students in self-evaluation and reflection.

Reeve and Jang (2006) identify controlling or autonomy-thwarting practices. These practices include spending a greater percentage of time engaging in teacher talking rather than allowing for student talk, holding and controlling classroom materials, giving solutions and answers instead of guiding students to them, giving commands and directives, asking controlling questions, criticizing students, and using praise to control behavior.

Generosity

Mrs. Philsinger communicates caring in her words and actions right from the beginning of the school year. Caring is a powerful theme throughout the year. By Mrs. Philsinger's modeling of caring, as well as encouragement for caring for each other, students will experience the benefits of the giving of oneself. The spirit of generosity involves the sense that one can and should contribute to the community, consider the welfare of others, and share personal and human resources. The opportunity to help and give to others in the community can increase the sense of self-worth in children and youth, foster a commitment to caring for others (Brendtro et al., 1990), and nurture social responsibility (Berman, 1990). Providing learners with an opportunity for giving to the lives of others and improving the community around them and the world builds self-esteem.

Opportunities for generosity can be powerful learning experiences and leave students feeling empowered and competent (Muscott, 2000). Curwin (1993) reported on the remarkable results of seeing difficult youth, including many who had been involved in gangs, make significant changes in attitudes and behaviors after being given responsibility as caretakers, tutors, and helpers of people in need. Those who are helped don't see the helping students as failures, so the attitudes of all concerned change and those changes lead to hope.

In a study of Japanese schools, Lewis (1995) concluded that students succeeded in academic achievement because of the schools' attention to children's need for belonging, contribution, and competence. She described the program as value-rich and the community as caring and supportive, with an emphasis on learning to live in groups. She reported a common end-of-day question: "Did our group members do something kind for one another today?" (p. 39). However, as Lipsitz (1995) notes, American schools themselves are rewarded for individual academic achievement and not for creating caring communities.

Opportunities for students to demonstrate caring and to participate in helping relationships with peers or adults are scarce, constrained by structured transition times and limited opportunities within a class (Bosworth, 1995). Teachers and programs that do provide a chance for one student to help another strongly favor the students who are academically stronger (Bosworth, 1995; McNamara, 1996). However, with careful planning, opportunities for nurturing generosity can be built into the school day.

Developing Generosity

Teachers are often concerned with students' self-esteem and self-worth. Typical beginning-of-the-year activities, especially in elementary schools, include activities that help children define why they are "special" in an effort to make students feel good about themselves. While these activities are well intentioned and may serve to help teachers get to know their students and for students to get to know each other, a sense of self-worth may be more easily and genuinely accomplished by providing opportunities for helping others (Brendtro & Longhurst, 2005).

For students to learn to help others, to contribute to the good of the school, and to care about people other than friends, we must provide opportunities to develop these values through shared rituals, routines, and discussions (Noblit, Rogers, & McCadden, 1995). For example, one classroom practice that can cultivate altruism is cooperative learning. In a study of cooperative learning, Guilles (2002) found evidence that learners who work in cooperative groups are more attuned to each other's needs and are more willing to give help when asked than those who aren't given the same opportunity.

Robinson and Curry (2006) provide specific suggestions for encouraging altruistic behaviors. First, teachers can provide opportunities for helping through activities such as peer tutoring, projects that involve a service to the school or community, and engaging students in solving community problems such as having students identify a way to recognize and appreciate school staff or finding ways to assist families in need. Second, engaging children in tasks that serve the classroom community can foster generosity. Learners can have classroom or school responsibilities that provide service or assistance where needed. Third, in addition to opportunities for helping and giving, time must be made for open discussions of values and issues (Curwin, 1993; Robinson & Curry, 2006) related to altruism and social responsibility.

Service learning provides another vehicle of engaging youth in generous behavior. Service learning is a service experience that includes intentional learning goals (Billing, 2000). According to her review of research, Billing concludes that when service learning involves an authentic need and includes meaningful planning, service, reflection, and celebration, learners become actively engaged. Other research indicates that youth who volunteer are less likely to engage in risky behavior (Mueller, 2005). Student choice, responsibility, and decision making are also key factors in successful service learning.

THE CIRCLE OF COURAGE AND THE POWER OF SOCIAL INTERACTION

As mentioned previously, for social constructivist theorists, social interaction is a key means of learning. The four spirits of the Circle of Courage, which represent basic human needs, are either enhanced or broken through our interactions and communication with others. In the classroom, it is the interactions of learners and their teachers and peers that develop the spirits of belonging, mastery, independence, and generosity. When schools and classrooms attend to those spirits, youth may not feel the need to rebel, bully, or avoid learning. For example, Siris and Osterman (2004) document how attention to belonging, competence, and autonomy assisted an elementary school in New York not only to address a growing bullying problem, but also to create a more positive learning environment overall. In this study, teachers intentionally observed their own classrooms for opportunities for choice and autonomy. Prior to the observations, the teachers claimed that these opportunities were plentiful, but their own observations revealed that they were few and far between. In addition, teachers discovered that students who were victims of bullying had fewer opportunities for competence building; they received less positive attention for their accomplishments than their peers. It is interesting that opportunities for caring and helping other students were attributed to helping students gain a sense of belonging. In other words, in many instances, the need for belonging, competence, independence, and generosity were missing, but when it was addressed, children flourished.

Communication with learners can help build the spirits represented in the Circle of Courage. Language that communicates competence, autonomy, belonging, and generosity can be as important as actions.

Communicate Competence
Teachers can use language that fosters a sense of competence in the face of frustration. For example, a teacher may be tempted to say, "Todd, come on, this isn't hard for you, you are such a bright boy." A comment such as this one may lead Todd to think that since a task is hard for him, he must not be that bright. Instead, a teacher may say, "This is hard, but I think if you keep trying, you will get it."

Communicate Belonging
The language we use can reinforce to learners that they are an important member of the community. Statements such as "We missed you yesterday and are happy you are back with us." "What ideas do you have to make our classroom more comfortable?" "How can we welcome new students to our class?" communicate that everyone belongs.

Communicate Independence
Language which conveys that the learner is responsible and can make decisions can foster independence. Questions like "What would be the best way to make sure we leave our classroom clean every afternoon?" "How would you like to present your project?" "What solutions can we find to this problem?" show respect for learner autonomy and an expectation of responsibility.

Communicate Generosity
Statements that acknowledge instances of caring in the classroom can generate generosity. Such statements could include "I appreciate how you helped Charlie with his math." "Sally feels hurt, what can we do to make her feel better?"

CONSTRUCTIVISM AND THE POWER OF PERSPECTIVE

For constructivist theorists, individual perceptions of events and experiences provide powerful information (Rodgers, 2006). Social constructivist theorists acknowledge the contributions of the school curriculum, the classroom and school environments, and the broader culture and community in forming the perceptions of learners in the classroom

(Cook-Sather, 2002). Although students in the classroom may experience the same activities, each student may create different meaning. Constructivist teachers understand the process by which different perceptions are generated by the same instructional activities to help them better plan and manage instruction (Hutchinson, 2006).

The perceptions of learners are important because to the learners they are reality. Teachers and administrators may have good intentions when developing management and discipline programs to control aberrant student behavior and increase academic achievement. However, if those programs are not perceived as helpful, fair, and respectful by the students, they often are not successful. If students perceive themselves as incompetent and perceive unnecessary control, alienation, and lack of purpose, the best ideas of teachers may only further frustrate and alienate them. Students are the ones most affected by educational policies and practices. Gaining and using student perspective can serve to empower students, convey trust, and help shape practices most conducive to student learning (Cook-Sather, 2002). Hence, gaining student perspective with regard to their experiences of mastery, independence, belonging, and generosity is essential in a constructivist classroom. Chapter 6 deals in depth with student perspectives and how to obtain them.

RESEARCH-BASED PRACTICES

With No Child Left Behind (NCLB) legislation and increasing demands for school accountability, school professionals have a growing concern that teachers use "evidence-based" practices, particularly those that result in increased student achievement. Classroom management practices can affect the amount of time that students are engaged in learning, their attitudes toward learning, their motivation, and their willingness and ability to collaborate with each other. As mentioned in Chapter 1, research that informs classroom management draws from many disciplines, including education, psychology, and sociology. Classroom practices that support the areas of the Circle of Courage, as well as enhance academic achievement, engagement, attitudes, motivation, and prosocial behavior, are well documented in professional literature. Figure 2.1 includes practical examples of practices from applied classroom research for each area of the Circle of Courage that align with constructivist philosophy.

SUMMARY

Mrs. Philsinger's classroom, described at the beginning of this chapter, illustrates what constructivist classroom management practices look like. This chapter deals with the constructivist view of classroom management. Classrooms are, by their nature, inherently social places where children and youth form much of their identity. According to constructivist theory, it is that social interaction that creates learning, motivation, and behavior. Taking advantage of that social interaction to help students develop belonging, mastery, independence, and generosity, can enhance motivation, engagement, achievement, and prosocial behavior. Learners themselves are the experts with regard to their school experiences. Gaining their perspective allows teachers to understand what learners may need to be engaged, motivated, socially appropriate, and socially responsible.

REFERENCES

Anderman, L. H. (2003). Academic and social perceptions as predictors for change in middle school students' sense of school belonging. *Journal of Experimental Education, 72*(1), 5–22.

Aronson, J. (2004). The threat of stereotype. *Educational Leadership, 62*(3), 14–19.

Aronson, J., & Steele, C. M. (2005). Stereotypes and the fragility of human competence, motivation, and self-concept. In C. Dweck & E. Elliot (Eds.), *Handbook of competence and motivation* (pp. 436–456). New York: Guilford.

Bandura, A. (1994). Self-efficacy. In V. S. Ramachaudran (Ed.), *Encyclopedia of human behavior,* 4, (pp. 71–81). New York: Academic Press.

Bandura, A. (1995). *Self-efficacy in changing societies.* New York: Cambridge University Press.

Bandura, A., Barbaranelli, L., Caprara, G. V., & Pastorelli, C. (2001). Self-efficacy beliefs as shapers of children's aspirations and career trajectories. *Child Development, 72*(1), 187–206.

Billing, S. H. (2000). Research on K–12 school-based service-learning: The evidence builds. *Phi Delta Kappan, 81*(9), 658–664.

Blum, R. (2005). A case for school connectedness. *Educational Leadership, 62*(7), 16–20.

Blum, R. W., McNeely, C., & Nonnemaker, J. (2001). Vulnerability, risk, and protection. In Fischhoff, B., Nightingale, E. O., & Iannotta, J. G. (Eds.), *Adolescent risk and vulnerability: Concepts and measurement.* Washington, DC: National Academy Press.

Blum, R. W., McNeely, C., & Nonnemaker, J. (2002). Promoting school connectedness: Evidence from the National Longitudinal Study of Adolescents. *Journal of School Health, 2*(4), 138–146.

Bosworth, K. (1995). Caring for others and being cared for. *Phi Delta Kappan, 76*(6), 686–693.

Bouffard, T., Boisvert, M., & Vezeau, C. (2002). The illusion of incompetence and its correlates among elementary school children and their parents. *Learning and Individual Differences, 14*(1), 31–47.

Bouffard, T., Marcoux, M., Vezeau, C. & Bordeleau, L. (2003). Changes in self-perceptions of competence and intrinsic motivation among elementary schoolchildren. *British Journal of Educational Psychology, 73*(2), 171–186.

Bowlby, J. (1969). *Attachment* (Attachment and loss series). NewYork Basic Books.

Brendgen, M., Vitaro, F., Turgeon, L., Poulin, F., & Wanner, B. (2004). Is there a dark side of positive illusions? Overestimation of social competence and subsequent adjustment in aggressive and nonaggressive children. *Journal of Abnormal Child Psychology, 32*(3), 305–320.

Brendtro, L. K., Brokenleg, M., & Van Bockern, S. (1990). *Reclaiming youth at risk: Our hope for the future.* Bloomington, IN: National Education Service.

Brendtro, L. K., Brokenleg, M., & Van Bockern, S. (2002). *Reclaiming youth at risk: Our hope for the future* (Rev. ed.) Bloomington, IN: National Education Service.

Brendtro, L., & Long, N. (1995). Breaking the cycle of conflict. *Educational Leadership, 52*(5), 52–56.

Brendtro, L. K., & Longhurst, J. E. (2005). The resilient brain. *Reclaiming Children and Youth. 14*(1), 52–60.

Bruner, J. (1986). *Actual minds, possible worlds*. Cambridge, MA: Harvard University Press.

Bruner, J. (1990). *Acts of meaning*. Cambridge, MA: Harvard University Press.

Carlsson-Paige, N., & Lantieri, L (2005). A changing vision of Education. *Reclaiming Children and Youth, 14*(2), 97–103.

Caprara, G. V., Barbaranellie, L., Pastorelli, C., & Cervane, D. (2004). The contribution of self-efficacy beliefs to psychosocial outcomes in adolescence: Predicting beyond global dispositional tendencies, *37*(4), 751–763.

Catalano, R. F., Haggerty, K. P., Oesterle, S., Fleming, C. B., & Hawkins, J. D. (2004). Importance of bonding to school for healthy development: Findings from the Social Development Research Group. *Journal of School Health, 74*(7), 252–261.

Cook-Sather, A. (2002). Authorizing students' perspectives: Toward trust, dialogue, and change in education. *Educational Researcher, 31*(4) 3–14.

C., Kevin. (1994). My independence day. *Journal of Emotional and Behavioral Problems, 3*(2), 35–40.

Curwin, R. L. (1993). The healing power of altruism. *Educational Leadership, 51*(3), 36–39.

Dam, G. T., & Volman, M. (2004). Critical thinking as a citizenship competence: Teaching strategies. *Learning and Instruction, 14*(4), 359–379.

Deci, E. L. & Ryan, R. M. (2000). The "what" and "why" of goal pursuits: Human needs and the self-determination of behavior. *Psychological Inquiry, 11*(4), 227–268.

Flannery, D. J., Torquati, J. C., and Lindemeier, L. (1994). The method and meaning of emotional expression and experience during adolescence. *Journal of Adolescent Research, 9*(1), 8–27.

Fleury-Roy, M.-H., & Bouffard, T. (2006). Teachers' recognition of children with an illusion of incompetence. *European Journal of Psychology of Education, 21*(2), 149–162.

Furrer, C., & Skinner, E. (2003). Sense of relatedness as a factor in children's academic engagement and performance. *Journal of Educational Psychology, 95*(1), 148–162.

Guillies, R. M. (2002). The residual effects of cooperative-learning experiences: A two-year follow-up. *The Journal of Educational Research, 6*(1), 15–20.

Hamm, J. V., & Faircloth, B. S. (2005). The role of friendship in adolescents' sense of belonging. *New Directions for Child and Adolescent Development,2005*(107), 61–78.

Hanze, M., & Berger, R. (2007). Cooperative learning, motivational effects, and student characteristics: An experimental study comparing cooperative learning and direct instruction. *Learning and Instruction, 17*(1), 29–41.

Henry, K. L., & Slater, M. D. (2007). The contextual effect of school attachment on young adolescents' alcohol use. *Journal of School Health, 77*(2), 67–74.

Hill, L. G., & Werner, N. F. (2006). Affiliative motivation, school attachment, and aggression in school. *Psychology in the Schools, 43*(2), 231–246.

Hughes, J. N., Zhang, D., & Hill, C. R. (2006). Peer assessments of normative and individual teacher–student support predict social acceptance and engagement among low-achieving children. *Journal of School Psychology, 43*(6), 447–463.

Hutchison, C. B. (2006). Cultural constructivism: The confluence of cognition, knowledge creation, multiculturalism, and teaching. *Intercultural Education, 17*(3), 301–310.

Jacobs, J. E., Lanza, S., Osgood, D. W., Eccles, J. S., & Wigfield, A. (2002). Changes in children's self-competence and values: Gender and domain differences across grades one through twelve. *Child Development, 73*(2), 509–527.

Jacobs, J. E., Vernon, M. K., & Eccles, J. S. (2004). Relations between social self-perceptions, time use, and prosocial or problem behaviors during adolescense. *Journal of Adolescent Research,19*(1), 45–62.

Johnson, D. W., & Johnson, R. T. (2004). Implementing the "teaching students to be peacemakers" program. *Theory into Practice, 43*(1), 69–79.

King, K. A., Vidourek, R. A., Davis, B., & McClellan, W. (2002). Increasing self-esteem and school connectedness through a multidimensional mentoring program. *Journal of School Health, 72*(7), 294–300.

Klem, A. M., & Connell, J. P. (2004). Relationships matter: Linking teacher support to student engagement and achievement. *Journal of School Health, 74*(7), 262–273.

Kukla, A. (2000). *Social constructivism and the philosophy of science.* New York: Routledge.

Landau, B., & McEwan, G. P. (2000). Creating peaceful classrooms. *Phi Delta Kappan, 81*(6), 450–454.

Lewis, C. C. (1995). The roots of Japanese educational achievement: Helping children develop bonds to schools. *Educational Policy, 9*(2), 129–133.

Lipsitz, J. (1995). Prologue: Why we should care about caring. *Phi Delta Kappan, 76*(9), 665–666.

Marks, H. M. (2000). Student engagement in instructional activity: Patterns in the elementary, middle, and high school years. *American Educational Research Journal, 37*(1), 153–184.

Marrais, P. (1996). *The politics of uncertainty: Attachment in private and public life.* London: Routledge.

McNamara, K. (1996). Bonding to school and the development of responsibility. *Reclaiming Children and Youth at Risk, 4*(4), 33–35.

McNeely, C.A., J.M. Nonnemaker and R.W. Blum (2002) Promoting Student Connectedness to School: Evidence from the National Longitudinal Study of Adolescent Health. Journal of *School Health, 72*(4): 138–146.

McNeely, C., & Falci, C. (2004). School connectedness and the transition into and out of health-risk behavior among adolescents: A comparison of social belonging and teacher support. *Journal of School Health, 74*(7), 284–292.

Mueller, A. (2005). Antidote to learned helplessness: Empowering youth through service. *Reclaiming Children and Youth at Risk, 14*(1), 16–19.

Muscott, H. (2000). A review and analysis of service-learning programs involving students with emotional/behavioral disorders. *Education and Treatment of Children, 23*(3), 346–368.

Noblit, G. W., Rogers, D. L., & McCadden, B. M. (1995). In the meantime: The possibilities of caring. *Phi Delta Kappan, 76*(9), 680–685.

Osterman, K. F. (2000). Students' need for belonging in the school community. *Review of Educational Research, 70*(3), 323–367.

Pajares, F. (1996). Self-efficacy beliefs in academic settings. *Review of Educational Research, 66*(4), 543–578.

Palincsar, A. S. (1998). Social constructivist perspectives on teaching and learning. *Annual Review of Psychology, 49*(1), 347–375.

Patterson, P., & Elliot, L. N. (2006). Struggling reader to struggling reader: High school students' response to a cross-age tutoring program. *Journal of Adolescent and Adult Literacy, 49*(5), 378–389.

Prawat, R. S., & Floden, R. E. (1994). Philosophical perspectives on constructivist views of learning. *Educational Psychologist, 29*(1), 37–48.

Reeve, J., & Jang, H. (2006). What teachers say and do to support students' autonomy during a learning activity. *Journal of Educational Psychology, 98*(1), 209–218.

Reeve, J., Jang, H., Carrell, D., Jeon, S., & Barch, J. (2004). Enhancing student motivation by increasing teachers' autonomy support. *Motivation and Emotion, 28*(2), 147–169.

Reid, R., & Nelson, J. R. (2002). The utility, acceptability, predictability of functional behavioral assessment for students with high-incidence problem behaviors. *Remedial and Special Education, 23*(1), 15–23.

Reynolds, R. E., Sinatra, G. M., & Jetton, T. L. (1996). Views of knowledge acquisition and representation: A continuum from experience centered to mind centered. *Educational Psychologist, 31*(2), 93–104.

Robinson, E. H., & Curry, J. R. (2006). Promoting altruism in the classroom. *Childhood Education, 82*(2), 68–73.

Rodgers, C. R. (2006). Attending to student voice: The impact of descriptive feedback on learning and teaching. *Curriculum Inquiry, 36*(2), 209–237.

Rutter, M. (1987). Psychological resilience and protective mechanisms. *American Journal of Orthopsychiatry, 57*(33), 316–331.

Siris, K., & Osterman, K. (2004). Interrupting the cycle of bullying and victimization in the elementary classroom. *Phi Delta Kappan,* 288–291.

Steele, C. M., & Aronson., J. (1995). Stereotype vulnerability and the intellectual test performance of African Americans. *Journal of Personality and Social Psychology, 69,* 797–811.

Stefanou, C. R., Perencevich, K. C., DiCintio, M., & Turner, J. C. (2004). Supporting autonomy in the classroom: Ways teachers encourage student decision making and ownership. *Educational Psychologist, 39,* 97–110.

Summers, J. J., Schallert, D. L., & Ritter, P. M. (2003). The role of social comparison in students' perceptions of ability: An enriched view of academic motivation in middle school students. *Contemporary Educational Psychology, 28*(4), 510–523.

Thornton, A., Orbuch, T. L., & Axim, W. G. (1995). Parent–child relationships during the transition to adulthood. *Journal of Family Issues, 16,* 538–564.

Tollefson, N. (2004). Classroom applications of cognitive theories of motivation. *Educational Psychology Review, 12*(1), 63–83.

Urdan, T., & Midgley, C. (2001). Academic self-handicapping: What we know, what more is there to learn? *Educational Psychology Review, 13*(2), 115–138.

Usher, E. L., & Pajares, F. (2006). Sources of academic and self-regulatory efficacy beliefs of entering middle school students. *Contemporary Educational Psychology, 31*(2), 125–141.

Valentine, J. C., Dubois, D. L., & Cooper, H. (2004). *The relation between self-beliefs.*

Vansteenkiste, M., Lens, W., & Deci, E. L. (2006). Intrinsic versus extrinsic goal contents in self-determination theory: Another look at the quality of academic motivation. *Educational Psychologist, 41*(1), 19–31.

Vieno, A., Perkins, D. D., Smith, T. M., & Santinello, M. (2005). Democratic school climate and sense of community. *American Journal of Community Psychology, 36*(314), 327–341.

Vygotsky, L. S. (1962). *Thought and language.* Cambridge, MA: The M.I.T. Press.

Vygotsky, L. S. (1978). Mind in society: The development of higher psychological processes. Cambridge, MA: Harvard University Press.

Weitzman, J., & Cook, R. E. (1986). Attachment theory and clinical implications for at-risk children. *Child Psychiatry and Human Development, 17,* 95–103.

Werner, E. E. (1995). Resilience in development. *Current Directions in Psychological Science, 4*(3), 81–85.

Werner, E. E., & Smith, R. S. (1982). *Vulnerable but invincible: A longitudinal study of resilient children and youth.* New York: McGraw–Hill.

Whitlock, J. L. (2006). Youth perceptions of life at school: Contextual correlates of school connectedness in adolescence. *Applied Developmental Science, 10*(1), 13–29.

Wolters, C. A. (2004). Advancing achievement goals theory: Using goal structures and goal orientations to predict students' motivation, cognition, and achievement. *Journal of Educational Psychology, 96*(2), 236–250.

BEHAVIORAL THEORY

Behavior is determined by its consequences.
B. F. Skinner

Mr. Clark starts the school year by posting a list of rules on the board. He talks to the students about why each rule is important. The rules cover any behavior that would interfere with learning. He demonstrates examples of following the rules and examples of behaviors that would be considered rule breaking. He informs learners of consequences for breaking the rules, but assures that those who follow the rules will be rewarded. He monitors the room frequently and praises many instances of good behavior that he catches by making specific comments about their behavior and their work. He drops a marble in a jar anytime he notices prosocial behaviors that he is especially trying to encourage. He explains to the class that when the jar is full, they will have a pizza party. When needed, Mr. Clark reminds students of the rules and redirects them back to their schoolwork. He applies consequences fairly and consistently. He watches for negative behavior patterns that may arise and adjusts classroom schedule, seating order, and so forth so that distractions to learning will be minimal. For example, he notices two students who appear to get each other off task when they are assigned seat work. He moves the students so that they are not sitting next to each other and therefore are not tempted to distract each other.

Mr. Clark tells learners that while they will have many opportunities for fun, work will always come first and fun will follow when the work is completed. He distributes a survey to ascertain students likes and dislikes, interests, and so forth. He will use the information to identify possible rewards and fun activities to reinforce desired behaviors. He had heard that this particular group had an aversion to math the year before. He takes a proactive approach to this concern by starting math with fun math games and easy math work to relieve the anxiety of the group and allow them to associate math with more positive feelings.

Mr. Clark is beginning his school year from the perspective of behavioral theory. He recognizes that he can control events in the classroom in ways that will optimize learning. Behavioral strategies in the classroom are intended to produce positive changes in the social and academic behavior of students. According to this theory, proactive classroom management involves arranging antecedents and consequences to promote positive behavior and eliminate or reduce inappropriate behavior. Many classroom teachers translate this theory into the use of rewards and sanctions in the classroom. However, appropriate use of behavioral theory requires a much broader understanding of theory and the application of its principles. Misuse of behavioral theory can be counterproductive as it may deter internal motivation and individual self-responsibility. Even without conscious application, the behavioral principles of classical conditioning, negative and positive reinforcement, and punishment may be unintentionally at work in the classroom. Understanding how these principles can shape behavior in the classroom can assist a teacher regardless of his or her philosophical perspective. Understanding of basic behavioral principles and cautious application can provide the classroom teacher with useful insights and strategies, especially when dealing with the challenges that some children bring to the classroom.

In this chapter, I describe applied behavioral techniques for managing student behavior. One part of this chapter is devoted to classical conditioning, with an emphasis on how students' feelings toward school, both positive and negative, are learned emotional responses to experiences in school. In addition, the uses and misuses of positive reinforcement, negative reinforcement, and punishment are discussed. I also compare and contrast, in summary form, the philosophical premises of behaviorism with those of social constructivism.

BEHAVIORAL PRINCIPLES

Behavioral theory views behavior as a learned response that is dependent on antecedent events and resulting consequences in the environment. In other words, behavior is viewed from a functional perspective in terms that are both measurable and observable. The origins of the behavioral model have their basis in the research of many prominent theorists who empirically derived scientific principles of learning. Each of these principles can be at work in the classroom with both positive and negative outcomes for learners.

Classical Conditioning

Mr. Clark learned that math might be particularly anxiety producing for his group of learners. To help disassociate math from negative feelings, Mr. Clark starts the year by setting the stage for fun and success with math.

Classical conditioning occurs when one neutral stimulus is paired with another stimulus that causes a physiological response that is involuntary. Soon the neutral stimulus begins to illicit the same physiological response as the one with which it is paired. The response then becomes controlled by the neutral stimulus. The famous psychologist Pavlov demonstrated this principle by conditioning dogs to salivate at the sound of a bell by pairing the bell with the presentation of raw meat. Eventually, Pavlov's dogs began to salivate when they heard the bell (the neutral stimulus). Classical conditioning isn't reserved for animals; humans respond to it as well. Advertisers often pair their product with beautiful women, fun, excitement, peacefulness, and so forth. In this way, individuals are conditioned to associate a product with a certain feeling, looking younger, having fun, relaxing, and more. Hence, classical conditioning connects feelings with environmental cues and with behaviors, and can be a form of influence in the classroom, both negative and positive.

When students are humiliated or made to feel anxious, they can be conditioned to feel anxiety and despair when faced with academic challenges. When tasks are presented as sanctions or punishment and their absence as a reward, students may become conditioned to dread school tasks. On the other hand, students can experience academic tasks and contexts that cause or encourage pleasant emotions. They can be conditioned to feel enthusiasm, excitement, or enjoyment. When academic tasks are presented as a challenge, privilege, or opportunity, then students begin to associate pleasant feelings with academic work. Consider the following examples, both positive and negative, of classical conditioning in the context of the classroom.

Negative Examples of Classical Conditioning
By pairing academic tasks with a negative association, children may be conditioned to dread assignments. For example, when his classroom or certain students in his room misbehave, Mr. Berry requires students to stay in at recess and write spelling words in sentences. The writing of spelling words in sentences is paired with the loss of recess. Consequently, students associate spelling with the bad feeling they have when they are being punished or reprimanded. The sound of the word "spelling" begins to cause dread.

Teachers can condition students to view academic work as undesirable. For example, Mrs. Little gives passes excusing students from homework or other academic tasks as a reward for good behavior. Avoidance of work is paired with reward and recognition from the teacher. Students begin to associate academic work avoidance as pleasurable.

Children who meet with ridicule or failure are conditioned to dread or avoid academic settings and tasks because of the negative feelings associated with them. Albert is ridiculed by his classmates when he reads aloud. Anthony begins to feel anxious when the teacher calls him to the reading table. Because ridicule (causing feelings of anxiousness) is paired with reading, Albert begins to dread reading.

Positive Examples of Classical Conditioning
Students can be conditioned to see academic work such as a math problem as a challenge and an exciting opportunity when the presentation is paired with enthusiasm and encouragement by the teacher. In Mr. Clark's room, he begins math with fun games in which students experience success. He is intentionally trying to break the pattern of math anxiety that the students experienced the year before. In another classroom,

Mrs. Patnic presents a math problem as a puzzle to be solved; mistakes and multiple ways of solving it are allowed. She states that students can use their recess time or lunch time to continue their work on it or talk to their friends about it if they wish. Students come to associate math with fun and challenge.

Operant Conditioning

While classical conditioning forms an association between two stimuli, operant conditioning forms an association between a behavior and a consequence, either positive or aversive. Reinforcement and punishment are at work in operant conditioning. Positive reinforcement is providing something positive to increase the likelihood that a behavior will occur again. Negative reinforcement is the removal of something aversive that increases the likelihood that a behavior will reoccur. Punishment is the presentation of something aversive or the removal of something pleasant to decrease the likelihood that a behavior will reoccur. It is important to note that behavioral theory indicates that a stimulus is defined as reinforcement or punishment based on its effect on behavior.

Positive Reinforcement

Praise, contingent attention, and rewards are three common uses of the principle of positive reinforcement. Used appropriately, they can have a good effect; however, if misused, they have unintended consequences.

Praise.   For children desiring positive teacher attention, praise can be powerful. Appropriate use of praise is discussed in Chapter 6. Despite considerable research attesting to the effectiveness of contingent praise, in their extensive review, Beaman and Wheldall (2000) found little evidence that teachers systematically use praise as positive reinforcement. Teachers tend to respond more frequently with disapproval of behaviors that they would like to decrease than with approval of appropriate behaviors. This response pattern can discourage inappropriate behavior. However, the contingent use of praise has repeatedly been shown to increase positive behavior.

While praise from teachers can be a positive reinforcer, praise from peers can also have a positive effect on behavior. Several studies document the positive effect of favorable peer reporting, a strategy that encourages peers to report the positive behavior of their peers (Moroz & Jones, 2002; Morrison & Jones, 2007; Skinner, Cashwell, & Skinner, 2000). Positive peer reporting is described in Figure 3.1.

Attention.   Contingent use of teacher attention has also been shown to have a powerful effect on student behavior (Alber & Heward, 1999; Beaman & Wheldall, 2000; Craft, Alber, & Heward, 1998). Unfortunately, students may not be discriminating customers when it comes to teacher attention. That is, attention via teacher disapproval can maintain behavior as well as teacher approval or praise. Hence, teachers who use high rates of disapproval may provide students with positive reinforcement in the form of negative attention and consequently increase student misbehavior. As mentioned earlier, stimulus

Figure 3.1   In the Classroom

Tootling

What is the opposite of tattle? Tootle! (Skinner, Cashwell, & Skinner, 2000). Also known as positive peer reporting, tootling involves teaching students to praise each other.

How it's done

- Teach students to recognize the prosocial behavior of their peers.
- Give students examples of prosocial behaviors such as lending a pencil, helping to carry books. Ask students to give examples of how they help at home and how they help at school.
- Give students an index card and ask them to watch for and report the prosocial behavior of their peers.
- Place a tootle box in the room to collect the tootles.
- Create a chart that shows the number of tootles each day.
- Set a goal (e.g., 100 tootles); when the goal has been reached, celebrate and set a new goal.
- Read the tootles aloud at the end of each day.

Advantages

- Gives students an alternative to tattling.
- Gives students recognition and praise from their peers.

For whom

- This strategy and variations of it have been used successfully with elementary-aged students and adolescents.

Evidence

- Jones, Young, & Friman (2000) used a version of tootling with adolescents and documented a decrease in inappropriate behavior of targeted students at risk for special education referral.
- Moroz and Jones (2002) used positive peer reporting to increase social involvement of elementary-school-aged children who were socially withdrawn.
- Morrison and Jones (2007) used postive reporting to reduce critical incidents of inappropriate behavior in elementary classrooms.

---

is defined by its effect on behavior. What a teachers sees as punitive (a reprimand) may be a reinforcer (attention) to the student.

On the other hand, positive attention from the teacher in terms of individual time, positive feedback, or individual assistance can improve behavior. For example, Mrs. Marshall keeps a chart of the students in her high school social studies classroom. She checks each time she attends to an individual student by giving assistance or feedback or showing concern. She refers to the chart daily to ensure that each student is receiving her attention over a week's time. Consequently, the group that tends to be unruly for other teachers is well behaved for Mrs. Marshall.

Rewards.   Rewards can also be used to modify behavior (Stage & Quiroz, 1997). Rewards such as stickers, a special activity, or tokens that are then exchanged for small prizes can be used as reinforcers. Many researchers caution about rewards and their effect on intrinsic motivation (Deci, Koestner, & Ryan, 2001). If used inappropriately, rewards can make it unlikely that students will engage in the desired behavior when the rewards are removed. Used sparingly, appropriately, and cautiously however, rewards can be used to support and encourage positive behavior (see Positive Behavior, Chapter 12) and motivate reluctant learners (see Motivation, Chapter 6). Teachers wary of using rewards due to their effect on intrinsic motivation often rely on punitive measures instead (Maag, 2001). Most experts agree that careful use of rewards is preferable to punishment.

Negative Reinforcement

Negative reinforcement is the removal of an aversive stimulus that results in an increase in a behavior. For example, the child who has a temper tantrum is given an ice cream cone and this stops the temper tantrum. The caregiver has unwittingly experienced negative reinforcement. The temper tantrum (the aversive stimulus that is removed) increases the likelihood of the caregiver giving into a child's demand for ice cream in the future. Like positive reinforcement and classical conditioning, negative reinforcement may be unintentionally at work, influencing the behavior of the student and/or the teacher in the classroom (Gunter & Coutinho, 1997; Harrison & Gunter, 1996). Consider the following examples:

> Johnny has difficulty with oral reading. When called to the reading table, his behavior becomes disruptive and unruly. The teacher sends Johnny back to his seat, where he puts his head down and remains quiet. In this example, reading (an aversive stimulus for Johnny) is removed, increasing the likelihood that he will repeat his unruly behavior at the reading table. The teacher may also be experiencing negative reinforcement—Johnny's unruly behavior (an aversive for the teacher) is stopped by sending Johnny back to his seat, increasing the likelihood that the teacher will send Johnny to his seat during reading in the future.
>
> When Mary, a high school student, uses offensive language in class, the teacher sends her to the office. Mary has effectively escaped the classroom situation and the teacher has effectively escaped the offensive language. Hence, the chances of the same scenario reoccurring are increased.

Punishment

Punishment is the presentation of an aversive stimulus that decreases the likelihood of a behavior reoccurring. Maag (2001) contends that punishment is often used in the classroom because it is easy to administer and works in the short term with many students. Teachers are often negatively reinforced for its use (a quick removal of aberrant behavior). However, most professionals agree that punishment is a short-term solution that brings many undesirable side effects (see Chapter 11).

Antecedents

Kern, Choutka, and Sokol (2002) describe how antecedents can influence behavior in the classroom. Antecedents are events or stimuli that occur before a behavior. One type of antecedent is a discriminative stimulus, or an event that signals a particular behavior to occur. In Mr. Clark's classroom, described at the beginning of the chapter, two friends sitting next to each other may have been the discriminative stimulus for the two to begin talking with each other instead of completing their work. By changing the seating arrangement, Mr. Clark has removed the discriminative stimulus for talking.

Another type of antecedent event is an establishing operation or an event or activity that occurs that may trigger a particular response. For example, skipping breakfast may be an operating event that causes a student who typically stays on task to be unable to complete an assignment. Ensuring that the child has something to eat each morning will improve his or her attention to task. Teachers can recognize how antecedents can influence behavior and use them to their advantage (Kern et al., 2002). For example, Allday and Pakurar (2007) describe a study in which antecedents were changed for three students identified for a study of off-task behavior. In each classroom, the students' on-task behavior during the first 10 minutes of class increased when teachers greeted the students as they entered the classroom. The authors note the simplicity of an intervention that merely engages teachers in positive interactions prior to the beginning of class.

COGNITIVE BEHAVIOR MODIFICATION

Classical and operant conditioning focus on observable behaviors and environmental events and tend to ignore the thinking or cognitive aspect of behavior—an unobservable process. In more recent years, behavioral theory has evolved to include the role of cognition. Cognitive approaches to altering behavior include cognitive behavior modification (CBM) strategies first introduced by Meichenbaum (1977). Many researchers contend that typical operant and classical conditioning strategies do not have as lasting an effect as cognitive approaches that emphasize self-control (Robinson, Smith, Miller, & Bronwell, 1991). Self-instruction and self-monitoring are two CBM procedures that have been effective in altering behavior in the classroom, especially for students who are hyperactive, impulsive, and aggressive (Robinson et al., 1999; Swaggart, 1998). Such procedures have been used successfully in general education classrooms with adolescents (Freeman & Dexter-Mazza, 2004; Hughes et al., 2002) and elementary-school-aged children (Levondeski & Cartledge, 2000).

Self-Monitoring

In self-monitoring, students are given a simple recording sheet on which to record the presence or absence of certain behaviors. For example, Crum (2004) provided a third grader with a chart with instructions to, when prompted by the teacher, record a "+" in a square if he was working or studying or a "0" if he was off task and not working. This student increased his on-task behavior considerably and was eventually engaged in setting his own goals for his behavioral improvements.

Self-Instruction

In self-instruction, students are taught to quietly verbalize the steps necessary to complete particular social or academic tasks (Swaggart, 1998). To use self-instruction appropriately, a teacher models thinking aloud the steps to the problem, has the student repeat the steps, rehearse the steps, and apply the steps, in context. In a meta-analysis of studies, Robinson et al. (1991) indicate that CBM that uses self-instruction can be used successfully in the classrooms to improve behavior.

TOOLS FOR THE CLASSROOM

Mr. Clark uses the principles of behavioral theory as a tool in his classroom to create a high level of on-task behavior and a positive classroom climate, and to promote appropriate behavior. As mentioned, knowledge of the principles of behavioral theory can assist teachers in arranging classroom conditions to be conducive to learning and the development of social skills. Tools that stem from behavioral theory are functional assessment and positive behavior support. Functional assessment involves determining the function or purpose of a behavior for students (e.g., avoiding work or gaining stimulation). Functional assessment assists a classroom teacher in demystifying the behavior of individual children who present classroom challenges despite a teacher's best efforts. Information from a functional assessment can be used to develop a positive behavior support plan. Positive behavior support involves changing antecedents and consequences to promote appropriate behavior. Considering functional assessment and positive behavior support from a behaviorist perspective, as well as a constructivist perspective, can assist the teacher in addressing the most disconcerting classroom behaviors. Functional assessment and positive behavior support are considered from an integrated perspective in Chapter 12.

APPLICATION OF BEHAVIORAL THEORY IN THE CLASSROOM

Many traditional classroom management practices come from a behaviorist perspective. However, without appropriate application of behaviorist principles, they fail in helping students learn prosocial behavior. For example, many classrooms use a system in which rules are posted and punishments are put in place for students who break the rules (Henington & Skinner, 1998). While these types of systems work for some students, when teachers rely on a set system of rules and consequences, they may neglect considering the classroom practices that may contribute to inappropriate behavior. They may fail to look at variables such as the appropriate level and relevance of assignments, appropriateness of classroom materials, classroom arrangement, and also forth. Skinner, Cashwell, and Skinner (2000) identify two other limitations of such approaches. First, some students, although they still engage in inappropriate behavior, become very adept at avoiding punishment by engaging in inappropriate behavior when the teacher isn't looking. When the behavior goes unnoticed by an adult, peers are put in the tenuous situation of being tattlers and adults are put in the position of having to judge whether tattlers are accurate. In

Table 3.1   Research-Based Practices that Support the Circle of Courage

	PRACTICE	DESCRIPTION	EVIDENCE	HOW IT PROMOTES
Belonging	Praise, teacher attention	Teachers give students positive attention and praise contingent on appropriate student behavior.	Allday and Pakurar (2007)	Promotes a positive student–teacher relationship
Independence	Self-monitoring	A behavior is identified and during regular intervals, a student marks a chart indicating whether or not he or she has engaged in the behavior.	Patton, Jolivette, & Ramsey (2006)	Students are taught to monitor their own specific behaviors
Competence	Peer tutoring, peer-assisted learning	Students take reciprocal roles in tutoring each other.	McMaster, Fuchs, & Fuchs (2007)	Students engage in the practice of academic skills with feedback
Generosity	Positive peer reporting	Students are taught to recognize and praise incidents of prosocial behavior by their peers	Morrison and Jones (2007)	Students help their peers learn prosocial behaviors

addition, the tattlers can become the victims of the perpetrator's revenge for tattling, which then perpetuates bullying behavior. Second, appropriate behavior often goes unnoticed and unrecognized. Even though teachers are trained to "catch students being good," their energy is often spent on the more punitive aspects of the system. Hence, students learn that appropriate behavior isn't valued. Despite the popularity of the above-mentioned system, many positively based behaviorist practices exist. While the primary emphasis of this book is a constructivist approach to classroom management, many behaviorist practices can promote belonging, competence, independence, and generosity and are supported by empirical research. Table 3.1 provides examples of these practices.

BEHAVIORIST VERSUS CONSTRUCTIVIST

Teachers must recognize the contributions from multiple theoretical perspectives. While many of the foundations of the behaviorist perspective oppose those of the constructivist, the wise teacher can find some points in common. For example, both behavioral theory and constructivist theory recognize the positive interactions of teacher and student as key to encouraging appropriate behavior. The behaviorist view encourages praise and attention contingent on appropriate behavior, while the constructivists see good listening and communication and taking the learner perspective as key to building relationships.

In addition to points of agreement, there are points of departure as well. The behaviorists view the teacher as the mediator of the environment. Through manipulation of antecedent events and contingent reinforcement, the teacher controls behavior. From a constructivist view, learners are regarded as proactive and self-regulating rather than as reactive and controlled by events that shape behavior. The self-beliefs of learners, such as self-efficacy beliefs, are critical; they allow learners some control over their thoughts, feelings, and actions (Pajares, 2003). The constructivist view of the classroom is child centered, with a focus is on the development of the capacity of learners to become self-disciplined, as well as supportive of the learning community.

From the behaviorist perspective, peers may be an important part of mediating reinforcement, but are not primarily seen as problem solvers. From the constructivist view, children learn to collaborate with each other, as well as with the teacher, to learn prosocial behaviors, to create an atmosphere conducive to learning, and to solve problems as they arise. From the behaviorist perspective, rewards can be useful in shaping behavior. The constructivist teacher is wary of rewards and punishments that "bribe" children to behave appropriately.

How does a teacher reconcile the differences or choose among the philosophies? Careful reflection regarding desired goals and outcomes and the approach or combination of approaches can help (discussed in Chapter 12). Regardless, the foundations of each perspective deserve careful consideration. For example, positive behavior support is grounded in behavioral theory, but can easily be applied through an integrated perspective that considers the need for belonging, mastery, generosity, and independence.

SUMMARY

Behavioral theory can inform classroom teachers in many ways. Operant and classical conditioning can be at work, both intentionally and unintentionally, to influence behavior and the way that children and adolescents feel about school. Awareness of these principles of learning are necessary for understanding classroom dynamics. In addition to the principles of learning, positive behavior support is a useful tool that is grounded in the behaviorist tradition. This tool can be used from multiple perspectives to understand difficult and challenging behavior and can aid teachers in finding ways to support all students in the classroom.

REFERENCES

Alber, S. R., & Heward, W. L. (1999). Teaching middle school students with learning disabilities to recruit positive teacher attention. *Exceptional Children, 65*(20), 253–258.

Allday, R. A., & Pakurar, K. (2007). Effects of teacher greetings on student on-task behavior. *Journal of Applied Behavior Analysis, 40*(2), 317–320.

Beaman, R., & Wheldall, K. (2000). Teacher's use of approval and disapproval in the classroom. *Educational Psychology, 20*(4), 431–447.

Craft, M. A., Alber, S., & Heward, W. (1998). Teaching elementary students with developmental disabilities to recruit teacher attention in a general education classroom: Effects on teacher praise and academic productivity. *Journal of Applied Behavior Analysis, 31*(3), 399–415.

Crum, C. (2004). Using a cognitive-behavioral modification strategy to increase on-task behavior of a student with a behavior disorder. *Intervention in School and Clinic, 39*(5), 305–309.

Deci, E. L., Koestner, R., & Ryan, R. M. (2001). Extrinsic rewards and intrinsic motivation in education: Reconsidered once again. *Review of Educational Research, 71*, 1–27.

Freeeman, K. A., & Dexter-Mazza, E. T. (2004). Using self-monitoring with adolescent disruptive classroom behavior. *Behavior Modification, 28*(3), 402–420.

Gunter, P. L., & Coutinho, M. J. (1997). Negative reinforcement in classrooms: What we're beginning to learn. *Teacher Education and Special Education, 20*(3), 249–264.

Harrison, J. S., & Gunter, P. L. (1996). Teacher instructional language and negative reinforcement: A conceptual framework for working with students with emotional and behavioral disorders. *Education and Treatment of Children, 19*(2), 183–197.

Henington, C., & Skinner, C. H. (1998). Peer-monitoring. In K. Topping & S. Ehly (Eds.), *Peer-assisted instruction* (pp. 237–253). Hillsdale, NJ: Erlbaum.

Hughes, L., Copeland, S. R., Agran, M., Wehmeyes, M. L., Rodi, M., & Presley, J. A. (2002). Using self-monitoring to improve performance in general high school classes. *Education and Training in Mental Retardation and Developmental Disabilities, 37*(3), 262–271.

Jones, K. M., Young, M. M., & Friman, P. C. (2000). Increasing peer praise of socially rejected delinquent youth: Effects on cooperation and acceptance. *School Psychology Quarterly, 15*(1), 30–39.

Kern, L., Choutka, C. M., & Sokol, N. G. (2002). Assessment-based interventions used in natural settings to reduce challenging behavior: An analysis of the literature. *Education and Treatment of Children, 25*(1), 113–132.

Larson, P. J., & Maag, J. A. (1998). Applying functional assessment in general education classrooms: Issues and recommendations. *Remedial and Special Education, 19*(6), 338–350.

Levondeski, L. S., & Cartledge, G. (2000). Self-monitoring for elementary school children with serious emotional disturbances: Classroom application for increased academic responding. *Behavioral Disorders, 25*, 211–224.

Maag, J. (2001). Rewarded by punishment: Reflections on the disuse of positive reinforcement in schools. *Exceptional Children, 67*(2), 173–186.

McMaster, K. L., Fuchs, D., & Fuchs, L. S. (2007). Research on peer-assisted learning strategies: Promises and limitations of peer-mediated instruction. *Reading and Writing Quarterly, 22*(1), 5–25.

Meichenbaum, D. H. (1977). *Cognitive-behavior modification: An integrative approach.* New York: Plenum Press.

Moroz, K. B., & Jones, K. M. (2002). The effects of positive peer reporting on children's social involvement. *School Psychology Review, 31*(2), 235–245.

Morrison, J. Q., & Jones, K. M. (2007). The effects of positive peer reporting as a class-wide positive behavior support. *Journal of Behavioral Education, 16*(2), 111–124.

Pajares, F. (2003). Self-efficacy beliefs, motivation, and achievement in writing: A review of the literature. *Reading and Writing Quarterly, 19*(2), 139–158.

Patton, B., Jolivette, K., & Ramsey, M. (2006). Students with emotional and behavioral disorders can manage their own behavior. *Teaching Exceptional Children, 39*(2), 14–21.

Robinson, T. R., Smith, S. W., Miller, M. D., & Bronwell, M. T. (1999). Cognitive behavior modification of hyperactivity—Impulsivity and aggression: A meta-analysis of school based studies. *Journal of Educational Psychology, 91*(2), 195–202.

Ruef, M. B. (1998). Positive behavioral support: Strategies for teachers. *Intervention in School and Clinic, 34*(1), 12–21.

Skinner, C. H., Cashwell, T. H., & Skinner, A. L. (2000). Increasing tootling: The effects of a peer-monitored group contingency program on students' reports of peers' prosocial behaviors. *Psychology in the Schools, 37*(3), 263–271.

Stage, S. A., & Quiroz, D. R. (1997). A meta-analysis of interventions to decrease disruptive classroom behavior in public education settings. *School Psychology Review, 26*(3), 333–369.

Swaggart, B. L. (1998). Implementing a cognitive behavior management program. *Intervention in School and Clinic, 33*(4), 235–239.

Acquiring multiple Perspectives

STUDENT PERSPECTIVES

4

We all suffer from misconceptions and stereotypes and risk wallowing in them unless we remain vigilant. It is necessary both to respect the conceptions that students of all ages bring to the schools and to be aware of our own predilections toward strongly held but unfounded beliefs . . . . We must place ourselves inside the heads of our students and try to understand as far as possible the sources and strengths of their conceptions. (Gardner, 1991, pp. 252–253)

Learners may experience schools in ways that the professionals who structure their experiences may overlook, undervalue, or fail to understand. Suggestions from practitioners, administrators, and higher education for school reform, classroom management, and character development abound in professional literature. Only recently have the voices of students been sought to inform classroom and school practices. In this chapter, the benefits of seeking student voice, examples of how students can inform management practices, and guidelines for seeking student voice are presented. Wise teachers take seriously the advice of Gardner (1991) and attempt to "place ourselves inside the heads of our students and try to understand as far as possible the sources and strengths of their conceptions" (p. 253).

BENEFITS OF LISTENING TO STUDENTS

The school curriculum, the classroom, the teacher, school environments, and the broader culture and community form the perceptions of students regarding their school experiences. Because of the uniqueness of circumstances in each classroom, each student and each group of students experience school in different ways. Furthermore, students' perspectives and teachers' perspectives of the classroom experience can differ (Allen, 1995; Farrell, Peguero, Lindsey, & White, 1988). Programs, practices, and curricula thoughtfully designed to be helpful may not be perceived as such by students and hence often are not successful. Gaining the student perspective brings numerous benefits, including enhancing belonging and commitment to classroom goals, preparing students for participation in a democratic society, enhancing dignity and respect, and providing insight into the quality of the educational experience of students.

Place attachment refers to the notion that individuals associate meaning and significance to places and that their actions reflect their affiliation and bonding with places (Swaminathan, 2004). Place literature suggests that the environment is cognitively mediated. That is, an individual's experience of place that does not engender positive feelings leads the individual to engage in activities that make a place more inviting or relevant. For example, children who do not feel connected to a school or classroom may attempt to form an identity or connection in the classroom by marking their names on the desks or walls or other vandalous actions designed to mark their spot (Langhout, 2004). According to Swaminathan (2004), "If we are to facilitate students in finding an affinity to school, the concept of attachment needs to be moved towards place identity. It needs to keep student perspectives central, and find ways to empower and facilitate students in their search for their 'place.' It is important to find out what it is about schools that students value as providing that 'homeplace'" (p. 39). Hence, understanding and gaining the student perspective allows us to understand how learners mediate the environment to create positive feelings. It gives an understanding of the kind of place that students want school to be for them.

In addition to enhancing belonging, listening to and honoring their voices empowers students and prepares students for active participation in a democratic society. As noted by Allen (1995), this empowerment moves students from seeing school as something done to them to having the right, ability, and responsibility to participate in decisions that affect their lives. Engaging students in dialogue about their school and ways to improve it can get students to take their own education more seriously (Noguera, 2007). Students can be collaborators in school and classroom reform efforts.

Furthermore, student voice is one vehicle for determining if school improvement plans, curricular decisions, and classroom management designs are having the desired effect. As Wilson and Corbett (2001) demonstrate in their qualitative study of urban schools, if true school reform occurs, the things that children say about school change, as do other measures. Learners' perceptions of school and classroom climate, teacher–student relationships, classroom practices, and so forth can provide important information for teacher and schoolwide reflection and action.

Finally, attending to the voices of students enhances the student–teacher relationship. Hutchinson (1999) describes the power of listening to students' stories in preventing marginalization of children, enhancing dignity, and understanding the sense that children are making of their lives. Gaining student perspective through their "stories" of their experiences allows the teacher to relate to each student as a unique individual and affirms for children that their lives are important, meaningful, and worthy of attention.

WHAT STUDENTS SAY ABOUT SCHOOL

The four spirits of the Circle of Courage can provide a framework for exploring how students experience school. Research that has sought to gain the perspective of students can inform how students experience belonging, competence, independence, and generosity, as well as informing the students' suggestions for encouraging these areas. Although treated here as discrete topics, each area is interrelated and intertwined. From the students' perspective, each area affects the other and they are hard to distinguish from one another.

Belonging

What do students say that helps them feel a sense of attachment and connection to school? Students talk about physical space, relationships with teachers, and opportunities for social interaction.

Physical Space

The physical space of the classroom may have an effect on student behavior and achievement (Sanoff, 2001; Uline, 2000; Ulrich, 2004). Classroom density, seating arrangements, physical arrangements, and décor affect the atmosphere and conditions for learning. For example, a high classroom density—low ratio of space to number of students—can adversely affect both achievement and behavior (Uline, 2000). In addition, students respond more positively to "soft classrooms" or classrooms that are flexible and responsive with warm colors, soft furniture, and soft flooring as opposed to hard environments that do not allow for human imprint. Sommer and Olsen (1980) discovered that students participated more in class discussions when they were in "soft" rooms and rated their classrooms significantly higher when soft features were added.

In studies by Swaminathan (2004), Langhout (2004), and Maxwell (2000), students identified characteristics of spaces they liked and those they did not. Students like physical spaces that are clean and organized, and where they have space to be creative. They prefer spaces that are open, inviting, and uncrowded. In addition to cleanliness, orderliness, and spaciousness, children and adolescents like to have a place within the school or classroom to call their own, a place that is a sanctuary where they can work, think, and keep their belongings safe. Having a space to call one's own that is marked personally through displays of a student's work or through something that identifies the student contributes to "place identity."

In contrast, students dislike spaces that are crowded, chaotic, and unclean. In referring to spaces they disliked, students made comments like "Most of the time the tables and benches, they aren't clean at all, there's stuff all over them" and "It's messy—the floors, the desks . . . The teacher's desk is junky too" (Langhout, 2004, p. 120). Some adolescents contend that school has "few places where you can be by yourself," making it difficult to "concentrate on what you are doing" (Sanoff, 2001).

Relationships with Teachers
Positive connections with adults at school encourage belonging. In most, if not all studies of student perspectives, including those of students from differing cultural and ethnic backgrounds, students identify positive relationships with teachers as key to positive
school experiences (Allen, 1995; Bloom & Habel, 1998; Certo, Cauley, & Chafin, 2003;
Fránquiz & del Carmen, 2004; Freed & Smith, 2004; Habel, Bloom, Ray, & Bacon, 1999;
Howard, 2002; Nieto, 1994; Swaminathan, 2004; Pomeroy, 1999; Wilson & Corbett,
2001). In the same studies, students also make reference to teachers who don't care,
have negative dispositions, and seem to dislike their charges. Students have much to say
about the type of teachers they want and don't want. When students talk about positive
experiences with teachers, they focus on relationships with teachers and administrators
that are characterized by care, trust, personal regard, affection, and fairness. Students
also identify fairness and a willingness to push students as desirable teacher characteristics that help students connect to school.

Teachers Who Care.   One defining feature of a good student–teacher relationship
that enables teachers to communicate caring is dialogue. Students in many studies refer
to teachers who took time to listen to and understand the students' perspective, who
knew them, and who would talk to and explain things to them. As one student said, "I
like someone who puts themselves into our shoes" (Wilson & Corbett, 2001, p. 87). Another said about caring teachers, "The teachers really listen to you when you have problems" (Allen, 1995, p. 290). In fact, listening is often identified as a sign that teachers
care, and students can tell when a teacher listens. As one student said, "You can tell
when they [teachers] listen when they ask you questions back and that gives you a hint
that they're listening" (Habel et al., 1999, p. 97).

Students talk about teachers who show regard for students' success and well-being.
"They show it. You might see them in the hallway, and they ask you how you're doing. How
was your last report card? Is there anything you need? Or, maybe one day you're looking a
little upset. They'll pull you to the side and ask you what's wrong. Is there anything I can
do? They just show a real concern for us students" (Certo et al., 2003, p. 715).

In interviews by Nieto (1994), students talked about caring teachers who used their
student's lives and experiences in their teaching: "[Most teachers] are really caring and
supportive and are willing to share their lives and are willing to listen to mine. They
don't just want to talk about what they're teaching you; they also want to know you."
(p. 407)

Teachers Who Don't Care.   In an analysis of factors that cause schools to be
sources of stress for students, Elias (1989) identified disconnectedness from significant
others as a primary factor. This disconnectedness can be prevalent because some school
personnel tend to take the position that stress is person centered—a problem of the
child who is experiencing stress. The school makes available palliatives in the form of
guidance and counseling, and special education services are available, but nevertheless,
according to Elias, it places the onus squarely on the child to shape up and manage the
stress. Teachers in such schools fail to listen to and show concern for student needs. In

some studies, students speak of the disconnectedness they experience at school when they describe teachers who fail to listen to them and appear uncaring. For example, in a study by Habel et al., (1999), when asked, "Is there a time when you thought a teacher or an administrator did listen to you?" students' responses included the following:

"Not anybody here."

"If they [teachers] agree, they listen to you."

And when you try to tell them, they say, "No, I don't want to hear it." That's the way . . . [a teacher] was this morning. I was in there and I wasn't arguing with the teacher or nothing. I was just telling her I didn't understand what she was saying. And I asked if she could explain and she said, "Just write him up and send him to the office and don't worry about it." Makes me so mad I can't see straight. (p. 98)

Examples of comments from students in other studies include

"She never comes in with a smile, she is always evil." (Wilson & Corbett, 2001, p. 55)

"He doesn't care. All he does is give us worksheets and we sit at our desk." (Certo et al., 2003, p. 725)

Teachers who disregard culture or fail to make curricula relevant to student culture are also perceived as uncaring. As one student noted,

I used to have a lot of problems with one of my teachers 'cause she didn't want us to talk Spanish in class and I thought that was like an insult to us, you know? Just telling us not to talk Spanish, 'cause they were Puerto Ricans and, you know, we're free to talk whatever we want . . . I could never stay quiet and talk only English, 'cause sometimes . . . words slip in Spanish. You know, I think they should understand that. (Nieto, 1994, pp. 399–400)

In one word, school was boring: Boring, boring, boring. Nothing year after year. The only Black people I ever heard about were Rosa Parks and Martin Luther King. Also, nothing they taught had anything to do with life. I saw it as being irrelevant. I felt no one was listening to what *I* wanted to know about. (Swaminathan, 2004, pp. 45–46).

In a study by Nieto (1994), when asked what the school could do to help Puerto Ricans stay in school, a student said, "Hacer algo para que los boricuos no se sientan aparte (Do something so that the Puerto Ricans wouldn't feel so separate)" (p. 411).

Justice

In addition to caring relationships with teachers, when learners make reference to schools, teachers, and classrooms they dislike, they include instances of abuse of power and injustice on the part of the teacher (Allen, 1995; Habel et al., 1999; Langhout, 2004; Wilson & Corbett, 2001). Examples from interviews of students include

"Like kids talk, and if one talks, he blame the whole class. He screams at us. He threw a desk." (Wilson & Corbett, 2001, p. 76)

"No teacher is fair." (Habel et al., 1999, p. 98)

"She makes us stand in the corner on one leg. I don't like the atmosphere when people are being punished." (Langhout, 2004, p. 120)

In several studies, students report unfair treatment of students of different ethnic groups (Freed & Smith, 2004; Howard, 2002; Langhout, 2004; Miron & Lauria, 1998; Phelan, Davidson, & Yu" 1994). For example, students interviewed in a study by Langhout (2004) reported unfair treatment of students, especially African Americans. In referring to a detention room, one student said that he sees "mostly black [kids here]" and when asked if it is just the Black kids that act up? The student responds, "No, they're the ones who get into trouble." (p. 121)

Relationships with Peers

In addition to the student–teacher relationship, peer relationships influence a student's sense of belonging in school. Having friends at school is positively related to achievement and prosocial behavior (Wentzel, Barry, & Caldwell, 2004). From the students' perspective, school is as much about time with friends as it is about learning. In studies of student perspectives, students discuss the importance of their relationships with peers and time for socializing with regard to a sense of belonging, as well as the social alienation felt by some and the existence of cliques and clans.

Many students feel that time for socialization in school is scarce. Students in the report from Bloom and Habel (1999) expressed comments such as

"During school, you don't do nothing except sit in desks most of the day, and go to lunch; then, if you talk to one of your friends in class, you've had it. You get to go see [the principal]." (p. 100)

"I wish we had more social time." (p. 100)

"There could be more activities during the day instead of at night whenever they play sports . . . All we do is sit in desks most of the day." (p. 100)

Many students express the idea that opportunities for socialization are what they like best about school. In Certo et al.'s (2003) study, students report, "I like to come to school, the social part of meeting with my friends everyday." (p. 716) "I get to see everyone because, you know, in the summertime I don't see everyone but I'd like to, and being at school you're kind of all here together and you can see everybody and that's nice. You know, I enjoy most of my classes and it's kind of fun, you know, it's usually just the student body that really keeps me coming". (p. 716)

Students acknowledge the existence of cliques and clans. Excerpts from Bloom and Habel (1998) include

[T]he school wants us to everybody be together, right? That's not gonna work. I mean, it would be nice if it would work. But not everybody agrees on the same things. Pretty much, the people that stand there on the crosswalks pretty much agrees on the same things. We do not like the way other groups treat other groups. But we, speaking of the

rednecks, we sit down there and we talk and we have a good ol' time, and the administration or the principals and everything try to get us to go back up there where everybody else is standing. We don't like to go up there because we are constantly made fun
of. They try to get our tempers flared up. They know we are short-fused. And then when
they do get our tempers flared up and there is a fight or something, we get all the blame,
every single square inch of the blame. (p. 101)

The hippies are in a clan . . . the rednecks are in a clan . . . the preps, they're just all over.
(p. 101)

In this school, we got gangs. Really bad. There's the Crips—so stupid—and the forgotten
cowboys. I think the gangs are stupid. People come from big cities where there's gangs
all around . . . and they try to bring it here. They want to be macho like them people up
there. (p. 101)

I understand that everybody doesn't get along with everybody and they feel better with
people that they do get along with, like their own group of friends. So I understand that's
how it is. (Certo et al., 2003, p. 715)

Some students feel a sense of isolation. Those that experience isolation and get
picked on tend to not be a part of any group.

There are a lot of people that get picked on . . . and they might make it a whole lot worse
in the future for everyone. (Certo et al., 2003, p. 716)

Because, like popularity for me has always been a problem. I used to not fit in that well.
I've a little bit more friends now, but it's kind of like, some of the groups. They don't accept you. Like, they remember you as like some child that was like not the prettiest little thing, or popular. (Certo et al., 2003, p. 718)

When they close it . . . what's there to belong to? (Habel et al., 1999, p. 97)

While there would be no specific recipe for enhancing belonging from the student
perspective, studies that have sought the student perspective identify aspects of teacher
characteristics and school practices that are perceived as enhancing belonging. Attending to physical space, caring for students, treating students fairly, and providing opportunities for positive relationships with peers are all important to students.

Mastery

Of course, the student perspective regarding experiences with mastery are varied and
complex. For many successful school students, a sense of competence is a natural outcome
of school; for some students, mastery is not a given; and for some students, lack of challenge is a source of discouragement. Research indicates that a perception of competence
is essential to engagement and motivation. In a study of third and fourth graders who
had above-average achievement, Miserandino (1996) found a great disparity in how

children perceive their own ability. Children who felt competent also said that they felt more curious and participated more in school tasks, enjoyed school tasks more, and persisted longer. On the other hand, children who were uncertain or felt less competent lost interest in school; didn't take part in as many activities; felt angry, anxious, and bored; and their school performance declined. Regardless, students have ideas about what teachers can do to enhance learning in the classroom.

Student Perception of Competence
Habel et al. (1999) report from students who feel less than competent in school. The following are excerpts from their interviews.

> When the teacher goes and tells me to do an assignment, like answer some questions, it's hard to go and find questions and answers. Everybody else is okay, but it takes me all the class time to answer one question. I have to go back and read the chapter over and over. (p. 98)

> I try my damnedest to make good grades, and I end up with C's and D's and I'm busting my ass. Some people don't even try, they don't get their homework in, don't do anything, hardly anything, and they don't turn homework in, and then they make a 100 on the quiz and then they get an A for the year. And here I am, stuck with a C or D. (p. 99)

> The day comes when I'll be successful, I'll be dead in my grave.

> I'm going to be walking down the road in about 20 years. I'm going to say "Hi," [the student referring to himself by name], and I'm not going to recognize him. He will be a drunk sitting on the side of the road. (p. 99)

When a feeling of competence is absent, students may appear failure oriented and unmotivated (Brendtro et al., 1990). Students say,

> I'm waiting till I'm 16 and I'm outta here. (Habel et al., 1999, p. 99)

> I can't pass all of my classes . . . . No, but I'm almost out of here. I've got 3 months left here, and in another 3 months, I'm out of here. (Habel et al., 1999, p. 99)

> Giving all these teachers paychecks. That's all we're here for. (Habel et al., 1999, p. 99)

> I worked good all the way up to fifth grade. Then I moved on to sixth grade. I didn't get work done. I had conflicts with school counselors, teachers, and the principle [sic], which resulted in me failing the sixth grade. [This forced me] to be in the same grade as my little brother. From the sixth grade up to the ninth grade, the years have been horrible in my life. (Freed & Smith, 2004, p. 26)

Encouraging Competence
An overwhelming theme in the literature with regard to what students see as encouraging competence is help from the teacher. Students cite positive examples of teachers

who help, as well as examples of teachers who do not. Student comments about getting help from teachers include

> A good teacher takes time out to see if all the kids have what they're talking about . . . and cares about how they're doing and will see if they need help. (Wilson & Corbett, 2001, p. 81)

> When you ask for help and you get it. Or whenever a teacher sees that you need help and you don't have it and she helps you without asking. That can be helpful. (Habel et al., 1999, p. 100)

Students often identify unhelpful teachers as well:

> In one class, my teacher has a bad attitude. He takes out his anger on you. He barely teaches. All we do is read books. If we don't know something, all he says is just "figure it out yourself." In my other class, we learn how to do letters. She wants to teach us what we don't know. If you raise your hand, she will explain it to us and show us how to do it. Some teachers just teach more. (Wilson & Corbett, 2001, p. 38)

> At times, she just say, "Don't bother me: I've told you once. Ask your classmates for help." She says to call your "study buddy." She don't like to help or care for some people. She only cares about nice, quiet people who do all their work. (Wilson & Corbett, 2001, p. 56)

> There's nobody that's going to help me. Calculus, no. And the teachers, they don't even care what kind of grade you get. They don't want to help you if you ask for it. (Certo et al., 2003, p. 715)

> I wasn't getting the help I needed from the teachers only because the classes were to [sic] full so they ran out of time to help me. I'm not saying this to make longer school hours, but we need more teachers so everyone can get help when they need it. (Freed & Smith, 2004, p. 25)

From the students' perspective, pushing and challenging on the part of the teacher is a characteristic of caring and is helpful for success.

> One of my teachers really push kids to do work. She is the most caring teacher. She really wants you to do the work. Sometimes that make me mad but I still try to do the work. It nice to know you got a teacher who cares. (Wilson & Corbett, 2001, p. 89)

> It's kinda like they're saying that you're not smart enough to do it, so they'll just go ahead and do it for you. . . . I'm not the smartest kid on earth by far, but I still know that when a teacher sits down with me and helps me do it instead of doing it for me, I know they really care about me learning it. But when a teacher sits down and does it for me, that just tells me they just want me out, to pretty much get out of their class. (Habel et al., 1999, p. 100)

> When they push me, it makes think I can do the work: I'm glad they're trying to teach me instead of ignoring me, thinking I can't do it. (Wilson & Corbett, 2001, p. 90)

In addition to perceiving pushing as a positive teacher behavior, students also desire challenge and dread the boredom that school can present.

> Boredom in school is just sitting there when the teacher is babbling, listening to lectures . . . I'm being bored sitting there twiddling my thumbs, being class clown, figuring out ways to stump the teacher . . . It's agitating; it's frustrating to be bored . . . (Kanevsky & Keighley, 2003, p. 25)

> The only thing you do at school is memorize. That's all they expect you to do. They don't understand. They just want you to remember that $2 + 2 = 4$ and not tell you why. We're never asked, we were never questioned, never inspired to ask why does this work? It was just, you know, do the work, hand it in. I'll make it. You'll get a grade, that was it. (Kanevsky & Keighley, 2003, p. 26)

Perhaps even more important than helping and challenging, students make numerous references to teachers who are good teachers because they break things down, put things in their own words, and use a variety of teaching strategies, such as hands-on and project-based learning, and fun games like learning activities.

> Just make it fun. Just make learning fun and all. I just like to come to school because my friends are there. . . . I just would like it, to make it fun . . . like that school that did the drawing . . . on the football field of the whole United States and . . . your teacher would say, "Oh, Michigan" and you'd run to Michigan and whoever didn't get there loses and gets out. Like this game that [a teacher] showed us that I like to play a lot now is that you pull down the map of the United States and . . . one person calls out a state and . . . whoever points to that state first wins. (Habel et al., 1999, p. 99)

> Doing things with my hands. Depends on experience with being able to hear it, see it, touch it. You know you can learn something a good deal by reading books. But not all learning comes from reading. You've got to have experience. (Habel et al., 1999, p. 99)

> I prefer projects, doing group projects because they are more fun; and working in a group, you have more people to help you. (Wilson & Corbett, 2001, p. 85)

> My favorite subject is math 'cause she made our work into games and I caught on real fast doing it that way. (Wilson & Corbett, 2001, p. 85)

> All the first teacher did was write on the board and make us copy. Now my favorite teacher is teacher #4-B. That teacher can do more things with us, like experiments. We did starfish, looked through a microscope, cut open a pig's eye, and the teacher already ordered the frogs. (Wilson & Corbett, 2001, p. 85)

> Everybody like the new teacher. The ol' teacher never did experiments. The new teacher don't yell. She just look at you and everybody be quiet 'cause they wanna do it. She brought in mice, a snake, a pig. (Wilson & Corbett, 2001, p. 86)

> What is your definition of a good teacher? Someone who knows how to break down explanations. Teachers who understand when kids have questions. (Wilson & Corbett, 2001, p. 60)

I learn better with experiments 'cause we really learn stuff. Copying from the board is doing what somebody else already did. (Wilson & Corbett, 2001, p. 60)

The teachers are real at ease. They take their time, you know, go step-by-step. We learn it more. It seems like they got the time to explain it all. We don't have to leave anyone behind. (Wilson & Corbett, 2001, p. 82)

Students also make reference to strategies they find not helpful.

Teachers could encourage you more . . . . They could say, "Good job!" and instead of saying, "You better do this now," they get to say, "Take your time and think about it hard." (Habel et al., 1999, p. 99)

He don't teach us in his own words. I don't understand. He teach us out of the math book. Whatever he says, he says from the book and if it is easy, he make it complicated. (Wilson & Corbett, 2001, p. 38)

With regard to mastery, students are able to identify teaching styles that they perceive as most helpful. According to students, teachers who help and persist until students learn; teachers who are encouraging, challenging, and hold high expectations; and teachers who use a variety of teaching strategies are most likely to encourage mastery.

Independence

With regard to independence, students want choices and to be treated respectfully as responsible learners. In both elementary and high school students, perceptions of autonomy support are positively related to grades, strategy use, and adaptive student motivation (Greene, Miller, Crowson, Duke, & Akey, 2004). Again, as with positive student–teacher relationships, the desire for autonomy through choices and responsibility appears as a theme in many of the studies of student perspectives (Allen, 1995; Bloom & Habel, 1998; Habel, Bloom, Ray, & Bacon, 1999; Howard, 2002; Kanevsky & Keighley, 2003; Langhout, 2004; Wilson & Corbett, 2001).

Choice
Students express a desire for choice. Representative excerpts from student interviews include

We get to pick out [reading] what we want. Its pretty cool 'cause we don't get bored so soon. (Habel et al., 1999, p. 12)

I had one [teacher] in Florida. I made real good grades in his class and I really tried and all that. He's a funny teacher. 'Cause we decided what we wanted to do that time. If we just wanted to have snacks, or if we wanted to go outside or. . . . Maybe it was because he was the only teacher to give us a choice. (Habel et al., 1999, p. 102)

Why are they [his grades] so poor if I'm so smart? . . . Because in high school, it's not like it's your opinion, you have to write what the teachers tell you to write and I really don't want to . . . I've been told [that] to pass through high school you have to jump through hoops and I don't want to. I want to make my own hoops. (Kanevsky & Keighley, 2003, p. 24)

Responsibility

In addition to choices, students want to be treated as responsible learners, capable of making decisions and learning from mistakes. They express a clear need for being treated with respect. The students had some clear ideas on how school could encourage independence. They had examples of respectful treatment and being treated as irresponsible.

> Give us the respect we deserve as young adults. They're trying to prepare us for the world. They need to let us make our own mistakes and learn from our mistakes. I mean, how are we going to know what's right and wrong? We're young adults. We're gonna make mistakes, let us learn from them. But don't stay on our backs trying to make us learn something that we haven't even made a mistake about. . . . If you're never gonna make any mistakes then you're perfect and you don't need school. (Habel et al., 1999, p. 102).

> They listen to us, but our opinions don't make a difference. (Habel et al., 1999, p. 102).

> Well, it doesn't really belong to the kids who go there. There are all these stupid rules . . . we had no say—nothing. Who sets the rules? All the time there's rules that tell you what you can't do. I spent more time in the office than in class and where's the sense in that? I'm late for class, and then I miss the whole class by waiting in the office and get even more behind in that class than I was. What am I going to do? I skip the whole thing—that's what. I remember one time some students go together and asked if we could get a room for us to generally hang out in, y'know, and it was like, no, no, who knows what you might be doing in there. So kids hang out in corridors and in parts of the playground. Nobody trusts us in school. We are supposed to trust all the teachers and the principal, but no one trusts us. (Swaminathan, 2004, p. 50)

> And another thing, we were treated like kids—don't do this, you can't do that. And we were NOT kids. It was supposed to be high school, and in middle school we could do things we suddenly couldn't do at high school. (Swaminathan, 2004, p. 50)

> Baba Jones get mad with us, but he never disrespects us, he explains why he is mad, what we did that made him upset, what he expected, and how we should do it the next time. After we deal with it (the problem), then we just move on. (Howard, 2002, p. 383)

Like belonging and competence, students have suggestions for teachers with regard to independence. Students want choices in the curriculum, to be trusted to make decisions and to act responsibly, and to be treated with respect.

Generosity

Descriptions of students' experiences with, and perspectives on, generosity are not found as frequently as are references to belonging, mastery, and independence. The paucity of references to generosity may be a function of the type of questions asked by researchers or a scarcity of opportunities to contribute to the school or classroom in meaningful ways, to care for others, or to be generous with time or materials. Even so, in at least three studies, students relate experiences with helping others and making contributions to the school as positive aspects of school (Habel et al., 1999; Langhout, 2004; Swaminathan, 2004). Swaminathan (2004) describes students' positive experiences with community service learning. In a study by Langhout (2004), students identify opportunities for helping as an aspect of school that they like. In a study by Habel et al., (1999), students found that opportunities for helping, although rare in school, were positive. Representative comments included

> I help the other kids because most of the shorter kids play on that [hang glider], and they can't get that. So I have to get that hang glider thing, so that makes me feel good. (Langhout, 2004 p. 119)

> I feel good [when I help other kids out]. I feel like a terrific kid all over again. (Habel et al., 1999, p. 101)

When asked how they feel when they do things to help the school, one student's response is,

> I don't know, I never felt it. (Habel et al., 1999, p. 101)

> Most of the time you help your friends out when they need help. The ones you don't like too good, you don't feel like helping them. . . . Most of the time we don't help them. (Habel et al., 1999, p. 101)

Although they perceive these opportunities to be rare, students feel good when they have the opportunity to help others and make a contribution to the classroom community. Along with the good feeling of being a helper or leader with important contributions to make, opportunities for generosity may also increase a perception of competence and belonging: "I feel like the terrific kid all over again."

In summary, studies that have sought to gain the perspective of students give us an idea of how students experience school; the kinds of schools, classrooms, and teachers that they like and don't like; and their ideas for school improvements. Their perspectives fit well with the Circle of Courage. Figure 4.1 summarizes student perspectives with regard to the spirits of belonging, mastery, independence, and generosity.

Figure 4.1   Student Perspectives of the Circle of Courage

SPIRIT	WHAT STUDENTS SAY	WHAT TEACHERS CAN DO
Belonging	Prefer open, uncluttered, comfortable, clean spaces. Like to have a space of their own	Keep classroom clean and organized. Allow space for movement. Allow students to mark a space of their own in an appropriate way.

(Continued)

Figure 4.1 (*Continued*)

SPIRIT	WHAT STUDENTS SAY	WHAT TEACHERS CAN DO
	Caring relationships with teachers are important.	Show care by listening. Ask students about their lives. Show concern for well-being.
	Teachers should be fair.	Apply rules and consequences consistently; help all learners.
	Opportunities for positive peer relationships are important.	Provide time for socialization.
	Gangs and cliques are a part of school life. Many do not feel a sense of belonging.	Develop a sense of community and strategies for problem solving for conflicts between students and groups.
Competence	Want to feel competent, but many students do not.	Build opportunities for success.
	Some teachers are helpful and some are not.	Encourage students. Push students, avoid doing work for students. Communicate high expectations. Provide help as needed until the light bulb goes on.
	Some teaching styles are preferred; others are boring.	Explain in many different ways. Don't leave anyone behind. Use project-based learning, hands-on learning, fun learning activities, and provide choices.
Independence	Want choices, want to be treated as responsible.	Provide choices throughout the day.
	Want to be respected.	Allow students to have a say in classroom matters. Trust students and expect responsibility. Treat students with respect in all matters, including discipline.
Generosity	Helping feels good. Few opportunities for generosity.	Allow students to be leaders and helpers and contribute to the classroom, school, and community in various ways.

GAINING STUDENT PERSPECTIVE

The studies referenced in the previous section provide some useful insights. However, it is important to note that for each learner, the school experience is unique. From a constructivist perspective, gaining student perspective is an intentional part of the classroom or school management plan. Engaging students in meaningful dialogue regarding their school experiences and perceptions of helpful and unhelpful programs, policies, and practices, as well as classroom management strategies, can take many forms—from—informal conversations to more structured strategies. Student perspective can be gained through a variety of activities, such as individual interviews with students, classroom meetings, suggestion boxes, "getting to know you" activities, and so forth. These strategies are discussed in Chapter 8. Two other strategies that hold promise are discussed in this chapter—dialogue journals and student advisory boards. Regardless of the means for gaining perspective, attention to the types of questions asked can also be helpful.

Interviews

Teachers can interview students either formally or informally to gain their perspectives about school in general or to gain feedback regarding certain aspects of school or classroom life. Done either formally or informally, interviews of students can be quite revealing and participating can be empowering. For example, Jonnie Walkingstick asked her students what they would like to change about school. The following are simple guidelines for conducting individual or small group interviews with students.

Dialogue Journals

Teachers can gain the student perspective through written conversation in a dialogue journal. Dialogue journals have been used with young children (Hannon, 1999; Waters, 1999), middle schoolers (Regan, 2003), and high school students (Hudson, 1995), and can inform teachers about student growth in writing, as well as provide a vehicle for students to tell their stories about school and life outside of school. According to Young and Crow (1992), through dialogue journals, students can share privately with the teacher their reactions, questions, and concerns about school and personal matters, enhancing the teacher–student relationship and giving a real life purpose to the academic skill of writing. Other benefits cited by Young and Crow are that dialogue journals help in classroom management (Staton, 1988), seem to raise the self-esteem of the students involved (Staton, 1988), and help students deal with personal and social problems, providing an outlet for talking about and thinking through problems (Manzo & Manzo, 1990) and empowering students to think critically about their environment and express these thoughts to their teacher (Bode, 1989).

The following excerpt from Hudson (1995), who used dialogue journals with high school students in a rural school, indicates the power of journals to provide a window into the experiences of students, both in and out of school.

People join gangs because they are confused or need someone to care about them, give 'em loving. When times are bad, like at my home or your peers they turn on you because of some reason, then you get lonely and then you turn to a gang and then all of your g's will give you some lovin'. The main thing they get out of it is love. Some gangs, they give you a gun when you join, and I know some people who did it just for that purpose. When you belong to a gang, you got to really worry about being faded in the territories you don't control. Also, fell gang members can turn on you and you are nuttin' left but memories. Once you are in a gang, the only way out for good is to die out. (p. 6)

Mrs. W is the meanest teacher around. She more mean than Mr. J. I was just wearing my hat down the hall and she compaskated ma hat. I wish I could kick her right swuatre in the head until she bleeds. I'm going to kill her. Mrs. W is annoying as hell. She's always the one starting shit. She's trying to get me in trouble all the time. When I grow up, I want to become a tool and die maker and make a lot of money. I don't want to be a truck driver like my dad because he's only home on the weekends so I only see him two days out of seven. (p. 60)

Some general guidelines for dialogue journals include the following:

- Allow for free writing. Dialogue journals can be ungraded and students should not feel pressured to use perfect spelling or grammar. Doing so may unnecessarily limit what students say.
- Statements or questions can be used to prompt writing if needed, especially if a teacher is seeking perspective on a particular topic. Examples include the following: Students are treated fairly in my school. Tell about your favorite part of school.
- Respond in writing on a regular basis. Although dialogue journals can be time consuming, students need to know that they are being read and that the teacher is willing to respond.
- Be sure that teacher responses are nonjudgmental, reflective, empathetic, and/or informative (i.e., the reason for that school rule is . . .).
- If sensitive issues arise in a student's journal, give the student an opportunity for a private conversation with the teacher and/or counselor.
- Ensure students that their entries are confidential.
- One common classroom journal can provide an alternative to individual journals for teachers seeking student perspective on classroom issues. It can be placed in a writing center or other easily accessible area.

Advisory Boards

Advisory boards have also been used successfully to gain student perspective and allow for student input (e.g., Bacon & Bloom, 2002; Howard, 2002). Bacon and Bloom (2000) used advisory boards with elementary through high school students in several different schools. The students who were asked to serve on the advisory board were either identified as behavior disordered or deemed at risk for that identification. Students were asked questions such as "What do students worry about most?" "What kinds of problems do students at your school have?" "What are your suggestions for solutions?" and "What kind of programs could teachers, parents, and students set up to help students get through school and learn?" Through the advisory boards, students identified relationships with peers, relationships with teachers, and academic work as sources of concern.

Their suggested solutions varied, but each was highly successful. At one elementary school, students and teachers launched a conflict mediation program to address student concerns about fighting. At another, they created a mentor program that involved students at an adjacent middle school who taught their buddies how to be cool and fit in without breaking school rules. At a middle school, they persuaded the administrators to create a safe space, a composure room, where a student could go voluntarily to cool down when agitated. And at a senior high school, they created an in-school factory to make designer T-shirts—a good way to prove their work skills to prospective employers.

Bacon and Bloom (2000) offer the following suggestions for convening and conducting student advisory boards:

- Formally invite students to be a member of the advisory board. Explain to the students and their parents that you are going to use their ideas as the basis for new programs at school.
- Be sure to invite the students who are least likely to have an opportunity to have a voice in the school. Low achievers, relationship-reluctant children, low-income children, and children from varying ethnic backgrounds will all have useful ideas about school improvement.
- Convene the meeting of the students in a comfortable safe place. Provide refreshments.
- Treat the students as though they were adults and members of an important advisory board.
- Listen to their concerns and solicit all of their ideas. Don't negate their experiences by offering countering opinions like "Oh, the rules here aren't really enforced unfairly."
- Accept their ideas without judgment. Don't say, "Policy prohibits that"; don't be defensive. Remember, you are in the business of reforming your classroom or school.
- Record the ideas. Discuss the next steps. Reconvene to discuss progress in carrying out the ideas.
- Thank the students. Keep their faith by demonstrating good-faith action on your part.

INQUIRIES

In student interviews, dialogue journals, student advisory boards, and other means of gaining perspective, open-ended inquiries that allow children to describe their experiences can give more insight than other types of inquiries. These open-ended inquiries might include some like the following:

"Tell me about a time that you felt like you belonged (didn't belong) in school."
"Tell me about a time that you were (or were not) successful in school."
"Tell me about a time when a teacher really helped you learn."

Figure 4.2   Guidelines for Talking with Students About Their School Experiences

- Take care to let the students know the purpose and confidentiality of the interviews.
- Ask open-ended questions that require students to describe specific school experiences (e.g., "Tell me about a time when you felt successful at school") can generate rich answers that provide insight into how students experience school. On the other hand, questions that require a yes or no response or a one-word answer provide little information (e.g., "Do you like school?").
- Follow up open-ended questions with probing questions such as "How did that make you feel?" and "Can you tell me more about that?"
- Follow up student suggestions if possible. Let the students know what suggestions or concerns have been addressed. Doing so lets students know that their input is valued.
- Some interviews, especially group interviews, can turn into a gripe session. It is important for students to know that what they have to say is important and sometimes students want the opportunity to vent. However, if "venting" becomes unproductive, suggest that they focus on solutions and/or ask for what students like about their classroom or school.

Some students are reluctant at first to share their experiences, especially when they have perceived school personnel to be less than trustworthy. When students give short replies, the adult can follow up with probing inquiries such as "Tell me more about that." "Tell me what that was like." "Tell me how that made you feel." Summarizing is also helpful in that it ensures understanding and lets the student know that he or she is being heard. In addition, students often want to be negative at first. The teacher should let students know that they are willing to listen to student complaints. After students have aired their grievances, teachers should direct them toward constructive solution-oriented comments. This can be done through questions like "How can we solve that?" "What would you like to see happen?" "What could make that situation work better?" Figure 4.2 includes guidelines for talking with students about school.

SUMMARY

A discussion of the student perspective is not intended so that students have the final say as to how schools operate. According to Nieto (1994), "suggesting that students' views should be adopted wholesale is to accept a romantic view of students that is just as partial and condescending as excluding them completely" (p. 397). But to provide a place where students want to be, to empower students and teach decision making, and to give dignity to students necessitates gaining their perspective, understanding their conceptions, attending to their concerns, and collaboratively reforming the classroom and school.

REFERENCES

Allen, J. (1995). Friends, fairness, fun, and the freedom to choose: Hearing student voices. *Journal of Curriculum and Supervision, 10*(4), 286–301.

Bacon, E., & Bloom, L. (2000). Listening to student voices: How student advisory boards can help. *Teaching Exceptional Children, 32*(6), 38–43.

Bloom, L. A., & Habel, J. (1998). Cliques, community, and competence of students with behavioral disorders in rural communities. *Journal of Research in Rural Education, 14*(2), 95–106.

Bode, B. A. (1989). Dailogue journal writing. *Reading Teacher, 42,* 568–571.

Brendtro, L. K., Brokenleg, M., & Van Bockern, S. (1990). *Reclaiming youth at risk: Our hope for the future.* Bloomington, IN: National Education Service.

Certo, J., Cauley, K. M., & Chafin, C. (2003). Students' perspectives on their high school experience. *Adolescence, 38*(152), 705–725.

Elias, M. J. (1989). Schools as a source of stress to children: An analysis of causal and ameliorative influences. *Journal of School Psychology, 27*(4), 393–407.

Farrell, E., Peguero, G., Lindsey, R., & White, R. (1988). Giving voice to high school students: Pressure and boredom, ya know what I'm sayin'? *American Educational Research Journal, 25*(4), 489–502.

Fránquiz, M. E., & del Carmen Salazar, M. (2004). The transformative potential of humanizing pedagogy: Addressing the diverse needs of Chicano/Mexicano students. *High School Journal, 87*(4), 36–54.

Freed, C. D., & Smith, K. (2004). American Indian children's voices from prison: School days remembered. *American Secondary Education, 32*(3), 16–33.

Gardner, H. (1991). *The unschooled mind: How children think and how schools should teach them.* New York: Basic Books.

Greene, B. A., Miller, R. B., Crowson, H. M., Duke, B. L., & Akey, K. L. (2004). Predicting high school students' cognitive engagement and achievement: Contributrions of classroom perceptions and motivation. *Contemporary Educational Psychology, 29*(4), 462–482.

Habel, J., Bloom, L. A., Ray, M. S., & Bacon, E. (1999). Consumer reports. What students with behaviour disorders say about school. *Remedial and Special Education, 20*(2), 93–105.

Hannon, J. (1999). Talking back: Kindergarten dialogue journals. *Reading Teacher, 53,* 200–204.

Howard, T. C. (2002). Hearing footsteps in the dark: African American students' descriptions of effective teachers. *Journal of Education for Students Placed at Risk, 7*(4), 425–444.

Hudson, N. A. (1995). The violence of their lives: The journal writing of two high school freshmen. *English Journal, 84*(5), 65–71.

Hutchinson, J. N. (1999). *Students on the margin: Education, stories, dignity.* Albany: State University of New York Press.

Kanevsky, L., & Keighley, T. (2003). To produce or not to produce? Understanding boredom and the honor in underachievement. *Roeper Review, 26*(1), 20–29.

Langhout, R. D. (2004). Facilitators and inhibitors of positive school feelings: An exploratory study. *American Journal of Community Psychology, 34*(1/2), 11–127.

Manzo, A. V., & Manzo, U. C. (1990). *Content area reading: A heuristic approach.* Columbus, OH: Merrill.

Miserandino, M. (1996). Children who do well in school: Individual differences in perceived competence and autonomy in above average children. *Journal of Educational Psychology, 88*(2), 203–214.

Maxwell, L. E. (2000). A safe and welcoming school: What students, teachers, and parents. *Journal of Architectural and Planning Research, 19*(2), 176–178.

Miron, L. F., & Lauria, M. (1998). Student voice as agency: Resistance and accommodation in intercity schools. *Anthropology and Education Quarterly, 29*(2), 189–213.

Nieto, S. (1994). Lessons from students on creating a chance to dream. *Harvard Educational Review, 64*(4), 395–427.

Noguera, P. A. (2007). How listening to students can help schools improve. *Theory Into Practice, 46*(3), 205–212.

Phelan, P., Davidson, A. L., & Yu, H. C. (1994). Navigating the psycholigical pressures of adolescence: The voices and experiences of high school youth. *American Educational Association, 31*(2), 415–447.

Pomeroy, E. (1999). The teacher–student relationship in secondary school: Insights from excluded students. *British Journal of Sociology of Education, 20*(4), 465–482.

Regan, K. S. (2003). Using dialogue journals in the classroom. *Teaching Exceptional Children, 36*(2), 36–42.

Sanoff, H. (2001). *A visioning process for designing responsive schools.* Washington, D.C.: National Clearinghouse for Educational Facilities. Retrieved July 11, 2005, from http://www4.ncsu.edu/unity/users/s/sanoff/www/schooldesign/visioning.pdf

Sommer, R., & Olsen, H. (1980). The soft classroom. *Environment and Behavior, 12*(1), 3–16.

Swaminathan, R. (2004). It's my place: Student perspectives on urban school effectiveness. *School Effectiveness and School Improvement, 15*(1), 33–63.

Uline, C. L. (2000). Decent facilitites and learning: Thirman A. Milner Elementary School and beyond. *Teachers College Record, 102*(2), 442–461.

Ulrich, C. (2004). Children and the physical environment. *Human Ecology, 32*(2), 11–14.

Waters, R. (1999). Teachers as researchers: Making sense of teaching and learning. *Language Arts, 77*(1), 44–47.

Wentzel, K. R., Barry, C. M., & Caldwell, K. A. (2004). Friendships in middle school: Influences on motivation and school adjustment. *Journal of Educational Psychology, 96*(2), 195–198.

Wilson, B. L., & Corbett, H. D. (2001). *Listening to urban kids: School reform and the teachers they want.* Albany: State University of New York Press.

Young, T. A., & Crow, M. L. (1992). Using dialogue journals to help students deal with their problems. *Clearing House, 65*(5), 307–411.

TEACHER PERSPECTIVES: ESTABLISHING COMMUNITIES OF PRACTICE

If students insult each other, it is easier for us to try to make each students act more courteously them it is to ask which elements of the system might have contributed to the problem. . . . It is obviously more convenient for us to address each individuals who says something insulting than it is to track down the structural contributors to such behaviors. . . . The status quo has no more reliable ally than the teacher of coping skills, becasue whatever is to be coped with is treated as something to be accepted rather than changed. (Alfie Kohn, 1997, p. 15)

In 1996, I had the opportunity to work with an amazing group of third grade teachers who worked in a school with primarily Native American children on nearby Native American land. The teachers left the isolation of the classroom to work collaboratively to transform their classrooms, grade block, and school. The following are two excerpts from a summary of their work written by Jonnie Walkingstick, one of the teachers:

> In the spring of 1996, an idea formed among a group of third grade teachers that would take common beliefs and make them reality. We wanted to create a community in our classrooms and utilize classroom councils and at the same time, satisfy a North Carolina Standard Course of Study social studies goal for third grade. This was not a new idea to us or even to the teaching field. As a matter of fact, the idea of classroom councils or governments has been around for quite a while. All of us had read books, professional articles, and attended workshops/seminars that encouraged the use of such practices. We, as classroom teachers, had each in our own way incorporated many practices in our classes such as more choice and more use of cooperative learning across the curriculum that moved us nearer to the community/classroom council approach. It was when we came together as a "community of classroom teachers" willing to work together and to discuss what

was happening in our classes and ways to make it better that we were able to take the next step of building a strong classroom community. Our classes were missing something that we couldn't put our finger on, but we knew that what was happening in our classrooms was merely on the surface, therefore, any solutions for problems in our classes were quick fixes, not truly meaningful or changes that would last.

. . . With all this changing or transforming our classrooms, I have left out a most important element of the teaching profession—the teacher. I am a strong believer in teacher shift, not student shift. It is my belief that the teacher has the responsibility of adapting to the needs of children, to their strengths and learning styles. The children should not have to adapt to my needs, strengths, and teaching styles to have the "right" to learn. As a teacher, I am a public servant, offering my services for the good of the community. What the other teachers or I did not realize was how much of an effect it would have in our lives and ideas about teaching. We all had different strengths in our teaching and were ready (somewhat) to encompass "Peacekeepers," the name this group of teachers gave to their third-grade block and community building practices. We were pleased with what we found and at times surprised. Knowing how differently we were affected and the shift we had to make for the children and the good of the community proved that the best results come as teachers shift, not students.

In this third grade block, in this small school, the teachers took on the role of professionals. They recognized that the routines that had been recommended to them were not addressing the needs they recognized for their children. They were critically reflective about their classroom practices and made decisions to change their practices for the good of their learners. I have worked with Mrs. Walkingstick for more than 10 years. Peacekeepers not only continues to evolve, the model has influenced many other classrooms—from kindergarten to 12th grade in the school. Peacekeepers represents a set of practices (described in Chapter 8) that were created by a team of professionals who considered not only their own perspectives, but the perspectives of their students, their culture, and the community.

In the quote at the beginning of this chapter, Alfie Kohn (1998) suggests that the climate and rules in many schools actually contribute to many of the behaviors of students that teachers consider irresponsible or disrespectful. Kohn argues that too often, students are judged to be irresponsible or disrespectful simply because they fail to do what they are told by those in authority. "Students are typically expected to follow the rules regardless of whether the rules are reasonable and to respect authority regardless of whether that respect has been earned" (Kohn, p. 4). Kohn wants schools to abandon the time-honored position that places the blame for misbehavior squarely at the feet of the child and implicates, to lesser degrees, the teacher and/or the family. As an alternative, he joins others with constructivist, child-centered views of education (Freiberg, 1999; McCaslin & Good, 1992; Weinstein, 1999) in arguing that it is the broader school context in which efforts to "manage" students' behavior—to increase desired behaviors and/or decrease undesirable behaviors—take place that often creates the misbehavior.

Cultivating the kinds of conditions within a school that foster belonging, competence, responsibility, and generosity takes the concerted effort of all members of the school community. Hence, management must occur at the school level, as well as at the classroom level. This premise is based on a systems view of the school and the classroom, acknowledging that both are complex systems that cannot be separated from other systems, including the families of students and the sociocultural milieu. Schools in which teachers experience a sense of professionalism through encouragement and time for reflection, collaboration, and team participation around curricular goals, as well as social and emotional goals, foster healthy climates for all. In Mrs. Walkingstick's third grade block, it was the professionalism, collaboration, systems perspective, and critical reflection that led to positive changes in the school and the classroom.

In this chapter, the structural elements of school that encourage teacher professionalism through reflection, team participation, and systems thinking are presented. This reflective practice, both as the process by which individual teachers try to make sense of their own experiences and as a collaborative process involving small groups of teachers, is presented. Examples of teachers working together in teams and engaging in reflection about their own practices in light of their goals are presented. I also discuss the creation of communities of practice within schools to bring professionals together to generate innovative responses to predicaments in classrooms and schools and to engage in collaborative decision making, creativity, and problem solving.

THE STRUCTURE AND CLIMATE OF THE SCHOOL

A systems view of the school and the classroom offers an interesting juxtaposition of contrasting centralist and populist concepts of school improvement (Clark, Hong, & Schoeppach, 1996). Advocates of reform simultaneously call for both centralization and decentralization of control in schools. Much of the decision-making power of local school boards has been usurped and centralized by state legislatures, which have established far-reaching standards for student and teacher performance. Moreover, recent Presidential administrations and a wide variety of professional and private organizations are pushing for the development of national standards. At the same time, advocates for site-based management of schools and for teacher empowerment take the populist position that ". . . empowering the individuals closest to the students to make the essential decisions needed to implement sound educational programs will indeed lead to greater satisfaction for those employees and, ultimately, to better education for students" (Clark, Hong, & Schoeppach, 1996, p. 596).

Educational theorists, policy makers, and practitioners have advanced many contrasting interpretations of teacher empowerment. One unifying theme in these interpretations is that the concept of empowerment is very different from traditional conceptions of power in schools. Traditionally, schools have been bureaucratic organizations, where decisions are made at the top. Legislators and their advisors, district-level supervisors, and building-level administrators have been the sources of regulations, procedures, and curricula, and teachers have been expected to comply with the requirements generated by these regulations, procedures, and curricula. Teachers are treated as technicians who are trained to apply practices informed by researchers who dwell outside the school. For those who wield power in the traditional bureaucracy of the school, power connotes "power over" and derives from the possession of the authority to control (Clark, Hong, & Schoeppach, 1996).

Maeroff (1988) cites similarities between teacher empowerment and professionalism. For him, empowerment connotes "working in an environment in which a teacher acts as a professional and is treated as a professional" (p. 6) and "the power to exercise one's craft with confidence and to help shape the way that the job is to be done" (p. 4). While recent legislation (e.g., the No Child Left Behind Act) calls for more stringent application of research-based practices, many reformers advise putting teachers in a professional role as problem solvers, as well as both producers and consumers of research (Liston, Whitcomb, & Borko, 2007).

Reflection is one aspect that distinguishes the role of teacher as the role of a professional, as opposed to the role of a technician. While the role of a technician is that of applying a known solution to a fixed set of problems, the role of a professional is that of applying reflection and judgment to predicaments within unique circumstances. Recently, the professional role of the teacher has been described as one of an adaptive expert (Darling-Hammond, 2006; Darling-Hammond & Bransford, 2005) who is able to solve problems, construct new knowledge, and, in turn, solve new problems, as opposed to a worker who engages in routine work. Anyone who has been in a classroom recognizes that the problems and predicaments encountered by teachers and schools do not present themselves in clear-cut routine fashion, but rather as messy situations and predicaments. Not only do teachers face messy situations each day, they often encounter "bumpy moments" (Romano, 2004) or incidents that require quick reflection and instantaneous decisions. According to Schön (1987), professions such as teaching hold that practitioners are instrumental problem solvers who select the technical means best suited to particular practices.

Collaboration with other teachers can further increase the professional status of teaching. In their review of literature about teacher empowerment and professional growth, Clark, Hong, and Schoeppach (1996) report that teachers today are more likely to be expected to be active participants in decisions that affect the entire school. No longer are teachers relegated to their individual classrooms, isolated from their colleagues, and disengaged from school-based management. Clark, Hong, and Schoeppach (1996) describe the new role of teachers in schools that emphasize teams of teachers:

> They [teachers] will be expected, in some manner or another, to participate in decisions concerning the broader school community of which they are a part. They are likely to be faced with conflict in these relationships, which will require them to work collaboratively in tense situations marked by sharp differences in values. This situation suggests that they will need to know how to resolve interpersonal conflicts. Moreover, it suggests they will need to be clear on their values and the purposes of schooling in a democratic society. Without being well grounded in such matters, it will be difficult for them to function in the emerging environment. (p. 612)

Clark, Hong, and Schoeppach (1996) note that professional reflection and teaming also require attention to the broader context of the school and the purpose of school. Scheffler as cited in Zeichner and Liston (1996) posits that

> Teachers cannot restrict their attention to the classroom alone, leaving the larger setting and purposes for schooling to be determined by others. They must take active responsibility for the goals to which they are committed, and for the social settings in which these goals may prosper. If they are not to be mere agents of others, of the state, of the military, of the media, of the experts and bureaucrats, they need to determine

their own agency through a critical and continual evaluation of the purposes, the consequences, and the social context of their calling. (p. 20)

In summary, from the teachers' perspective, reflection, teaming, and systems thinking are important elements for professional development and management at the school and classroom levels. These elements are explored further.

The Value of Reflection

Reflection is a valued quality of the teaching profession (Liston, Whitcomb, & Borko, 2007; Zeichner & Liston, 1996) and research suggests that a disposition toward reflection is positively related to effective teaching (Giovannelli, 2003). The constructivist teacher recognizes that with regard to classroom management and academic instruction, where each child and family is different and each classroom, school, and community is unique, reflection is invaluable. Merely applying a basket of technical tricks is insufficient in the predicaments encountered. Figure 5.1 represents an example of how one teacher used reflection in her classroom. Zeichner and Liston (1996) present an example of the difference between applying a technical solution and using reflection to understand and solve a classroom dilemma. In their example, a white prospective teacher in her early thirties is faced with a group of six children (five of whom are children of color from low-income families) who present problems during a 40-minute free-choice period. These students either sit and do nothing or get into arguments and disrupt the class and use "rough" language with each other. Both Rachel and the cooperating teacher value the idea of a period where students are allowed to choose what they want to do.

From a nonflective or technical stance, Rachel first locates the source of the problem within the students and seeks a technique to alter the behavior of the deviant students without questioning her assumptions or examining the context of the classroom and the interaction of the students' backgrounds within this context. From a reflective stance, Rachel examines her assumptions and motivations in the context of the classroom and the diverse cultural backgrounds of her students. She realizes from her reading and reflection that her "liberal" child-centered approach may not be effective for everyone in her room. Her resulting changes did not focus solely on modifying the behavior of the students, rather they focused on facilitating choices for students through closer planning for and monitoring of students during the independent study time.

Perspectives on Reflection

Schön (1983) described reflection as occurring in two phases: reflection-on-action and reflection-in-action. Reflection-on-action occurs during planning, as well as after an action, while reflection-in-action occurs during the action and so is also called on-the-spot reflection. Schön stresses the importance of reflective practitioners, such as teachers, framing and reframing problems in light of information gained from the settings in which they work. Schön (1987) believes that while educators and other professionals can acquire essential professional knowledge and technical skills from

Figure 5.1   Bumpy Moments In the Classroom

Romano (2004) describes a self-study of her classroom. This study involved the following:

- Audio tapes of her classroom
- Reviews of the audio tapes to identify "bumpy moments," or moments when problems arose and teaching was interrupted
- Analysis of bumpy moments:

    - 61% of bumpy moments were the result of management issues
    - 3% occurred during recess
    - 18% were the result of not being prepared
    - 18% were due to parent volunteers being late or not showing up

- Analysis of days without bumpy moments
- Analysis of her thoughts during the bumpy moments

Romano's analysis and reflection of bumpy moments allowed her to greatly reduce their occurrence. In her discussion, Romano captures the essence of the benefit of reflection:

> I found that the overwhelming number of management moments were presented in periods of time and could be improved and/or prevented with systematic reflection in and after practice. These types of moments tended to focus me inward, on myself, and my practice, making it difficult for me to see additional alternatives that might have improved the immediate situation. However, closer examination of the "bumpy moments" in my teaching helped me to systematically look at the events over time and offered a retrospective view of how I could handle things differently or make changes to my teaching. Because such moments are usually lost in the continuous activity of teaching, I cannot be sure that I would have been able to gain these insights had I not engaged in this form of action research. (p. 678)

"packaged" programs, in-service, and credit-granting courses, a second essential component of their learning comes through continuous action and reflection on the everyday predicaments that they encounter in practice. Schön holds that the information gained from this experience is often tacit and difficult to analyze. He does not refer to a cognitive knowledge base for teaching or other forms of professional practice; rather, he refers to an "appreciation system." This system contains a professional's repertoire of theories, practices, knowledge, and values that influence how situations are defined, what is noticed, and the kinds of questions one will form and decisions one will make about particular actions. According to Schön, reflection involves the framing of a problematic situation. Reflective teachers recognize that their existing frame of reference for understanding what happens in their classroom is only one of several possibilities. They scrutinize the assumptions that underlie their work.

According to Zeichner and Liston (1996), the five key features of reflective teaching are:

- Examining, framing, and attempting to solve the dilemmas of classroom practice.
- Being aware of and questioning the assumptions and values brought to teaching.
- Attending to institutional and cultural contexts.
- Taking part in curriculum development and involvement in school change efforts.
- Taking responsibility for professional development.

Zeichner and Liston's (1996) conception of reflection differs from that of Schön. According to these authors, Schön's conception of reflection-on-action and reflection-in-action ignores two aspects critical to reflective teaching. The first aspect involves the benefit of reflection as a social process taking place within a learning community. Schön presents reflection as a solitary act, while Zeichner and Liston maintain that teacher development is enhanced through discussion of ideas with others. Zeichner and Liston argue that teachers' ideas become clearer and more authentic when discussed with others. One team of teachers in a small rural school in western North Carolina recently transformed their classrooms from traditional teacher-directed classrooms to more child-centered classrooms. These teachers meet weekly. One teacher described this reflective group process as similar to the problem-solving meetings of her students: "We call each other to the carpet to discuss and solve problems. This is where we bare our souls, support and learn from each other."

In addition to the benefits of collaborative reflection, Zeichner and Liston (1996) maintain that Schön's conception of reflection only considers teaching practice at the level of the individual teacher and ignores the social conditions that frame and influence practice. They contend that teachers should be encouraged to focus both internally on their own practices, as well as on the circumstances of their practice. Reflective teachers seek to maintain a broad view of their work, examining their own practice, as well as the context and conditions of the school and community.

With respect to the school context, Jones (1996) posits, "It is impossible to separate management from such issues as school climate, structure, decision making, and the type of professional support that is provided within the building" (p. 508). As Jones notes, schools in which teachers work in genuinely collaborative ways to achieve clear goals have fewer student behavior problems and students learn better. A consideration of team structures and systems thinking can address the recommendation of Zeichner and Liston (1996) that reflective practice include collaboration among teachers and consideration of a broad view of teaching practice.

The Value of the Team Structure

The value of the team structure is in saying that all of us thinking together is better than one of us thinking alone.
Jane Belmore, Principal, Schenk Elementary School, Madison, Wisconsin

Friedman (1997) observes that while school teams, or communities of practice, have been increasingly advocated as a means to both structural and instructional improvement in schools, the record of teams in schools is disappointing compared with the experiences of manufacturing and service organizations. Friedman attributes the poor record of teams in schools to entrenched bureaucratic principles—specialization, standardization, control through hierarchy—that are intended to provide an efficient basis for large-scale schooling. The chief purpose of an emphasis on teams is to explore the team approach as a vehicle for involving teachers in governance and managing the change process at the school level. Richardson (1996) tells a story of successful school teams that illustrates how involving teachers in decision making can produce both structural and instructional improvement. When reading scores rose dramatically for third graders at Schenk Elementary School in Madison, Wisconsin, the school's team building program received the lion's share of the credit. Jane Belmore, Shenk's principal at the time, observed, "Moving the achievement required a significant reorganization at the school. Team building was the infrastructure for the changes that we made" (Richardson, p. 1). Establishing multi-age classrooms for first and second graders was the innovation by the team at Shenk that lead to the improvement in the reading scores of third graders.

Perspectives on Communities of Practice

The concept of community of practice in schools is based on contemporary theories of participatory management developed by Peter Drucker, E. Edwards Deming, and others. The basic assumption is that schools must be organizations in which conditions provide teachers, as well as students, with continuous intellectual and spiritual renewal. The concept of the adhocracy as a model for a community of practice at the level of the school is based, in part, on the work of Skrtic (1995a, 1995b). Skrtic (1995) contrasts the adhocratic configuration in school organization with the bureaucratic configuration and characterizes schools as professional bureaucracies that are "premised on the principle of standardization" and "configured to perfect the practices that they have been standardized to perform" (p. 202). Although these characteristics of schools reduce their ability to adapt to change and to innovate, schools, as public organizations, must respond to public demands for change. The most common way schools respond to change is by either adding subunits—programs and classrooms, for example—that require professionals with specialized knowledge or by targeting teachers for shot-in-the-arm in-service programs designed for giving prescriptions for effective teaching. These types of bureaucratic initiatives protect the organization from the need to engage in genuine reform.

The adhocracy emerges in an environment of uncertainty, innovation, and adaptation as an alternative to the bureaucracy (Skrtic, 1995). Adhocracies are "premised on the principle of innovation" and function as "problem-solving organizations that invent new practices for work" (Skrtic, p. 203) that are ambiguous and uncertain. Situations where school professionals, such as general and special education teachers, psychologists, counselors, and so forth, are asked to work together to meet the needs of diverse populations of learners lend themselves well to an adhocratic structure. Participants in an adhocracy cannot fall back on professionalism and specialization to divide work because no ready-made, standardized practices exist for the work that is required. Therefore, the success of the work of an adhocracy depends on the ability of those involved to collaborate on an ad hoc basis on creative efforts to determine responses to predicaments. Table 5.1 contrasts the adhocratic configuration in a school organization with the bureaucratic configuration.

Adhocractic structures can contribute to the knowledge base of effective practices for educating diverse learners at all levels. By participating, teachers become an integral part of planning, implementing, and evaluating practices. Teachers are no longer faced with the challenge of meeting the needs of diverse learners in isolation. Rather, as supportive groups of professionals meet, they can draw from their various areas of interdisciplinary expertise to respond creatively to the predicaments they face in their practice.

Table 5.1 Comparison of Adhocracy and Bureaucracy

Adhocracy	Bureaucracy
Premised on the principle of innovation	Premised on the principle of standardization
Function as problem-solving organizations that invent new practices for work that are ambiguous and uncertain	Configured to perfect the standardized practices that they have been established to perform
Emerges in an environment of uncertainty, innovation, and adaptation	Reduces schools' ability to adapt to change and to innovate
Teachers work collaboratively in tense situations marked by sharp differences in values	Responds to change by adding subunits—programs and classrooms, for example—that require professionals with specialized knowledge
Participants cannot fall back on specialization to divide work because no ready-made, standardized practices exist for the work that is required	Responds to change by targeting teachers for shot-in-the-arm in-service programs designed for giving prescriptions for effective teaching
Success depends on the ability of all involved to collaborate on an ad hoc basis on creative efforts to determine responses to predicaments	Bureaucratic initiatives protect the school from the need to engage in genuine reform
Power lies in opportunities to exercise one's craft with confidence and to shape the way that the job is to be done	Decisions are made at the top; power connotes "power over" and control

Purpose of Communities of Practice

In their review of literature about teacher empowerment and professional growth, Clark, Hong, and Schoeppach (1996) observe that a major transformation in the role of the teacher is in full swing. They report that teachers today are more likely to be expected to be active participants in decisions that affect the entire school. No longer are teachers relegated to their individual classrooms, isolated from their colleagues, and disengaged from school-based management. Clark, Hong, and Schoeppach (1996) describe the new role of teachers in schools that emphasize teams of teachers:

> They [teachers] will be expected, in some manner or another, to participate in decisions concerning the broader school community of which they are a part. They are likely to be faced with conflict in these relationships, which will require them to work collaboratively in tense situations marked by sharp differences in values. This situation suggests that they will need to know how to resolve interpersonal conflicts. Moreover, it suggests that they will need to be clear on their values and the purposes of schooling in a democratic society. Without being well grounded in such matters, it will be difficult for them to function in the emerging environment (p. 612).

Birchak, Connor, Crawford, Kahn, Kaser, Turner, and Short (1998) describe the challenges and promises of establishing a community of practice:

> As teachers, we have experienced how difficult it is to find time to reflect on our teaching or to engage in a meaningful conversation with a colleague. We race from meeting to meeting, from student to student, and from one crisis to another. And that's all in the course of a normal day.
>
> Our interest in study groups developed out of a need to talk with colleagues about professional issues—to stop running past each other in hallways and to actually take time to reflect and dialogue about teaching and learning.
>
> We would see each other in faculty meetings, child study sessions, and various school committees, but these meetings had particular agendas with specific items of business. We were incredibly alone in a school full of people. While it would seem natural for schools to be places where educators come together and share professional concerns, we had experienced only occasional collaboration with one or two colleagues.
>
> We began to raise questions about establishing a community of educators within a school. Could we find a way to make reflection and dialogue a part of our daily lives as professionals in schools? Was it possible to slow down long enough to think about how we "did" school? Could we productively talk about our differences as teachers and find ways to use those differences to build a stronger school? How could our voices as teachers become a stronger part of the curricular changes within the school and across the district? Were there other approaches to professional development beyond the one day "shot-in-the-arm" in-service that introduces a new approach by the newest expert? (p. 1)

Communities of practice can serve several purposes in the school. Communities of practice can give teachers relief from isolation, provide opportunities for conscious reflection and evaluation of teaching, and support teachers' efforts in action research.

One purpose of a community of practice is to give teachers relief from the isolation in which they often work. Even as inclusion becomes a more common practice, teaching remains an activity that teachers almost always do alone. Collaboration is a professional virtue, something that goes far beyond simple congeniality in the workplace or the class-room. When educators form a team, they can produce a sense of community and shared commitment and a willingness to pool their energies, to share their burdens, and to complement one another's strengths and weaknesses.

A second purpose of a community of practice is to provide teachers of children with opportunities to develop and refine their "appreciation systems," to recapture experience in the field, to think about it, mull it over, and evaluate it. While unconscious processes of learning and/or teaching do occur, it is important that this activity take place at a con-scious level. Unconscious processes do not allow one to make active and conscious deci-sions about our learning. It is only when one brings ideas to consciousness that one can evaluate them and begin to make choices about what one will and will not do.

A third purpose of a community of practice is to support teachers' efforts to improve their own practice through action research. (Chapter 13 contains a complete discussion of the practice of action research that is designed to improve professional practice.) With both the school and the teacher as the units of change, action research projects focus on teachers' actual work situations while being grounded in the research-based literature that addresses the situations. Action research is a form of inquiry that grants teachers a research role based on a vision of the committed professional investigating his or her own practice (Carr & Kemmis, 1988).

There is a moral dimension to the kind of "shared vision" that members of the community of practice are striving to achieve. They view themselves as something more than a collection of self-interested individuals driven by private goals; they also are a community of social individuals engaged in a search for shared meanings. Indi-vidual ends are intricately interrelated with the goals of their community, but the pri-mary concerns are for the moral quality of the social relationships among the members of the community and for establishing and maintaining both shared initia-tive and mutual responsibility.

The Practice of Systems Thinking in Schools

As Senge, Cambron-McCabe, Lucas, Smith, Dutton, and Kleiner (2000) observe,

> Most schools are drowning in events. . . . Each event seems to require an immediate re-sponse. . . . Each time, the superintendent (or some other staff member) does a heroic job of fixing the problem: making the fastest possible diagnosis and finding the most im-mediate solution. (p. 77)

However, these quick fixes are likely to do more harm than good in the long run be-cause establishing a pattern of solving problems quickly can create an "attention deficit culture" in the school (Senge et al., 2000, p. 77). When much of an educator's efforts in-volve moving rapidly from one crisis to another, the focus becomes solving crises rather than preventing them. Systems thinking provides an alternative way of looking at prob-lems and goals, not so much as isolated events, but as components of a whole whose el-ements have an underlying pattern that persists over time (Friedman, 1997; Gitlin, 1999; Senge et al., 2000; Skrtic, Sailor, & Gee, 1996).

Senge and colleagues (2000) have developed a four-step exercise, called "The Iceberg," to help educators in a given school to begin to acquire the building blocks of systems thinking. In the exercise, participants attempt to understand a particular event in a school or classroom from four different perspectives. Participants are led to view the event as "the tip of an iceberg," whose visible part looks huge and threatening. Most of the iceberg, however, lurks below the surface, and to navigate around it, participants must examine the hidden structure that allows the tip to remain visible.

The Iceberg: Introducing the Practice of Systems Thinking

STEP 1: Event

Name a crisis that emerged in your school or classroom in recent months. How have people tried to solve it?

STEP 2: Patterns and Trends

What is the history of the event you described in step one? When has it occurred before? Create a timeline and look for emerging patterns of behavior.

STEP 3: Systemic Structure

What forces seem to create the pattern of behavior described in step two? Many of these forces develop over time as a result of habitual responses to chronic problems. When identified, these structures reveal the points of greatest leverage, where effort can produce the greatest influence for change.

STEP 4: Mental Models

What is it about our thinking that causes the forces and structures identified in step three to persist? The pattern of forces and structures is built on a set of attitudes and beliefs—mental models about the way the world works—that may be counterproductive because they are tacit and remain unchallenged. If these attitudes and beliefs can be safely brought to the surface, they can be examined and change in behavior can ensue. (Senge et al., 2000, pp. 80–83)

Having identified strategic leverage points and having begun to uncover mental models that produce habitual responses to chronic problems, the next step is to create teams to develop ideas into projects. For Senge and colleagues (2000), the purpose of these teams is to create a vision for one particular area of the school, rather than actually implement policies. Teams proceed first by establishing a few critical initial goals; then they experiment with reaching those goals.

WHAT DO WE WANT TO CREATE?

. . . [A] vision can die if people forget their connection to one another. . . . Once people stop asking, "What do we want to create?" and begin proselytizing the "official vision," the quality of ongoing conversation, and the quality of relationships nourished through the conversation erode. One of the deepest desires underlying shared vision is the desire to be connected to a larger purpose and to one another. (Senge et al., p. 230)

Adhocractic structures—communities of practice—permit the question "What do we want to create?" to drive the practice of those involved. While these questions do not necessarily supplant the mission of the school and the covenants of the classroom, they focus professionals on the values and goals that drive their work. Teachers can engage in collaborative reflective thinking by considering their values and goals within the context of the community and the school in which they work.

Teachers as Models

Joseph Joubert, a French essayist, said,

"Children need models, not critics." As parents and teachers, the simple elegance and straightforward wisdom of this statement is striking. It is widely understood that all of us, not only children, learn by example. The work of Albert Bandura (1986), a pioneer in the development of the theory of social learning, demonstrates that adults who work co-operatively and are respectful of each other, as well as of children, are not only modeling a skill or behavior, they also are helping to arrange the psychological conditions for children to learn cooperatively and treat others respectfully. Many teachers who complain that children are irresponsible and "just won't follow directions" assume that children learn to be responsible and respectful by following directions—by being ordered around. With this focus on compliance with adults' demands and respect for authority, these teachers rarely, if ever, ask whether they have created an environment in which students' voices are valued and heard and where students' ideas matter. . . .

Making Schools Safe for Teams

Communities of practice can contribute to the knowledge base of effective practices for educating diverse learners at all levels. As members of communities, teachers need no longer be faced with the challenge of meeting the needs of diverse learners in isolation. Rather, as supportive groups of professionals meet, they can draw from their various areas of interdisciplinary expertise to respond creatively to predicaments they face in their practice and begin to develop a shared vision for their school. Genuine collaboration in the public school in the service of children has many dimensions, including

- good communication—mastering the practices of dialogue and discussion;
- what Senge (1990) refers to as "operational trust," a condition in which individuals remain conscious of those with whom they collaborate and can be counted on to act in ways that complement their actions;
- learning how to deal creatively with powerful forces opposing genuine collaboration in organizations. In a school, for example, various individuals can have conflicting views about complex and subtle issues;
- as Birchak, Connor, Crawford, Kahn, Kaser, Turner, and Short (1998) describe, learning how to productively talk about our differences as teachers and find ways to use those differences to build a stronger school; and
- slowing down long enough to make reflection and dialogue a part of our daily lives as professionals in schools.

Maeroff (1993) cautions that teams sometimes spend too much time learning how to be a team. He reminds us that the purpose of communities of practice is not simply to increase the likelihood that teachers will collaborate more effectively or like each other better. All of the plans and activities of teams need to be related to student learning.

On a similar note, Achinstein (2002) advises about the role of conflict in collaboration. She suggests that when teachers collaborate, they may run into conflicts over professional beliefs and values. Achinstein presents two case studies of urban middle schools that illustrate how collaboration can lead to conflict.

> By airing diverse perspectives in a collective setting, by raising expectations for teacher input, and by allowing teachers to debate what and how to do schooling, these schools generated new conflicts because of their commitment to creating community. Structures that fostered teacher–teacher collaboration, such as schoolwide decision making, made public collective decisions about practice that were, at times, at odds. Whereas historically, teachers could retain their private and diverse beliefs behind closed doors, innovations that supported collaboration opened up such differences for scrutiny and often resulted in conflict. (p. 440)

Achinstein contends that the manner in which teams mange conflict can determine the potential for organizational learning and change. Avoiding conflict for the sake of unity and harmony among a group of teachers can result in locating the sources of difficulties within the students and families to avoid exploring real issues or changes that could affect positive outcomes within the school. Embracing differences in opinions and perspectives can lead to opportunities for innovation and successful reform.

FINDING TIME FOR COLLABORATION

Many teachers lament about how difficult it is to find time to reflect on teaching, to build teams of teachers, or to engage in a meaningful conversation with a colleague. In the course of a normal day, teachers race from meeting to meeting, from student to student, and from one crisis to another. In our experience, teachers respond with genuine enthusiasm to efforts to promote teams, but their enthusiasm is tempered by their knowledge of the chief challenge to establishing and maintaining a community of practice—claiming and protecting time. Despite their awareness of time constraints, many teachers' enthusiasm for a community of practice grows out of their need to (a) stop running past each other in hallways and actually take time to reflect and talk about matters of concern, and (b) work in an environment in which they can help shape the way the job is done. Addressing these needs can be a powerful source of satisfaction for teachers.

While there are no easy answers to the issue of time, many teachers have been creative in carving time out of the week to meet in teams. In one example, one grade block can "double up" one afternoon every other week. In other words, fourth and fifth graders can meet together for cross-age peer tutoring, a peer buddy program, or something similar. One week, the fifth grade teachers can supervise so that the fourth grade teachers can meet. The next time, the supervision switches hands so that each grade block has an opportunity for an extended block of time. In another example, a music, art, physical education, or media specialist, or even the principal, can plan a special program for two or more classrooms of children to free up a small group of teachers for team work.

SCHOOLWIDE POSITIVE BEHAVIOR SUPPORT

Schoolwide positive behavior support provides one example of how professional reflection, collaboration, and systems-level thinking can work together to improve school climate. The goal of schoolwide positive behavior support is to reduce inappropriate behavior and increase appropriate behavior at a schoolwide or systems level by using a team process to develop a plan that considers the unique political, social, economic, and cultural characteristics of the school and the neighboring community. To accomplish this goal, a school team reviews several sources of information, including interviews of students, staff, and parents; observations of students; and office discipline data, including office referrals, suspensions, expulsions, detentions, and any other type of schoolwide consequences. These data are used to determine the extent and nature of discipline problems and the overall climate of the school. According to Sugai and Horner (2002), this information can then be used to (a) define a small number of positively stated expectations that apply to all students; (b) develop procedures for teaching and practicing these expectations; (c) develop a continuum of procedures for encouraging these expectations; and (d) develop a continuum of procedures for discouraging, responding to, and preventing rule violations and problem behaviors. The team evaluates progress and uses a team process to make adaptations and enhance schoolwide practices based on data.

By including the voices of students, parents, and school staff, the team can evaluate many aspects of school climate, including the school's responsiveness to student needs in terms of belonging, autonomy, mastery, and generosity. Positive schoolwide behavior support is proactive in nature and can be effective in enhancing a positive school climate and preventing many behavioral problems. While many students may benefit from its application, some groups of students and individual students will need increased levels of support. School teams that function as professional communities of practice can be instrumental in planning and implementing secondary and tertiary levels of support. These levels of support are described in Chapter 6.

SUMMARY

In a sense, the same school conditions we desire to create for students—conditions that foster a sense of belonging, competence, generosity, and autonomy—are appropriate for teachers. Being treated as a competent professional who makes appropriate decisions, who belongs to a professional community, and who contributes to school improvement can make the job of a teacher more satisfying, as well as unlock a valuable resource for schools. Under these conditions, constructivist teachers can seek to be reflective about classroom practices by identifying problems, questioning the assumptions about their teaching, developing their professional practice, and learning and helping each other.

REFERENCES

Achinstein, B. (2002). Conflict amid community: The micropolitics of teacher collaboration. *Teachers College Record, 104*(3), 421–455.

Bandura, A. (1986). *Social foundations of thought and action: A social cognitive theory*. Upper Saddle River, NJ: Pearson.

Birchak, B., Connor, C., Crawford, K. M., Kahn, L. H., Kaser, S., Turner, S., & Short, K. (1998). *Teacher study groups: Building community through dialogue and reflection*. Urbana, IL: National Council of Teachers of English.

Carr, W., & Kemmis, S. (1988). *Becoming critical: Education, knowledge, and action research*. Philadelphia: The Falmer Press.

Clark, R. W., Hong, L. K., & Schoeppach, M. R. (1996). Teacher empowerment and site-based management. In J. Sikula, T. J. Buttery, & E. Guyton (Eds.), *Handbook of research on teacher education* (pp. 595–616). New York: Macmillan.

Darling-Hammond, L. (2006). *Powerful teacher education: Lessons from exemplary programs*. San Francisco: Jossey–Bass.

Darling-Hammond, L., & Bransford, J. (2005). *Preparing teachers for a changing world: What teachers should learn and be able to do*. San Francisco: Jossey–Bass.

Freiberg, H. J. (1999). Sustaining the paradigm. In H. J. Freiberg (Ed.), *Beyond behaviorism: Changing the classroom management paradigm* (pp. 164–173). Boston: Allyn & Bacon.

Friedman, V. J. (1997). Making schools safe for uncertainty: Teams, teaching, and school reform. *Teachers College Record, 99*(2), 335–371.

Giovannelli, M. (2003). Relationship between reflective disposition toward teaching and effective teaching. *Journal of Educational Research, 96*(5), 293–309.

Gitlin, A. (1999). Collaboration and progressive school reform. *Educational Policy, 13*(5), 630–659.

Jones, V. (1996). Classroom management. In J. Sikula, T. J. Buttery, & E. Guyton (Eds.), *Handbook of research on teacher education* (pp. 503–521). New York: Macmillan.

Kohn, A. (1998). The limits of teaching skills. In *What to look for in classrooms . . . and other essays* (pp. 3–7). San Francisco: Jossey–Bass.

Liston, D., Whitcomb, J., & Borko, H. (2007). NCLB and scientifically based research. *Journal of Teacher Education, 58*(2), 99–107.

Maeroff, G. I. (1988). *The empowerment of teachers*. New York: Teachers College Press.

Maeroff, G. I. (1993). *Team building for school change*. New York: Teachers College Press.

McCaslin, M., & Good, T. L. (1992). Compliant cognition: The misalliance of management and instructional goals in current school reform. *Educational Researcher, 21*(3), 10–17.

Richardson, J. (1996). *Emphasizing team development can boost student learning.* Retrieved January 24, 2003, from http://www.nsdc.org/library/innovator/inn11-96rich.html

Romano, M. E. (2004). Teacher reflections on "bumpy moments" in teaching: A self study. *Teachers and Teaching: Theory and Practice, 10*(6), 663–680.

Schön, D. A. (1983). *The reflective practitioner.* New York: Basic Books.

Schön, D. A. (1987). *Educating the reflective practitioner.* San Francisco: Jossey–Bass.

Senge, P. M. (1990). *The fifth discipline: The art and practice of the learning organization.* New York: Doubleday.

Senge, P., Cambron-McCabe, N., Lucas, T., Smith, B., Dutton, J., & Kleiner, A. (2000). *Schools that learn: A fifth discipline field book for educators, parents, and everyone who cares about education.* New York: Doubleday.

Skrtic, T. M. (1995a). Special education and student disability as organizational pathologies: Toward a metatheory of school organization and change. In T. M. Skrtic (Ed.), *Disability and democracy* (pp. 190–232). New York: Teachers College Press.

Skrtic, T. M. (1995b). Deconstructing/Reconstructing public education: Social reconstruction in the postmodern era. In T. M. Skrtic (Ed.), *Disability and democracy* (pp. 233–273). New York: Teachers College Press.

Skrtic, T. M., Sailor, W., & Gee, K. (1996). Voice collaboration and inclusion: Democratic themes in educational and social reform initiatives. *Remedial and Special Education, 17*(3), 142–157.

Sugai, G., & Horner, R. (2002). Introduction to the special series on positive behavior support in schools. *Journal of Emotional and Behavioral Disorders, 10*(3), 130–136.

Weinstein, C. S. (1999). Reflections on best practices and promising programs: Beyond assertive classroom discipline. In H. J. Freiberg (Ed.), *Beyond behaviorism: Changing the classroom management paradigm* (pp. 147–163). Boston: Allyn & Bacon.

Zeichner, K. M., & Liston, D. P. (1996). *Reflective teaching: An introduction.* Mahwah, NJ: Lawrence Erlbaum.

COMMUNITY AND FAMILY INVOLVEMENT

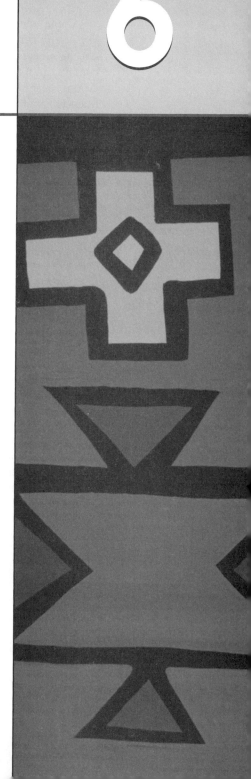

I wish that for just one time you could stand inside my shoes. You'd know what a drag it is to see you.
Bob Dylan, "Positvely, 4th Street"

In Jonnie Walkingstick's fifth grade classroom, learners are given an assignment to come up with a synonym for the word "said" for each letter of the alphabet so that they will have a wide range of words to use in their writing. While they are allowed to use a dictionary, a thesaurus, the Internet, and other resources, learners are encouraged to ask for help from members of their community and their family. Learners are asked to have each person who helps sign the back of their paper. They are instructed to thank those individuals for helping them learn. One student proudly shows his teacher the signature of the tribal chief. Others show the signatures of their parents, aunts, uncles, and neighbors. This is just one activity that this teacher uses to engage learners with families and community as the school year progresses.

On another day, Mrs. Walkingstick has a conference with a parent whose child has never brought in a homework assignment. She understands how this family has struggled in many ways. The mother is a single parent with many responsibilities, including a night job. Mrs. Walkingstick asks the parent and the student how many nights of homework they might be able to handle—if there was at least one night of the week they thought they could manage. The parent and the student agree that one night might be doable. This student, who has never turned in work, is now turning in homework at least one night a week. By recognizing that the family is overwhelmed, asking for their input, and establishing a manageable goal, she has engaged this previously uninvolved family in the student's education.

Communities, schools, families, and children function as parts of an ecological system often referred to as overlapping spheres of influence (Epstein, 1987). Children cannot be understood separate from their families, or families separate from their communities. Likewise, the school is an integral member of the larger community. Decisions regarding the school, classroom, and children must consider these spheres of influence. Family and community involvement are often valuable but untapped resources for schools that can make a difference in the climate of the school and classroom. Furthermore, community and parent participation has gained increasing prominence in school reform agendas, including the No Child Left Behind Act of 2001 (Bush, 2001). The constructivist teacher recognizes the interconnectedness and interdependence of the child, family, school, and community and seeks to use these relationships to enhance the student's educational experiences. In this chapter, I present the benefits of and barriers to family and community involvement, as well as strategies for inviting parents and the community to be partners in the school.

BENEFITS OF PARENTAL INVOLVEMENT

While students are likely to reap the most benefits from parental involvement, strong partnerships also bring advantages to parents, teachers, and schools.

Benefits for Students

Research and professional literature strongly suggest that parental participation has a positive effect on academic outcomes (Henderson & Berla, 1994; Pressini, 1998; Walberg & Wallace, 1992) and that "the more that parents are involved, the better students perform in school" (Henderson & Berla, 1994, p. 7). However, studies examining the effects of parental involvement on student achievement have not controlled for the different types of parental involvement (i.e., in school versus in-the-home involvement) or have used inconsistent definitions of student achievement such as grades, scores on standardized tests, or homework completion (Pressini, 1998). Consequently, the exact nature of the relationship between parental involvement and achievement, especially in middle school and high school and with regard to factors such as race, ethnicity, and socioeconomic status, is, as of yet, not clearly understood (Desimone, 1999; McNeal, 2001; Trivette & Anderson, 1995).

Despite the complex and unclear relationship between parental involvement and achievement outcomes, it is evident that parental involvement influences behavioral outcomes such as school attendance (Epstein & Sheldon, 2002) and classroom behavior (Comer & Haynes, 1992; Haynes & Comer, 1996; McNeal, 2001; Trusty, 1996), which in turn affect academic achievement. In addition, parental involvement fosters positive attitudes toward learning and school, as well as toward students' educational aspirations (Gonzalez, 2002; Greenwood & Hickman, 1991; Trivette & Anderson, 1995; Trusty, 1996, 1998).

Benefits for Parents, Teachers, and Schools

In addition to the positive influence of parental involvement on student outcomes, parental involvement can also have a positive effect on parents, teachers, and schools. For example, parental benefits include a better understanding of the school programs and policies and higher aspirations for their children (Epstein, 1986). Teachers may benefit in that when parents are involved in education, parents tend to have more positive attitudes toward their children's teachers (Christenson, 1995; Greenwood & Hickman, 1991). As for the school, those schools that actively engage parents outperform schools with little parental involvement (Epstein, 1987; Henderson, 1988).

BARRIERS TO FAMILY INVOLVEMENT

Generating positive relationships between families and schools is a complex task. Relationships between parents and school professionals can be tenuous and difficult to maintain. Attitudes and assumptions; role expectations; and family, student, and cultural factors can create barriers to effective partnerships. As the quote at the beginning of the chapter suggests, if parents and teachers could trade places, they may better understand possible sources of distrust and ill regard.

Attitudes and Assumptions

Attitudes and assumptions on the part of teachers, administrators, and parents often hinder effective family and school partnerships. Raffaele and Knoff (1999) suggest that when parents do not become actively involved in their children's school, teachers and administrators may assume that they are unable to participate, not interested in participating, or apathetic regarding their children's education. Furthermore, teachers may believe that parents are to blame for their children's academic failure and/or behavioral difficulties. However, Raffaele and Knoff (1999) identify several reasons that parents may fail to become involved, including family factors, as well as school factors. For example, some parents had negative school experiences themselves and consequently do not trust that teachers have their children's best interests at heart. Others may see themselves as being "different" from their children's teachers and may perceive that their cultural values are not accepted or appreciated by teachers and administrators. Some parents may be uncertain of what they can contribute to their children's education. They may feel overwhelmed, as well as powerless, with regard to the traditional bureaucracy operating in many school systems.

Role Expectations

Problems with inaccurate and/or inappropriate assumptions and attitudes among school players can be compounded by incongruent expectations regarding the roles of parents. Nakagawa (2000) describes how parents are often confused by the role they should play in their children's education.

Parents are placed in a protector/instigator bind, making it unclear how they should best help their children in relation to school: Should they assert their rights as parents to protect their children's interests, or should they follow the directions of the school system? Parents are told that they are a valuable tool, but are also told that they are the cause of why schools are not doing better. Parents can turn the schools around, but first they must take time off work and learn what they are supposed to do. In either case, parents must act in ways that are validated by the school system, or their participation is not recognized or may be resented. The good parent is construed as one who follows the lead of the school, who is involved but not too involved, and who supports but does not challenge (Nakagawa, 2000, p. 456).

School professionals often enter into relationships with parents from a hierarchical position of authority (Epanchin, Townsend, & Stoddard, 1994), contributing to the belief that professionals are more knowledgeable and objective than parents on matters related to children and schooling, and that parents should be willing to learn from professionals and return home to teach their children. From the hierarchical viewpoint, parents are expected to take and implement professional advice, often without question, and defer most educational decision making to school personnel. When they do this, they are considered cooperative, positive parents. When they do not do so, they are often termed "noncompliant." This view of the relationship of teachers and administrators to parents ignores the potential contributions of parents by virtue of their intimate and historical relationship with their children.

Family Factors

The effects of parental involvement are also mitigated by various family factors, such as social class and family structure (Nakagawa, 2000). Low-income and single-parent families are at a disadvantage because schools often provide fewer opportunities for their involvement. Middle-class parents are better able to fulfill the school's expectations for involvement and are seen as "good" parents. Consequently, parental involvement may further the inequalities between students of low-income parents and those of wealthier parents. As an alternative, Nakagawa suggests that it be conveyed to parents who have limited opportunities to be in the school that "a parent who provides a model for the importance of education and lifelong learning also may be termed an involved parent. (p. 466)"

Cultural Factors

Many families from culturally diverse populations may be more passively involved in the education of their children (Matuszny, Banda, & Coleman, 2007) and/or at odds with the school (Harry, Klinger, & Hart, 2006). Factors that may discourage the active involvement of culturally diverse families include language differences, perceived discouragement from teachers or administrators, the perception that their opinions are not valued, unfamiliar or intimidating school systems, and incongruent role expectations (Matuszny, Banda, & Coleman, 2007; Vazquez-Nuttal, Li, and Kaplan, 2006). Vazquez-Nuttal et al. give examples of how cultural mismatches can cause difficulty. In one example, they explain that in American culture, teachers expect parents to speak freely at conferences. However, in some cultures (e.g., Hmong, Hispanic), teachers are seen as the authority and parents are expected to listen—a behavior that may be interpreted as apathy by the teacher. In another example, in some cultures, saying "yes" may have a different meaning—"I heard you," as opposed to "I agree." Hence, teachers may be frustrated when families say "yes" to a teacher request, but do not follow through.

Student Factors

Generating parental involvement in high school and middle school may be even more challenging than in the elementary grades. Adolescents who are seeking to establish autonomy from their parents may discourage their parents from volunteering in school or even attending parent–teacher conferences. Furthermore, parents of middle school and high school students often feel less able to help and spend less time helping their children with homework (Balli & Demo, 1998). While most parents of high school students tend to agree that greater involvement would be beneficial, many are never contacted by the school (Sanders & Epstein, 2000). Due to constraints on time and resources and the responsibility for large numbers of students, high school teachers are less likely to encourage active family involvement (Dornbusch & Ritter, 1988).

FOSTERING PARENTAL INVOLVEMENT

The discussion regarding parental involvement in school-reform literature recognizes the need for not only increasing the level of parental participation in school activities, but also developing meaningful partnerships in which parents are active and informed participants (Baker, Kessler-Sklar, Piotrkowski, & Parker, 1999). The National Parent Teacher Association (PTA) developed the following standards for parental involvement programs:

- Communicating—Communication between home and school is regular, two way, and meaningful.
- Parenting—Parenting skills are promoted and supported.
- Student learning—Parents play an integral role in assisting student learning.
- Volunteering—Parents are welcome in the school and their support and assistance are sought.
- School decision making and advocacy—Parents are full partners in the decisions that affect children and families.
- Collaborating with community—Community resources are used to strengthen schools, families, and student learning.

Epstein and Dauber (1991) identify six types of parental involvement that contribute to meaningful partnerships (summarized in Figure 6.1). Partnership programs must be well planned and comprehensive in that they reach out to all families, not just those who are easily contacted (Henderson & Berla, 1994). In their review of studies on family involvement, Henderson and Mapp (2002) found that schools that succeed in involving families from diverse backgrounds share three key practices. They build trusting and collaborative relationships among teachers, families, and community members. They recognize and respect the class and cultural differences and attend to families' needs. They embrace the ideas of shared power and responsibility in developing partnerships.

Inviting, encouraging, and maintaining these types of partnerships requires effective two-way communication, providing opportunities for meaningful involvement through sincere efforts to elicit family input in behavior management, curriculum, and instruction; considering family needs with regard to homework; and allowing and encouraging a variety of ways for parents to contribute to student learning and volunteering in the school and/or classroom.

Figure 6.1   Six Types of Parental Involvement

1. Family obligations: Families should provide safe, healthy homes for children and develop positive parenting skills that maintain healthy child development. Families should also develop positive home conditions that support academic and social learning across the school years. Schools can support families in these endeavors by providing parent training, family support programs, and workshops that assist families in understanding ways to support their children at each grade level.

2. School obligations: Schools should design effective forms of school-to-home and home-to-school communications about school programs and children's progress with such practices as a regular schedule of useful notices, memos, phone calls, newsletters, and other communications.

3. Parental involvement at school: Recruit and organize the parents' help and support. Parents and families can volunteer to provide assistance to administrators and teachers. They can also provide an audience for support of student performances, sports, and other school events. Schools can organize volunteers, train volunteers to maximize their usefulness in the classroom, and vary the schedules of school events so that more families can participate.

4. Parental involvement at home: Families need information and ideas about how to best assist with homework, maintain high aspirations for their children, encourage their children, and reinforce and support what their children are learning at school. Provide information and ideas to families about how to help students at home with homework and other curriculum-related activities.

5. Parental involvement in decision making and governance: Include parents in school decisions, developing parent leaders and representatives. PTA/PTO and other parent groups should not only be involved in fund raising, but also should be encouraged and supported in having a voice in all school matters.

6. Community connections: Schools can assist parents in tapping into community resources by identifying and integrating resources and services from the community, such as after-school care, health services, and recreational and summer programs.

Source: Information taken from Epstein & Dauber (1991).

HOME–SCHOOL COMMUNICATION

Two-way communication is key to the development of a productive home–school partnership (Watkins, 1997). Fuerenstein (2000) found that just by increasing the number of contacts made by the school, parental volunteerism increased. Upon initial contact with the family (whether that be at the open house at the beginning of the school year or through individual conferences), the teacher can communicate to families the importance of developing a collaborative relationship with them and the teacher's willingness to be accessible for conferences when needed. Families should feel that initiation of contact with the teacher is available, welcome, and expected, and that flexibility is not a problem.

Many modes of communication are readily available to teachers: telephone contact, personal conferences (both open school nights and scheduled/unscheduled conferences), and notes sent home. But with the growing diversity of the population and the increased demands on families, these more conventional methods do not suit all families' needs. Teachers must be both creative and flexible in keeping open the lines of communication with families. Upon first meeting families, the teacher can establish the mode of communication that would be most useful and convenient for both teacher and family. In order to maintain communication, families may need or prefer flexibility with time of day in scheduling, telephone conferences, e-mail, etc. There may be additional barriers to overcome, such as language differences and illiteracy, so accommodations should be made to meet the individual needs of each family whenever possible.

Examples of ways in which regular communication can be maintained between the classroom teacher and the family include the following.

Home/School Journal or Log

Many teachers, especially in the elementary grades, use folders, notebooks, or journals for quick daily communication with parents. Teachers can take the opportunity to make positive statements such as "David is doing so much better with his reading this week . . . " in the log or place a smiley sticker or star indicating good work for the day. Families can communicate events going on at home that may affect the child's performance at school. Homework assignments can be contained in this same folder so that parents are aware of what the child is supposed to be completing each night.

Newsletters

Newsletters can be produced for a single class, grade level, or the entire school, but the more personalized they are, the more beneficial they will be to the families. The content of newsletters can include

> Changes in services at the school
> Upcoming events and schedules

Tips to support and involve parents in childrens' education at home
Community opportunities for parents to share with their children
Accomplishments of students
Student essays, poetry, or other writing
Weekly or monthly themes or units planned for the classroom
Resources needed for the classroom that parents could contribute

Students, especially in the upper grades, can be involved in some aspects of producing the newsletter as a learning opportunity and as an audience for their written work. Working alongside students, parent volunteers can assist in the production of these newsletters. Newsletters can easily be made accessible via the Internet as well, for those with computer accessibility. If there is a significant minority population represented in the school/classroom, then efforts may be made to print a bilingual version.

Phone Calls

Traditionally, parents/caregivers of students have been accustomed to receiving the "dreaded phone call from the teacher." Teachers have overused the telephone as a means of communicating problems with student behavior or academic work to families. Making an effort to use the telephone as a tool for positive communication can open the way to developing positive relationships with families. These phone calls can be made on a regular basis, and families should be made aware of the plan to use them. A telephone schedule could be made in advance so that groups of parents/families know that they will be contacted during a particular week, or a specific time could even be established in advance to contact particular parents. Some topics that might be discussed during these "positive phone calls" could include

- discussing the child's progress—informing the parent(s)/family of special achievements or improvements made by the child;
- answering questions and discussing any concerns that the parent(s)/family may have about the child; and
- inviting the parent(s)/families to open houses, conferences, special events, parent education nights, volunteer opportunities, and other school activities.

An additional or alternative opportunity for communication by telephone is to provide a regularly scheduled call-in time ("open office hours") during each week in which parents/families can call and speak with teachers about concerns and ideas, or to schedule conferences. Announcing acceptable times for phone calls to the teacher may alleviate the trepidation that some parents may feel about calling a very busy teacher. For middle and high school students who have many different teachers, parents can be made aware of whom to call for general questions or concerns regarding their adolescent (visit http://www.ed.gov/pubs/ReachFam/oncom.html for more information).

Other

Additional means of communication might include the following:

- Send e-mail and post online Web pages.
- Develop a parent handbook to provide positive, practical information about the school and/or classroom. Include information on how parents can support their child's efforts to succeed. Involve veteran parents in the development of the handbook.
- Utilize translator liaisons during contact with families who do not speak English (or are not fluent). Also, these families can be partnered with another family in the classroom who is bilingual.
- Arrange alternative meeting places in neutral territory for parents who feel disenfranchised by the school (e.g., McDonald's on Saturday morning, a community center, etc.).
- Circulate a phone list containing students' names, parents' names, and phone numbers. Establish a "phone chain" for notification of timely information (e.g., reminders about field trips, etc.). Also, "homework buddies" can be established with this list so that students and/or parents have someone that they can call if there are any questions about assignments.

MEANINGFUL INVOLVEMENT

According to Comer and Haynes (1992), when parents have authentic roles and real responsibilities in the decisions that affect their child's learning, their ownership and support of school programs will flourish. For example, parent representatives may urge other parents to become active participants and to help develop solutions to obstacles that limit their participation. In addition, parents bring a community perspective to planning and management activities. They also bring an understanding of the needs and experiences of their own children that can help teachers plan age-appropriate and culturally appropriate social and academic programs in the classroom. At the school level, parents can be involved in helping to shape school policies, missions, goals, and desired outcomes through membership in the PTA or Parent Teacher Organization (PTO); through representation on advisory boards, curriculum committees, and interview committees for teaching and administrative vacancies and school improvement teams; and by having open and inviting lines of communication with school administrators. The National PTA provides the following examples of strategies for involving families in decision making:

- Share annual reports of school performance and program information with parents at an open meeting to review current progress and solicit input for future goals.
- Communicate school/program procedures for addressing parents' concerns, including appropriate contact person and the process for defining the problem and developing and implementing solutions. Publicize successful changes in the school or program as a result of parent initiation and involvement.

- Include a mini-poll (one question) of parents' opinions in each program newsletter covering a wide range of topics over time. Utilize parent feedback in making school/program decisions.
- Develop workshops or include parents in ongoing training on relevant topics such as developing parents as advocates, mastering skills for supporting learning, identifying and supporting learning styles, resolving difficulties, and fostering student achievement.

At the classroom level, meaningful involvement can mean including families in planning educational activities and development of the classroom management plan.

Educational Activities

Involving families in planning educational activities begins early in the year. Ideally, such planning is introduced at the open house (i.e., the first contact with parents as a group), and could be followed up with subsequent meetings with all interested family members. The teacher can evaluate the curriculum in advance of the meeting and identify what areas within the curriculum would be most enhanced by family contributions. The teacher will want to tap into the resources available and represented within the families (i.e., individual talents and skills, occupations, cultural practices, field trip opportunities related to occupations). This information can then be shared with the families at the meeting and a guided brainstorming session can follow in which suggestions can be contributed by the parents/families. Volunteers can be requested for various suggestions. From this, a list of plans can be developed and incorporated into the lesson plans for the year.

Behavior Management

In addition to involving families in educational planning, their input can be sought regarding behavior management. Seeking input on behavior management philosophy recognizes that the needs of the classroom and the school are quite different from the needs of families, children, and communities. Family behavior management philosophies are shaped by a number of factors, including parent–child relationships, cultural norms and traditions, living space, and the degree of adult supervision. In developing a home–school behavior management philosophy, the following variables should be considered:

- Each child's support system: The child's family may or may not be a parent or relative.
- Personal bias: Preconceived notions or expectations about the family and their style of interaction and behavior management approach may exist. Teachers should acknowledge and take care to reject negative biases.
- Culture, values, and beliefs: Teachers and families may not hold the same values and beliefs. Wise teachers are cautious about letting these differences influence their respect for and appreciation of the family.

Activities that can facilitate family involvement in the development of a behavior management philosophy and encourage appropriate classroom behavior can include

- Survey: Present at an open house after a brief discussion about how classroom rules are established at the beginning of the year (with student involvement and input), the general behavioral expectations of students, and so forth. Let them know (again) that you value their input and would like to know their opinions, management style, and expectations at home, etc.
- Solicit parents' assistance with encouraging appropriate classroom behavior: After classroom rules are developed and shared with families, develop a system of communication so that parents can be informed of students' progress with social skills and development of appropriate classroom behavior. Discuss with parents strategies such as praise and celebrations that they can use to recognize and encourage positive classroom behavior.
- Counselor (if available): Introduce at open house and let families know his or her role and availability to help with problems inside or outside of the school.
- Parent education classes: Assess for interest in, and involve parents in planning parenting classes to address positive ways to deal with behavioral issues at home.
- Epstein and Sheldon (2002) found that parent–school partnerships could effectively increase student attendance. These authors found the following strategies to be positively correlated with lower absentee rates for students: (a) communicating with parents about attendance, (b) providing a contact person for parents to call, (c) conducting workshops for parents, and (d) conducting home visits for students with high absenteeism.

FAMILY INVOLVEMENT IN STUDENT LEARNING

There are many ways that teachers can encourage and support parents/families in their involvement with student learning. Homework is only one way that families can support student learning and should not be the focus of family involvement in learning. Research suggests that other factors in the parents' control may have an even greater influence on academic performance, including student attendance, the variety of reading materials available in the home, and limitations on television viewing (Lewis, 1995). Figure 6.2 highlights one first grade teacher's project that applied research indicating the power of reading to children and the availability of reading materials in the home in the development of literacy (McCarthey, 2000). Some basic guidelines for involving parents in student learning follow:

- Inform parents of the expectations for students in each subject at each grade level.
- Report research findings in school newsletters about how parental involvement can promote student success.
- Sponsor workshops or distribute information to assist parents in understanding how students can improve skills, get help when needed, meet class expectations, and perform well on assessments.

Figure 6.2   Home-Based Literature Program

As a first grade teacher, my students have always had a book or two to take home each night to practice reading. They read books on their own level to practice fluency and reading strategies. However, I recently added another component to my take-home reading program. The students would have to continue to read to someone in their family each night, but the parents would also have to read to their child.

In all primary classrooms, teachers value reading to children. I make sure that my students are read to several times each day. I always read to my own children at home and it was easy to assume that all parents read to their children. Reading to children is just using good parenting skills! However, my experience has taught me that not all parents read to their children on a regular basis.

One day, in my first grade class, a boy, who is an excellent reader, brought his favorite book, *Thunder Cake,* to school. This book had been a gift to him from his grandmother. She was a member of a children's book club and he received a new book each month. We read this book and this led to a discussion of how much reading was done in each child's home. All of the students were reading their beginning readers to their parents at night and the parents were signing their homework logs. However, the better readers had parents who were reading to them at night. The better readers also had age-appropriate books in their homes.

In 1985, the Commission on Reading, which was organized by the National Academy of Education and the National Institute of Education and was funded under the U.S. Department of Education, issued a landmark report. After 2 years of studying 10,000 research projects to determine what really worked and what didn't in teaching a child to read, the commission's report, *Becoming a Nation of Readers*, stated, "The single most important activity for building the knowledge required for eventual success in reading is reading aloud to children."

This knowledge prompted me to develop a Home-Based Literature Program built around a classroom library of good children's literature that could be checked out by students in my class for their parents to read to them. The students continued to have their reading book, but now they would also be able to take home a book for their parent to read to them. The children loved the idea of their parents having homework too! Money was obtained through a local university to help with the purchase of books, volunteers were sought to make a cloth bag to carry the new books back and forth to school, the books were recorded on tape by graduate students working with the school, a log to record the books read was developed, and a system of checking out the books was put in place.

The final step was inviting the parents in to go over the importance of reading aloud to their child. Many felt that they were listening to their child read at night and wondered how reading to their child was going to improve their child's reading! I relied on Jim Trelease's book, *The Read Aloud Handbook,* for my arguments supporting reading aloud.

An end-of-year survey and anecdotal records indicated that the program was a success. Next year, I will continue to require my students to read to their parents each night, but I will also require the parents to read to their child each night!

Pam Douthit, First Grade Teacher, Cullowhee Valley School, Cullowhee, NC

- Involve parents in setting student goals each year and in planning for post-secondary education and careers. Encourage the development of a personalized education plan for each student, where parents are full partners.
- Provide information regarding how parents can foster learning at home, give appropriate assistance, monitor homework, and give feedback to teachers.

  Address the issue of homework assignments at the first meeting with parents (e.g., open house): what to expect, the use of homework assignment logs or notebooks, resources available for assistance, and so forth.

  Suggest that parents set clear rules and expectations with their children regarding completion of homework: where and when it is to be done, and so forth. Parents should provide a place without distractions and with good lighting where homework can be completed.

  Make sure that homework assignments aren't just "busy work." Neither should homework be introducing new material or used to teach a new concept, but rather it should be a review of material already presented.

  Regularly assign interactive homework that facilitates positive and fun family interactions. For example, instead of assigning a math worksheet, have students interview their parents about how they use math during the day.

  Provide guidelines for parents in helping students with a particular subject, for example, information that explains how to help a young child with reading unknown words or how to help a teen with a research project.
- Ask parents to take an active role in reviewing student progress toward learning goals. Parents have the opportunity to review expectations, discover their child's areas of strength, and gain insight into how to help their child improve.
- Create a resource bank of activities and supplies for fostering student learning that is accessible to parents.

Source: Information adapted from the National PTA

Parents as Volunteers

The presence of parents/families in the classroom is an invaluable asset. Not only are they ready hands to help, but more importantly, they offer an opportunity for students to see that the family values school. Some ways in which family members can participate in classroom experiences include

- reading individually with students;
- helping during special activities (class parties, presentations);
- chaperoning field trips;
- assisting with the preparation of classroom materials for lessons;
- providing telephone support to other parents;
- sharing experiences with students; and
- providing individual tutoring.

It is important to remember that all types of parental involvement are valuable and that most parents do not have the time and/or resources to devote long hours for volunteering. Every effort can be made to appreciate even the smallest of contributions to student learning. Even notes to busy parents that show appreciation for the smallest of contributions to student learning go a long way toward nurturing a positive relationship with a family.

CONSIDERATIONS FOR CULTURAL DIFFERENCES

Vazquez-Nuttal et al. (2006) explain that traditional practices for encouraging participation may be less effective with culturally diverse families than with White, middle class families. While caution about applying stereotypes to all families of a particular culture and/or assuming that there is a "one size fits all" approach to working with culturally diverse families is warranted (Vasquez-Nuttal et al., 2006), some general guidelines for practice can be gleaned from professional literature and research:

- Avoid assumptions regarding the parents' opinion about the value of education and their concern for their child's education (Harry et al., 2005).
- Ask parents about their concerns and perspectives through either surveys or interviews (Hope-King & Goodwin, 2002). Use this strategy to learn things like what language is spoken at home and what are the cultural practices in the home as a way to affirm their child's culture in the school.
- Assist teachers in learning about cultures represented in their school (Hope-King & Goodwin, 2002; Vasquez-Nuttal et al., 2006) by conducting in-service presentations and/or by providing cultural resource notebooks.
- Offer workshops to empower parents to work effectively with schools (Vasquez-Nuttal et al., 2006).
- Assign a culturally competent liaison for working with diverse families.
- Create a family room where parents can meet, read, and talk (Hope-King & Goodwin, 2002), and visit families in their home and neighborhood (Vasquez-Nuttal et al., 2006).
- Recognize the value of different kinds of parental involvement and recognize family strengths (Harry et al., 2005; Vasquez-Nuttal et al., 2006).

COMMUNITY INVOLVEMENT

As with family partnerships, a number of valuable resources can result from positive community–school relationships. As with school connectedness, youth who have positive connections with their community reap benefits. Research suggests that feelings of competence and well-being are correlated with community connectedness (Eccles & Gootman, 2002). Youth with a sense of community belonging are less likely to experience negative outcomes such as drug abuse (Resnick et al., 1997). In addition, Flanagan,

Cumsille, Gill, and Gallay (2007) found that regardless of age, gender, or ethnic background, youth with a sense of community connectedness were more likely to commit to democratic goals and believe that America is a just society.

Communities can provide mentors and volunteers, enrichment opportunities, businesses that offer work experience and career information, and agencies that provide social services for students and families. In addition, communities can offer after-school, summer learning, and recreation programs; locate library and cultural services near to schools; make neighborhoods safer and drug-free; support schools' efforts to develop challenging academic standards; and work to improve education in many other ways. Furthermore, through field trips to community businesses and organizations, as well as by asking community members to share their expertise as guest speakers, the community becomes a resource for learning that is real-world-based and sends both parents and students a message about the value of schooling and the work of the community. Efforts to establish community partnerships involve bringing the community to the school, as well as the school to the community.

St. Pierre (1996) asserts that keeping the community informed and involved will lead to increased public support and trust in the school. St. Pierre describes several strategies for enhancing community–school communication, including the following:

- Principal for a day. In this program, community members are invited to be principal for a day. Through the program, business and community leaders have the opportunity to experience the school setting. Participants gain an appreciation for what goes on in their local schools and they share their experiences with others in the community. Many beneficial partnerships may be formed or enhanced through the Principal for a Day program as participants see opportunities for supporting the school.
- Service clubs. Service clubs, such as Kiwanis and Lions, that meet weekly often welcome speakers at their meetings. Teachers, as well as their students, can take advantage of this opportunity by preparing short presentations that exhibit student work, inform the community of school activities, and showcase opportunities for service clubs to support the school. Service clubs can even be invited to meet at the school.
- Community forums. As with parents, some community members may want to provide input and be a part of the district's decision-making process. One way to do this is through community forums. Forums can be designed to discuss specific issues or to be more open-ended so that parents and community members can ask questions about various educational issues.
- Steering committees. Steering committees can involve parents, administrators, students, community members, and school personnel and can be used for short-term projects such as creating a mission statement or volunteer recruitment.
- Newspaper inserts. Local newspapers can be provided with short pieces describing special activities and student accomplishments. Businesses that support the school can also be recognized and shown appreciation through newspaper articles.
- Information booths at community events such as street fairs allow community members who are unable to visit the school to learn about the school's programs.

SUMMARY

As school professionals seek to develop meaningful relationships with the families and communities of the children they serve, they must keep in mind the possible tenuousness of the relationship due to attitudinal barriers and family, school, and community circumstances. However, nurturing and fostering a mutually respectful and meaningful relationship can only benefit all involved. There are many types of parental involvement that should be considered, nurtured, and valued to encompass the diversity of families and family experiences. Parents are vital to the success of our students. With their lives being more hectic and demanding than ever before, and with the added pressure of responsibility on so many single parents, they deserve all of the assistance we can give them to continue to support and participate in their children's education.

As families have become more diverse and complex, so have communities. Keeping the school alive in the hearts and minds of the community and seeking their assistance in the education of youth and the support of families is key to a successful school.

REFERENCES

Baker, A., Kessler-Sklar, S., Piotrkowski, C., & Parker, F. L. (1999). Kindergarten and first-grade teachers' reported knowledge of parents' involvement in their children's education. *The Elementary School Journal, 99*(4), 369–380.

Balli, S., & Demo, D. (1998). Family involvement with children's homework: An intervention in the middle grades. *Family Relations, 47*(2), 149–158.

Bowen, N. K. (1999). A role for school social workers in promoting student success through school–family partnerships. *Social Work in Education, 21*(1), 34–48.

Bush, G. W. (2001). Remarks on implementation of the No Child Left Behind Act of 2001. *Weekly Compilation of Presidential Documents, 38*(2), 36–39.

Christenson, S. L. (1995). Best practices in supporting home–school collaboration. In A. Thomas & J. Grimes (Eds.), *Best practices in school psychology III* (pp. 253–267). Washington, DC: National Association of School Psychologists.

Comer, J. P., & Haynes, N. M. (1992). Parent involvement in school: An ecological approach. *The Elementary School Journal, 91*(3), 271–278.

Desimone, L. (1999). Linking parent involvement with student achievement: Do race and income matter? *Journal of Educational Research, 93*(1), 11–33.

Dornbusch, S. M., & Ritter, P. L. (1998). Parents of high school students: A neglected resource. *Educational Horizons, 66*(2), 75–77.

Eccles, J. S., & Gootman, J. A. (2002). *Community programs to promote youth development.* Washington, DC: National Academic Press.

Epanchin, B. C., Townsend, B., Stoddard, K. (1994). *Constructive classroom management: Strategies for creating positive learning environments.* Grove City, CA: Brooks/Cole Publishing Co.

Epstein, J. L. (1986). Parents' reactions to teacher practices of parent involvement. *The Elementary School Journal, 86*(3), 277–294.

Epstein, J. L. (1987). Toward a theory of family–school connections: Teacher practices and parent involvement. In K. Hurrelmann, F. Kaufmann, & F. Losel (Eds.), *Social intervention: Potential and constraints* (pp. 121–136). New York: DeGruyter.

Epstein, J. L., & Dauber, S. (1991). School programs and teacher practices of parent involvement in inner-city elementary and middle schools. *The Elementary School Journal, 91*(3) 289–305.

Epstein, J. L., & Sheldon, S. (2002, May/June). Present and accounted for: Improving student attendance through family and community involvement. *Journal of Educational Research, 95*(5), 308–321.

Flanagan, C. A., Cumsille, P., Gill, S., & Gallay, L. S. (2007). School and community climates and civic commitments: Patterns for ethnic minority and majority students. *Journal of Educational Psychology, 99*(2), 421–431.

Fuerenstein, A. (2000). School characteristics and parent involvement: Influences on participation in children's schools. *The Journal of Educational Research, 94*(1), 29–40.

Gonzalez, A. R. (2002). Parental involvement: Its contribution to high school students' motivation. *The Clearing House, 75*(3), 132–134.

Greenwood, G. E., Hickman, C. W. (1991). Research and practice in parent involvement: Implications for teacher education. *Elementary School Journal, 91*(3), 279–289.

Harry, B., Klinger, J. K., & Hart, J. (2005). African American families under fire: Ethnographic views of family strengths. *Remedial and Special Education, 26*(2), 101–112.

Haynes, N., Comer, J. (1996). Integrating schools, families, and communities through successful school reform: The school development program. *School Psychology Review, 25*(4), 501–507.

Henderson, A. (1988). Parents are a school's best friends. *Phi Delta Kappan, 70*(2), 148–153.

Henderson, A. T., & Mapp, K. L. (2002). *A new wave of evidence: The impact of school, family, and community connections on Student achievement*. Austin, TX: National Center for Family and Community Connections with Schools Southwest Educational Development Laboratory.

Henderson, A. T., & Berla, N. (Eds.). (1994). *A new generation of evidence: The family is critical to student achievement*. Washington, DC: National Committee for Citizens in Education.

Hope-King, S., & Goodwin, A. L. (2002). *Culturally responsive parental involvement*. Washington, DC: American Association of Colleges for Teacher Education.

Lewis, A. (1995). Changing views of parent involvement. *Phi Delta Kappan, 76*(6), p 430–432.

Leyser, Y., & Abrams. P. (1982). Teacher attitudes toward normal and exceptional groups. *Journal of Psychology, 110*(2), 227–238.

Matuszny, R. M., Banda, D. R., & Coleman, T. J. (2007). A progressive plan for developing collaborative relationships with parents from diverse backgrounds. *Teaching Exceptional Children, 39*(4), 24–31.

McCarthey, S. J. (2000). Home–school connections: A review of the literature. *Journal of Educational Research, 93*(3), 145–145.

McNeal, R. B. (2001). Differential effects of parental involvement on cognitive and behavioral outcomes by socioeconomic status. *Journal of Socio-economics, 30*(2), 171–179.

Nakagawa, K. (2000). Unthreading the ties that bind: Questioning the discourse of parent involvement. *Educational Policy, 14*(4), 443–473.

Pressini, D. (1998). What's all the fuss about? *Teaching Children Mathematics, 4*(6), 320–326.

Raffaele, L., & Knoff, H. (1999). Improving home–school collaboration with disadvantaged families: Organizational principles. *School Psychology Review, 28*(3), 448–467.

Resnick, M. D., Bearman, P. S., Blum, R. W., Bauman, K. E., Harris, K. M., Jones, J. , et al. (1997). Protecting adolescents from harm: Findings from the National Longitudinal Study on Adolescent Health. *Journal of the American Medical Association, 278*(10), 823–832.

Sanders, M., & Epstein, J. (2000). The national network of partnership schools: How research influences educational practice. *Journal of Education for Students Placed at Risk, 5*(1/2), 1–61.

St. Pierre, J. (1996). Reach out & touch your community. *Thrust for Educational Leadership, 26*(3), 30–33.

Trivette, P., & Anderson, E. (1995). The effects of four components of parental involvement on eighth-grade student achievement. *School Psychology Review, 24*(2), 299–328.

Trusty, J. (1996). Relationship of parent involvement in teens' career development to teens' attitudes, perceptions, and behavior. *Journal of Research and Development in Education, 30*(1), 63–69.

Trusty, J. (1998). Family influences on educational expectations of late adolescents. *Journal of Educational Research, 91*(5), 260–271.

Vazquez-Nuttal, E., Li, C., & Kaplan, J. P. (2006). Home–school partnerships with culturally diverse families: Challenges and solutions for school personnel. *Journal of Applied School Psychology, 22*(2), 81–102.

Walberg, H. J., & Wallace, T. (1992). Family programs for academic learning. *School Community Journal, 2*(1), 12–28.

Watkins, T. J. (1997). Teacher communications, child achievement, and parent traits in parent involvement models. *Journal of Educational Research, 91*(1), 3–12.

CULTURAL PERSPECTIVES

7

We must treat all children with love, care and respect. We must make them feel welcomed and invited by allowing their interests, culture, and history into the classroom. We must reconnect them to their own brilliance and gain their trust so that they will learn from us. We must respect them so they will feel connected with us.

Lisa Delpit p. 48

If students insult each other, it is easier for us to try to make each student act more courteously than it is to ask which elements of the system might have contributed to the problem . . . . it is obviously more convenient for us to address each individual who says something insulting than it is to track down the structural contributors to such behaviors. . . . The status quo has no more reliable ally than the teacher of coping skills, because whatever is to be coped with is treated as something to be accepted rather than changed.

Alfie Kohn, The Limits of Teaching Skills, p. 6

Developing a classroom where all learners want to be, where they will thrive academically and socially, and develop positive attitudes about others necessitates consideration of cultural perspectives and development of management practices that are culturally responsive. As one aspect of multicultural education, culturally responsive classroom management can promote a sense of belonging and equal opportunity for learning in the classroom, as well as an appreciation of diversity.

Culturally responsive classroom management includes an understanding of the influence of culture, gender, ability, and socioeconomic status on students' communication, patterns of learning, and classroom behavior, as well as on teachers' expectations and interactions. Failure to address these influences results in inequitable treatment of students, as well as inequitable access to opportunities for learning. Understanding and planning for diversity can bring many benefits to all learners. With a focus on classroom management, this chapter explores the influence of culture on both teachers and learners and suggests strategies for meeting the needs of diverse populations of children and fostering an appreciation of diversity.

Nieto defines multicultural education as "antiracist and basic education for all students that permeates all areas of schooling; it is characterized by a commitment to social justice and critical approaches to learning" (1999, p. xviii). Her definition includes not only race, ethnicity, and language, but also gender, social class, sexual orientation, ability, and other differences. This definition of multicultural education and culturally responsive classroom management has much different implications for practice than what is typically played out in many classrooms. As Nieto (1999) asserts, multicultural education is often interpreted by teachers to mean a unit on civil rights, bulletin boards featuring Martin Luther King during Black History Month and the inclusion of Kwanza and Chanukah in winter décor and celebrations. However, multicultural education and, more specifically, culturally responsive classroom management are not just about presenting multicultural perspectives in lessons and celebrating diversity. For teachers, it means examining personal beliefs and biases, understanding behavior and communication patterns, and attending to classroom curriculum and materials.

This chapters starts by looking at how culture influences learners and teachers, and how, by ignoring cultural perspectives, learners can be left behind, disengaged, and disenfranchised. The chapter continues by presenting culturally responsive classroom management practices.

INFLUENCE OF CULTURE

Students bring to the classroom diverse characteristics that can be shaped by culture, family traditions, economic conditions, and previous school experiences. In addition, individual characteristics, such as activity levels and learning abilities and disabilities, contribute to the uniqueness of each learner. These variables can influence communication styles, social behaviors, approaches to learning, values, and motivation. For some students, the influence of culture, economic conditions, and disabilities can put them at a disadvantage in the classroom, especially when their characteristics are misunderstood or misinterpreted by the teacher.

Communication

Communication style is an important factor in the cultural climate of the classroom. According to Gay (2000), children of color whose communication styles are more representative of their cultural and ethnic traditions are more likely to be at a disadvantage than those whose communication styles approximate the mainstream cultural norms. A mismatch between the communication styles of teacher and learner can cause misinformation with regard to a student's achievement, as well as misunderstanding with regard to classroom behavior. Students may not be able to communicate, and/or their teachers may not be able to understand all students due to differences in communication styles. Furthermore, teachers may view some communication styles as disrespectful or disruptive.

Gay (2000) gives many examples of how communication styles can differ by culture and affect classroom dynamics. In one example, African American children may use a call–response style of communication. Call–response involves listeners responding to the speaker as they are talking by giving compliments, comments, and criticisms. In this communication style, the speaker "calls" or makes a statement and the listener responds with a vocal utterance and/or gesture. In addition, African American speakers may enter a conversation or "gain the floor" through assertiveness rather than waiting for permission to speak. These behaviors may be considered rude or disruptive by many teachers. As another example, many African American, Latino, Native American, and Asian American students tend to be more inductive, interactive, and communal in problem solving. They tend to work from the big or whole picture to the parts, working together to formulate an answer or a solution. These styles are in contrast to that of many teachers who ask convergent, single-answer questions and propose deductive problems that emphasize a part-to-whole way of thinking. Questions are answered by one individual at a time. The details and how they fit to form the whole are both important.

Nonverbal communication is another aspect of communication style that may be culturally influenced. Nonverbal communication includes facial expression, gestures, personal distance, and sense of time, as well as the degree of assertiveness in communicating. DuPraw and Axner (1997) describe how nonverbal communication can come into play. For instance, for some White Americans, a raised voice can be a sign of disagreement or conflict, while for some African, Jewish, and Italian Americans, a raised voice is a sign of enthusiasm and excitement in a conversation among friends. Thus, some White Americans may react negatively to a loud discussion, while members of some American ethnic or non-White racial groups may show no concern. In the classroom, the culturally responsive teacher uses caution in making assumptions about a student's tone of voice.

Learning and Motivation

According to DuPraw and Axner (1997), the ways that individuals approach task completion can vary by culture. For example, when it comes to working together effectively on a task, cultures differ with respect to the importance placed on establishing relationships. Individuals from Asian or Hispanic cultures tend to value establishing relationships early in the collaborative process and emphasize task completion toward the end. In contrast, European Americans tend to focus immediately on the task at hand, and let relationships develop as they work on the task. This does not mean that individuals from any one of these cultural backgrounds value relationships or commitment to tasks any more or any less; it means that they may pursue them differently.

According to Gay (2000), for African American and Latino cultures, problem solving is highly contextual and individuals with these cultural influences often engage in setting the stage prior to a performance or task. African American students in the classroom may be setting the stage when they spend a lot of time arranging their materials, sharpening their pencil, stretching, or socializing with their peers before getting started on a task. While these behaviors may be a way for these students to focus, they may be perceived as procrastination or wasting time by an unknowing teacher.

McCarthy and Benally (2003) identify the learning preferences of many Native American learners. They may have a preference for learning that more closely resembles learning in their homes and communities, including small group learning and getting assistance from peers, joint activities, and learning through observations of elders. In addition, Native American learners have a preference for learning that is visual, as well as holistic. Native Americans may respond with inattentiveness to whole-group instruction via lecture followed by independent work, as is found in many classrooms. Teachers may attribute the lack of attentiveness to lack of motivation or disregard for a lesson.

Students with behavioral disorders and students with learning disabilities often have low self-esteem and poor motivation (Friend, 2007). For example, students with learning disabilities often exhibit an external locus of control or the tendency to attribute their successes and failures to external forces such as luck rather than effort. Some students with learning disabilities also demonstrate learned helplessness by giving up on a task before they have even tried and/or by overdependence on the teacher for assistance, feedback, and attention. Students with behavior disorders and learning disabilities often experience low academic achievement (Friend, 2007). A history of failure can inhibit motivation and the willingness to take risks in the classroom. Students that experience repeated failure may give up or appear apathetic with regard to success or grades.

Values

Lambie (2005) provides an example of how African American cultural values can be in conflict with school values in high schools. According to her review of research, Lambie indicates that the value that African American girls place on motherhood often outweighs the value that they place on completing high school or college, resulting in a large number of African American girls who drop out of school to become mothers. Lambie suggests that an awareness of this issue can assist teachers in helping African American girls develop high self-esteem and competency early in the educational process, as well as helping girls identify academically successful role models.

La Roche and Shriberg (2004) identify three Latino cultural values that can affect school performance. *Respeto* is a cultural value characterized by obedience toward parents and elders. Many Latino children are taught not to make eye contact or question authority. This seemingly passive attitude may be interpreted as lack of interest on the part of the teacher. *Familismo* is characterized by loyalty and family attachment. Family relationships are valued over relationships outside the family. Hence, Latino children may be more likely to seek help from family members than from teachers or other school personnel. Again, this behavior may be interpreted by the school as lack of interest. *Allocentrism* is the tendency to value group goals rather than individual goals, and to emphasize social relationships. Many individuals of Latino descent value collaboration and group cohesiveness over assertiveness and competition. Therefore, Latino children may do better in classrooms with a strong sense of community and thrive less well in many typical classrooms that promote competitiveness and individual comparisons.

Native American learners often speak more quietly and look downward when responding to a teacher as a sign of respect (McCarthy & Benally, 2003; Sparks, 2000). In addition, in many Native American cultures, competition in the classroom is not valued. Achieving beyond the group's norms is frowned upon and the achievement of the group is more important than the achievement of the individual (Sparks, 2000; Swisher, 1991; Wilder, Jackson, 4 Smith, 2001). Hence, students may be reticent to answer questions in front of the class or correct the answer of one of their peers in front of the class, be the winner of an academic competition, or achieve high grades.

Behavior

Townsend (2000) explains how African American learners can be at a disadvantage because of their activity level. Many African American learners are more active in the classroom than their peers. African American cultures value activity, especially in boys, and characterize a high activity level as "verve." This activity level, which may be valued in a learner's home and community, can be a cause of concern for misinformed teachers. In addition to being more physically active, many African American learners are used to engaging in many activities and conversations simultaneously while in their home or community. In many classrooms, teachers reward individual activities and attention to one task at a time, as well as quiet work, putting African American learners at a disadvantage.

Students with disabilities often bring social characteristics and behaviors to the classroom that may be viewed negatively or misunderstood by the teacher. In addition to academic difficulties, low self-esteem, and low motivation, some students with disabilities, also have difficulty with social behaviors. For example, students with attention deficit disorders, learning disabilities, and behavior disorders often either lack social skills or the ability to recognize that different behaviors are required for different settings (Friend, 2007). Teachers can respond to students with disabilities with lowered expectations, a low tolerance for their behavior, and feelings of helplessness with regard to being able to teach these individuals. Studies of teachers' attitudes regarding individuals with disabilities indicate that when teachers lack preparation and knowledge about disabilities, they often have negative attitudes toward inclusion of those individuals in the general classroom (Van Reusen, Shoho, & Barker, 2001). The characteristics that many children and youth with disabilities exhibit may hinder their sense of belonging, independence, competence, and generosity.

INEQUITABLE TREATMENT OF LEARNERS

When multicultural perspectives are ignored, when discord exists between the teacher's culture and the student's culture, when children are all treated the same regardless of their individual differences, or when teachers treat students only from their own cultural frame of reference, children can be denied opportunities to learn and can become disenfranchised and disengaged. Teachers with limited knowledge of how culture can influence learning, communication, and behavior may confuse or misinterpret student learning and behavioral characteristics as a learning or behavior problem and/or a disability (Chamberlain, 2005; Gay, 2002; Gollnick & Chinn, 1991; Patton & Townsend, 1997). Years of data clearly indicate that discipline or punitive strategies such as office referrals, suspensions, and expulsions are disproportionately meted out in schools and classrooms. In addition, minority students are overrepresented in special education programs and underrepresented in programs for students who are gifted. They also experience higher dropout rates and lower academic achievement.

Inequities in School Discipline

While we would like to believe that classroom sanctions are meted out equitably based on objective standards for classroom behavior, research indicates otherwise. The doling out of sanctions in the form of suspensions, expulsions, reprimands, and so forth is highly contextualized and influenced by many factors, including race, gender, socioeconomic status, and ability. Teachers' perceptions of student behavior may be consciously or unconsciously biased by these factors. Several studies have documented racial, socioeconomic, disabled–nondisabled, and gender disparities in school discipline data (Drakeford, 2004; Johnson, Boyden, & Pittz, 2001; Skiba, Michael, Nardo, & Peterson, 2002). Data from these studies indicate that boys tend to be disciplined more than girls; children from low-income families tend to be disciplined more than children from high-income families; minority children, especially African American children, are disciplined with punitive strategies more frequently than White children; and children with disabilities are punished more often than their nondisabled peers.

African American males tend to bear the brunt of inequitable disciplinary procedures. In their study, Skiba et al. (2002) controlled for gender and economic status variables and found that African American males, regardless of their economic status, receive a greater portion of punitive measures than other groups. This study also suggests that while males tend to be disciplined more than females, they also tend to have higher rates of misbehavior. However, the same does not hold true with regard to African American males. Data did not indicate higher rates of misbehavior on the part of African American males than for other students. Data did suggest, however, that African American males tend to receive more severe punishment for less severe behavior, as well as for behavior that is subjectively defined. For example, African American males are likely to be referred to the office for behaviors such as disrespect, excessive noise, making threats, and loitering, while White students were referred for vandalism, leaving without permission, and smoking. In another study, Casteel (1998) found that in integrated classrooms, African American males have more negative interactions and receive less praise and positive feedback from White teachers.

Another group that tends to receive higher rates of punitive strategies is students with disabilities. The results from a study by Safran and Safran (1985) suggest that children with a reputation for being disruptive or who are labeled as such may receive disproportionate blame for classroom disorder. In addition, students with behavior disorders tend to be viewed negatively (Center & Wascom, 1987; Habel, Bloom, & Ray, Bacon, 1999; Leyser & Abrams, 1982; Safran & Safran, 1985) and experience rejection and low tolerance from many classroom teachers (Habel et al., 1999; Johnson & Blankenship, 1984; Ritter, 1989). They also experience higher rates of negative interactions with teachers. In their studies, Gunter & Jack (1994) found that negative interactions between teachers and behavior-disordered students occur 22% of the classroom time and positive interactions occur only 3% of the time.

Another group that may be disciplined through suspension and expulsion at higher rates are learners from low-income families (Brantlinger, 1991; Skiba, Michael, Nardo, and Peterson, (2002); Skiba, Peterson, & Williams, 1997). In a study by Brantlinger (1991), low-income adolescents reported a greater number and variety of penalties that seemed both disproportionate to the offenses and humiliating in nature. Brantlinger suggests that inequitable school conditions and disciplinary practices for low-income students influence their behaviors and contribute to their anger and alienation. With regard to low-income students, it is important to note that race is a more significant factor with regard to school discipline than is income. Studies that have controlled for poverty still show racial inequities in disciplinary procedures (Skiba et al., 2000).

Research indicates that gender can also influence classroom discipline. Years of study indicate that boys tend to be disciplined more frequently than girls and are more often suspended (Skiba et al., 2002). In a meta-analysis of studies of gender equity in the classroom, Jones and Dindia (2004) found that teachers initiate more negative interactions with male students than with female students. Robinson (1992) found that a teacher's notion of appropriate gender behavior plays a major role in determining the approach and response to the behavior of boys and girls in the classroom. Girls whose behavior deviates from stereotypical beliefs about girls and appropriate behavior risk conflict with the teacher and can result in the application of derogative labels regarding their character, which, in turn, can have a negative effect on girls' motivation and self-esteem.

Inequitable Learning Opportunities

Inequitable discipline can clearly lead to fewer learning opportunities and disengagement from school. Students who are suspended or expelled naturally miss opportunities for learning in the classroom. In addition, learners in the classroom can be given different treatment from their peers. In their study of students at risk for learning and behavior problems, Montague and Rinaldi (2001) found that children in the early grades (1–4) spent less time on task and received more negative and nonacademic responses from their teachers. Hence, these students also had negative perceptions of themselves and perceived their teachers as having negative expectations. Inequitable learning opportunities and discipline in schools can lead to underachievement and disengagement of learners.

Underachievement

Related to the issue of inequitable learning opportunities are the low-achievement and high dropout rates, and the overrepresentation of minority students in special education. A case in point is that African American males make up a disproportionately larger percentage of children and youth placed in special education, especially in the area of behavior disorders, than any other group (Duren Green, 2005; Salend & Garrick Duhaney, 2005). The behavior of African American learners may be perceived as problematic when viewed through the cultural lens of a White teacher; hence, referrals and placements for behavior disorders may be more likely (Webb-Johnson, 2002). Furthermore, if African American males are suspended, expelled, and sent to the office more frequently, they can miss instruction, feedback, and other learning opportunities. In addition to overrepresentation in special education, African Americans have higher dropout rates than Asian American and White students, as well as lower performance on standardized tests (National Center for Education Statistics [NCES], 2004).

Latino students, compared to White and Asian American students, have lower academic achievement and higher dropout rates (AFT Policy Brief, 2006), and are underrepresented in programs for gifted students. Interestingly, this group experiences overrepresentation in special education in a few states and urban areas (Artiles, Rueda, Salazar, & Higareda, 2005; Blanchett, Mumford, & Beachum, 2005; Conroy & Fieros, 2002) and underrepresentation in other areas, suggesting the possibility that these individuals may have unrecognized and unmet educational needs (Artiles et al., 2002). When Latino students, like African Americans, are identified for special education, they tend to be placed in more restrictive settings than their White counterparts (Conroy & Fieros, 2002).

Although less pronounced than with African American populations, Native Americans are also overrepresented in special education (Parrish, 2002). Native Americans experience higher dropout rates and lower academic achievement than White students (Kao & Thompson, 2003; Wilder et al., 2001). As with other minority populations, teachers can hold expectations and require ways of doing things that are different from what many Native American students have learned elsewhere (Wilder et al., 2001).

Children in low-income households often do not fair as well academically as their more affluent counterparts (Mahoney, Lord, & Carryl, 2005; Von Secker, 2004). Children from low-income households often start school with less preparation, experience lower academic achievement during elementary school, experience continued risk for academic failure during later years, and have higher dropout rates than students from middle- and upper-income households (Mahoney et al., 2005; NCES, 2004). In addition, children from low-income households may hold a relatively lower expectancy of success and lower intrinsic motivation for pursuing academic tasks (Mahoney et al., 2005; Tucker et al., 2002). According to their analysis of data regarding race, poverty, and overrepresentation in special education, Skiba, Poloni-Staudinger, Simmons, Feggins-Azziz, & Chung (2005) contend that with regard to placement in special education, the primary effect of poverty is to exacerbate existing racial disparities. While parental involvement can enhance academic achievement and foster positive attitudes toward school, low-income families often experience barriers to involvement in their children's education (Hill & Taylor, 2004).

Disengagement
Students from diverse cultural groups and students with disabilities who experience poor academic outcomes and disparities in discipline can easily become disengaged from school and at risk for dropping out. In a review of research on academic identification, Griffin (2002) found that students who experience low achievement over time may develop low self-esteem and low self-efficacy, leading to frustration with school. Students often demonstrate their frustration with oppositional behavior, absenteeism, apathy, and disenfranchisement. On the other hand, the more success a student experiences, the more identified with school the student becomes. African American and Hispanic

students tend to demonstrate higher levels of academic misidentification relative to Asian American and White students (Griffin, 2002).

RESPONSIVE CLASSROOM MANAGEMENT

The reasons for inequitable discipline and overrepresentation of minority students in special education are varied and complex. However, most experts agree that cultural mismatch between learners and the teacher can contribute to these patterns. Nieto (1999) cautions about basing purportedly culturally responsive teaching practices on a static view of culture. Although cultural attributes may apply to many, they do not apply to all, and their manifestations are mediated by social class, education, ethnic identification, and affiliation (Gay, 2000). Assuming that students of a particular background have a set of values and behaviors specific to that culture can lead to lists of characteristics being attributed stereotypically to all students and to the assumption that all students from the same cultural background learn in the same way. Nieto (1999) cites the example of teachers assuming that all Korean children prefer to work on their own. Truly responsive management takes into account the dynamic, complex, and multifaceted nature of culture and recognizes that each student brings his or her own perspective, personality, idiosyncrasies, cultural experiences, and so forth.

The myriad characteristics, abilities, experiences, and influences that learners bring to the classroom may seem overwhelming to consider in developing sound classroom management practices. Teachers may be tempted to develop a plan that treats all learners the same. In fact, a well-respected teacher, Jonnie Walkingstick, was speaking to a group of teacher education students discussing what it was like to be a student, to be Cherokee, and to teach children who are Cherokee. One future teacher in the audience spoke up and said that working with diverse populations would not be a problem because she would just treat everyone the same. This idealistic notion—that fair and equitable classroom management means treating everyone the same—fails to recognize the importance of multicultural perspective and the diverse needs of learners. As Walkingstick stated, "Everyone is not the same, and treating everyone as though they are the same would mean not meeting their needs." Nieto (1999) concurs, indicating that a refusal to acknowledge the influence of culture on learning and a commitment to treating everyone the same can be counterproductive and deny many students equal access to learning. Hence, culturally responsive teaching cannot be applied mechanistically and uncritically; instead, it involves continual critical reflection, awareness of personal biases, knowledge of students and their families, and practices that accommodate all learners.

Critical Reflection

Garmon (2005) posits that in order for teachers to develop culturally responsive classrooms, they must be willing to examine their beliefs, understand how their experiences influence those beliefs, and be critically reflective about their practices. Garmon identifies six factors that are essential to enhancing teachers' attitudes toward and beliefs about diversity: openness, self-awareness/self-reflection, a commitment to social justice, intercultural experiences, educational experiences, and collegial support.

Openness
Garmon characterizes openness as being receptive to new information, a willingness to consider others' ideas and arguments, and openness to different types of diversity. According to Garmon, a lack of openness can limit learning and understanding of cultural perspectives. Culturally responsive teachers learn about their students' community, family, culture, and heritage. They are willing to consider their learners' needs in light of their backgrounds.

Self-Awareness/Self-Reflection
Garmon defines self-awareness as having an awareness of one's own beliefs and attitudes. Self-reflection is the willingness and ability to think critically about one's actions, thoughts, and biases. Both are critical to culturally responsive classroom management. Culturally responsive teachers are willing to examine their own beliefs and biases and to be critical of their own practices. They examine practices for biases, assumptions, and possible inequities.

Commitment to Social Justice
Commitment to social justice, as defined by Garmon, is a deep concern for achieving equity and equality for all people. Along with being aware of the inequities in educational opportunities for minority children, culturally responsive teachers become advocates and agents for change in schools.

Intercultural Experiences
Garmon describes intercultural experiences as direct interactions with individuals from groups different from one's own. Diverse cultural experiences can enhance cultural understanding and foster positive attitudes about diversity.

Educational Experiences and Collegial Support
Teachers can learn from workshops, courses, and studies on diversity that provide rich experiences and opportunities for critical reflection and self-examination. Teachers can benefit from support groups of colleagues that provide continued opportunities for dialogue, reflection, and professional growth with regard to culturally responsive practices.

Culturally Responsive Practices

Knowledge of students' cultural orientations, communication patterns, behaviors, and learning preferences can assist teachers in developing responsive classroom management. Teachers can use their knowledge of students in planning lessons, developing classroom expectations and rules, responding to students in nonpunitive ways, and motivating students.

Curriculum Relevance

Making sure that the curriculum is relevant to learners is key to engaging and motivating youth. "Culturally relevant teachers utilize students' culture as a vehicle for learning" Ladson-Billings (1995, p. 161) by creating lessons that incorporate students' culture and heritage. In one example, Fránquiz & del Carmen Salazar (2004) describe the engagement of Latino students whose teacher taught English as a second language through Spanish literature and included study of individuals such as César Chávez and other American heroes who tackled social issues in nonviolent ways. Ladson-Billings (1995) gives the example of one teacher's artist/craftsman-in-residence program in which a parent was invited into the classroom for 2 days to teach students how to make sweet potato pies. In addition to learning to make the pies, students engaged in research about George Washington Carver and his research on sweet potatoes, ran taste tests, and developed marketing plans.

Ladson-Billings (1995) also suggests that a culturally relevant curriculum empowers students by involving them in critiquing cultural norms, values, mores, and institutions that perpetuate inequities. She gives an example of a group of students and teachers who examined out-of-date textbooks and wrote letters to the editor of the newspaper to inform the community of the inaccuracies in the textbooks and the inequities in how funds for textbooks were distributed so that middle class groups received newer ones.

Ignoring cultural relevancy in the curriculum can be disadvantageous for many learners. "When instruction is stripped of children's cultural legacies, then they are forced to believe that the world and all the good things in it were created by others. This leaves students further alienated from the school and its instructional goals . . . (Delpit, 1995, p.41). According to Delpit, having a culturally relevant curriculum does not mean that we should water down curricula, lower standards, or teach only what students are interested in; rather, we should start with student culture, heritage, and interest and build academic programs around them.

Classroom Materials

Classrooms can provide learners with physical evidence of belonging. In classrooms that are culturally responsive, classroom materials represent a rich array of diversity where learners can find many books, materials, and media, as well as décor, that are relevant to their culture (McKinley, 2003). Literature that has main characters with which students can identify and materials that acknowledge the diversity of students and families and that portray diverse individuals in nonstereotypical roles reinforce the message that everyone belongs. In contrast, in classrooms that include only token pictures or books that portray people who are ethnically and culturally diverse, token pictures of individuals with disabilities, token holiday decorations from various cultures, or a 1-week display of famous African Americans, learners may find little with which to identify and may consequently see school as irrelevant and their culture as undervalued.

In addition to relevant curriculum and materials, culturally responsive teachers model appreciation for diversity (Weinstein, Curran, & Tomlinson-Clarke, 2003). Culturally responsive teachers celebrate the diversity in the classroom and call attention to the richness that diversity adds to the classroom community.

Learning Focus

Keeping the focus on learning and academic engagement as opposed to behavior control can maximize learning and create a positive climate for all learners. Studies have shown that teachers vary in the amount of time spent on discipline matters versus time spent on academics. For example, Kamps et al. (1989) found that urban teachers make more comments related to management, while suburban teachers make more comments related to academics. Davis and Jordan (1994) found a relationship between higher rates of discipline and lower academic achievement. Time spent on controlling behavior may detract from academic engagement opportunities, especially for African American males. Because many subjective behaviors, such as "being disrespectful" and getting prepared for a task, become reasons for disciplining students (Skiba et al., 2002; Townsend, 2000), the manner in which these behaviors are perceived and handled can make a big difference in classroom climate and learning orientation.

Townsend (2000, p. 385) suggests using the "so what" test in developing classroom behavioral expectations. Teachers can use the "so what" test to determine what behaviors are most crucial to learning. Behaviors that are crucial to learning pass the test and hence remain as expectations, while those which fail are inconsequential to learning. For example, many students barely touch their seat while working on seat work, especially students with a high level of "verve." If barely touching the seat poses no threat to learning, it fails the "so what" test and should not be considered an appropriate expectation. Similarly, if talking with a peer while working does not interfere with learning, then keeping quiet during seat work activities should not be an expectation.

Accommodating Communication

In addition to avoiding controlling behavior, cultural styles can be incorporated into classroom instruction. For example, the "call and response" behaviors of learners can be incorporated into a lesson and used as a valid way to enhance learning (Monroe & Obidah, 2004). When teachers respond with reprimands or sanctions to "call and response" communication, it can strain the student–teacher relationship (Obidah, Teel, in Brown, 2003). Brown (2003) illustrates how one teacher reframes "call and response" communication so that it is not considered disruptive or inappropriate. A teacher in Brown's study reported, "Conversation is their primary priority. It's unconscious. They are from very verbal environments. I find that they can handle side discussions and engage in the main discussion at the same time. They're not talking to be disruptive." (p. 281)

As another example of accommodating differences in communication, teachers can attend to the way in which they communicate commands. African American learners may be more accustomed to straightforward commands from adults in authority rather than the indirect commands used by White teachers (Delpit, 1995). An African American learner might not respond to a direction put in the form of a question, such as "John, would you please finish your work?" although he may respond to a more direct command, such as "Get finished." Delpit recommends that teachers either change the way that directions are given or teach students the "code" so that they will understand how the teacher communicates a directive that is not optional.

McCarthy and Benally (2003) give an example of teachers whose middle school Navajo students won't respond with an alternative answer when a classmate gives an incorrect response because doing so would violate a cultural norm. Hence, awareness of those norms and values can assist teachers in designing appropriate instruction. Small-group work and cooperative learning, as opposed to didactic instruction, would accommodate a learner's reluctance to answer in front of the class. For another case in point, McCarthy and Benally (2003) indicate that individual reward systems can be ineffective with Native American students. Native American students share with their peers; hence, a reward earned by one becomes the reward of all, whether it was earned or not. Native American students may respond more favorably to opportunities for small-group work, cooperative learning, and peer tutoring.

Accomodating Behavioral Styles
Since there may be misunderstandings due to differences regarding views of appropriate behavior and communication patterns, Weinstein et al. (2003) encourage the use of clear expectations. Teachers can involve students in developing norms and expectations for the classroom community. Moreover, they can communicate and teach academic and behavioral expectations so that all learners understand the specific behaviors that are required in the classroom. Teachers can model and provide students with opportunities to practice these behaviors. Likewise, teachers can examine behaviors in light of cultural norms and values before determining if a behavior should be reprimanded or penalized.

Employing instructional tactics that allow for movement can minimize the amount of time and energy needed to control noise and activity in the classroom. One first grade teacher allows her students time to "set the stage for learning" during writing lessons by allowing students 5 minutes to talk with each other about what they are going to write and to share ideas with each other before they get started. Furthermore, cooperative learning, peer tutoring, and hands-on activities that capitalize on student strengths and interests and allow for conversation and movement accommodate the learning preferences of many cultural groups (Gay, 2000; Starnes, 2006; Townsend, 2000).

The Circle of Courage

A classroom where cultural perspectives are considered can be very conducive to enhancing the Circle of Courage. Lessons and materials that are culturally relevant and teacher–student relationships that respect culture and heritage enhance belonging. Strategies that recognize and incorporate communication, behavior patterns, and learning preferences enhance academic success. Discipline that considers students' perspectives and pedagogy that empowers learners to question inequitable treatment enhance independence. Finally, when all learners are valued and appreciated, when the heritage of all learners contributes to the richness of the classroom, and when all learners can share with and care for each other, generosity is nurtured. Figure 7.1 demonstrates how culturally responsive practices embrace the Circle of Courage.

	CULTURALLY RESPONSIVE PRACTICE	EXAMPLES
Belonging	Provide culturally relevant instruction and materials.	Present a unit on Thanksgiving that explores the holiday from the perspective of Native Americans. Provide books and materials that are representative of many cultures.
Independence	Understand the influence of culture on behavior and communication.	Learn about students' community, culture, and heritage. Participate in a book study with colleagues. Engage in reflection and dialogue with colleagues.
	Examine personal biases. Provide accommodations for behavioral and communication styles.	Allow for movement and active learning. Arrange desks in clusters. Incorporate "call and response" in instruction. Adjust communication to a style that is congruent with students' culture or teach students communication "codes."
	Empower learners to question inequities.	Engage learners in examining media for cultural biases. Allow them to present their findings to a community group.
Mastery	Attend to learning preferences.	Allow cooperative learning and peer tutoring.
Generosity	Allow for, acknowledge, and appreciate the contributions of all learners in the classroom.	Acknowledge the contributions of heritage to the richness of the classroom. Allow for caring and helping each other. Allow for the sharing of traditions and celebrations. Model appreciation of diversity.

SUMMARY

Culturally responsive classroom management involves a continual process of learning and reflection. Culture influences behavior, communication, motivation, and learning preferences. Wise classroom teachers recognize the importance of obtaining cultural perspectives. They understand how their biases and assumptions could lead to inequities in discipline and learning. They learn about the cultures and heritages of their students, incorporating those perspectives into their instruction and management practices. They create classrooms that model appreciation of diversity. The Circle of Courage is a natural fit for culturally responsive classroom management as students learn to respect and value diversity, engage in culturally relevant study, question injustice, and care for each other.

REFERENCES

American Federation of Teachers (AFT). (2006). *Where we stand: English language learners*. Washington, DC. American Federation of Teachers.

Artiles, A. J., Rueda, R., Salazar, J. J., & Higareda, I. (2005). Within-group diversity in minority disproportionate representation: English language learners in urban school districts. *Exceptional Children, 71*(3), 283–300.

Artiles, A. J., Rueda, R., Salazar, J. J., & Higareda, I. (2002). English-language learner representation in special education in California urban school districts. In D. J. Losen & G. Orfield (Eds.), *Racial inequity in special education* (pp. 117–136). Cambridge, MA: Harvard Education Press.

Blanchett, W. J., Mumford, V., & Beachum, F. (2005). Urban school failure and disproportionality in a post-Brown era. *Remedial and Special Education, 26*(2), 70–81.

Blum, R. (2005). A case for school connectedness. *Educational Leadership, 62*(7), 16–20.

Brantlinger, E. (1991). Social class distinctions in adolescents' reports of problems and punishment in school. *Behavioral Disorders, 17*(1), 36–46.

Brown, D. F. (2003). Classroom management in a diverse society. *Theory Into Practice, 42*(4), 277–282.

Casteel, C. A. (1998). Teacher–student interactions and race in integrated classrooms. *Journal of Educational Research, 92*(2), 115–121.

Center, D. B, & Wascom, A. (1987). Teacher perception of social behavior in behavior disorders and socially normal children and youth. *Behavioral Disorders, 12*(3). 200–206.

Chamberlain, S. (2005). Recognizing and responding to cultural differences in the education of culturally and linguistically diverse learners. *Intervention in School and Clinic, 40*(4), 195–211.

Conroy, J. W., & Fieros, E. G. (2002). Double jeopardy: An exploration of restrictiveness and race in special education. In D. J. Losen & G. Orfied (Eds.), *Racial inequity in special education*. Cambridge, MA: Harvard Civil Rights Project.

Curran, M., Tomlinson–Clarke, S., & Weinstein, C. (2003). Culturally responsive classroom management: Awareness into action. *Theory Into Practice, 42*(4), 269–276.

Davis, J. E., & Jordan, W. J. (1994). The effects of school context, structure, and experiences on African American males in middle and high schools. *Journal of Negro Education, 63*(4), 570–587.

Delpit, L. (1995). *Other people's children: Cultural conflict in the classroom.* New York: The New Press.

Delpit, L., & Dowdy, J. (Eds.). (2002). *The skin that we speak: Thoughts on language and culture in the classroom.* New York: The New Press.

Drakeford, W. (2004). *Racial disproportionality in school disciplinary practices.* Denver, CO: National Center for Culturally Responsive Educational Systems.

DuPraw, M. E., & Axner, M. (1997). Working on common cross-cultural communication challenges. Toward a more perfect union in an age of diversity: A guide to building stronger communities through public dialogue. Retrieved from http://www.p6s.org/ampu/crosscult.html, June 5, 2007.

Duren Green, T. (2005). Promising prevention and early intervention strategies to reduce overrepresentation of African American students in special education. *Preventing School Failure, 49*(3), 33–41.

Duren Green, T., McIntosh, A., Cook-Morales, V., & Robinson-Zanartu, C. (2005). From old schools to tomorrow's schools: Psychoeducational assessment of African American students. *Remedial and Special Education, 26*(2), 82–92.

Fránquiz and del Carmen Salazar. (2004). The transformative potential of humanizing pedagogy: Addressing the diverse needs of Chicano/Mexicano students. *The High School Journal, 87*(4), 36–53.

Friend, M. (2007). *Special education: Contemporary perspectives, for school professionals.* Boston: Allyn and Bacon.

Garmon, M. A. (2005). Six key factors for changing preservice teachers' attitudes and beliefs. *Educational Studies, 38*(3), 275–286.

Gay, G. (2000). *Culturally responsive teaching: Theory, research, and practice.* New York: Teachers College Press.

Gay, G. (2002). Culturally responsive teaching in special education for ethnically diverse students: Setting the stage. *International Journal of Qualitative Studies in Education, 15*(6), 613–629.

Gersten, R., & Brengelman, S. (1994). Effective instruction for culturally and linguistically diverse students: A reconceptualization. *Focus on Exceptional Children, 27*(1), 1–16.

Gollnick, D. M., & Chinn, P. C. (1991). Multicultural education for exceptional children. ERIC Digest # E498. Reston, VA: Council for Exceptional Children.

Greene, R., Beszterczey, S., Katzenstein, T., Park, K., & Goring, J. (2002). Are students with ADHD more stressful to teach? *Journal of Emotional & Behavioral Disorders, 10*(2), 79–89.

Griffin, B. W. (2002). Academic disidentification, race, and high school dropouts. *The High School Journal, 85*(4), 71–81.

Gunter, Philip L., & Jack, Susan L. (1994). Effects of challenging behaviors of students with EBD on teacher instructional behavior. *Preventing School Failure, 38*(3), 35–40.

Habel, J., Bloom, L. A., Ray, M. S., & Bacon, E. (1999). Consumer reports. What students with behaviour disorders say about school. *Remedial and Special Education, 20*(2), 93–105.

Hammond, H., Dupoux, E., & Ingalls, L. (2004). Culturally relevant classroom management strategies for American Indian students. *Rural Special Education Quarterly, 23*(4), 3–9.

Hill, N., & Taylor, L. (2004). Parental school involvement and children's academic achievement. *Current Directions in Psychological Science, 13*(4), 161–164.

Howard, G. (1999). *We can't teach what we don't know: White teachers, multiracial schools.* New York: Teachers College Press.

Johnson, L. J., & Blankenship, C. S. (1984). A comparison of label-induced expectancy bias in two preservice teacher education programs. *Behavioral Disorders, 9*(3), 167–174.

Johnson, T., Boyden, J., & Pittz, W. (2001). Racial profiling and punishment in U.S. public schools: How zero tolerance policies and high stakes testing subvert academic excellence and racial equity. (ERIC Document Reproduction Service No. ED461921)

Jones, S. M., & Dindia, K. (2004). A meta-analytic perspective on sex equity in the classroom. *Review of Educational Research, 74*(4), 443–471.

Jordan, A. (2005). Discourses of difference and the overrepresentation of black students in special education. *Journal of African American History, 90*(1/2).

Kamps, D. M., Cara, J. J., Delquadri, J. C., Arreaga-Mayer, C., Terry, B., & Greenwood, C. R. (1989). School-based research and intervention. *Education and Treatment of Children, 12*(35), 359–389.

Kao, G., & Thompson, J. (2003). Racial and ethnic stratification in educational achievement and attainment. *Annual Review of Sociology, 29*(1), 417–442.

Kunjufu, J. (2005). *Keeping black boys out of special education.* Chicago: African American Images.

Ladson-Billings, G. (1994). *The dreamkeepers: Successful teachers of African American children.* San Francisco: Jossey-Bass.

Ladson-Billings, G. (1995). But that's just good teaching! The case for culturally relevant pedagogy. *Theory Into Practice, 34*(3), 159–165.

Lambie, R. (2005). At-risk students and environmental factors. *Focus on Exceptional Children, 38*(4), 1–16.

La Roche, M., & Shriberg, D. (2004). High stakes exams and Latino students: Toward a culturally sensitive education for Latino children in the United States. *Journal of Educational and Psychological Consultation, 15*(2), 205–223.

Leyser, Y., & Abrams, P. D. (1982). Teacher attitudes toward normal and exceptional groups. *Journal of Psychology, 110*(2), 227–238.

Mahoney, J. L., Lord, H., & Carryl, E. (2005). An ecological analysis of after-school program participation and the development of academic performance and motivational attributes for disadvantaged children. *Child Development, 76*(1), 811–825.

McCarthy, J., & Benally, J. (2003). Classroom management in a Navajo middle school. *Theory Into Practice, 42*(4), 296–304.

McKinley, E. (2001). Cultural diversity: Masking power with innocence. *Science Education, 85*(1), 74–76.

McKinley, J. (2003). *Leveling the playing field and raising African American students' achievement in twenty-nine urban classrooms.* Retrieved August 10, 2005, from http://www. newhorizons.org/strategies/differentiated/mckinley.htm

Monroe, C., & Obidah, J. (2004). The influence of cultural synchronization on a teacher's perceptions of disruption: A case study of an African American middle-school classroom. *Journal of Teacher Education, 55*(3), 256–268.

Montague, M., & Rinaldi, C. (2001). Classroom dynamics and children at risk: A follow-up. *Learning Disability Quarterly, 24*(2), 75–84.

National Center for Education Statistics. (2004). *Status dropout rate.* Retrieved December 2, 2006, from http://nces.ed.gov/ssbr/pages/dropout.asp

Nieto, S. (1999). *The light in their eyes: Creating multicultural learning communities.* New York: Teachers College Press.

Obidah, J., & Teel, K. (2001). *Because of the kids: Facing racial and cultural differences in schools.* New York: Teachers College Press.

Parrish, T. (2002). Racial disparities in the identification, funding, and provision of special education. In D. J. Losen & G. Orfield (Eds.), *Racial inequity in special education* (pp. 15–37). Cambridge, MA: Harvard Civil Rights Project.

Patton, J., & Townsend, B. (1997). Creating inclusive environments for African American children and youth with gifts and talents. *Roeper Review, 20*(1), 13–17.

Ritter, D.R. (1989). Teacher perceptions of problem behavior in general and special education. Exceptional Children, 55(6), 559–564.

Robinson, K. H. (1992). Classroom discipline: Power, resistance and gender. A look at teacher perspectives. *Gender and Education, 4*(3), 273–287.

Safran, S. P., & Safran, J. S. (1985). Classroom context and teachers' perceptions of problem behaviors. *Journal of Educational Psychology, 85*(2), 237–243.

Salend, S., & Garrick Duhaney, L. (2005). Understanding and addressing the disproportionate representation of students of color in special education. *Intervention in School and Clinic, 40*(4), 213–221.

Skiba, R. J., Michael, R. S., Nardo, A. C., & Peterson, R. L. (2002). The color of discipline. *Urban Review, 34*(4), 317–343.

Skiba, R. J., Peterson, R. L., & Williams, T. (1997). Office referrals and suspension: Disciplinary intervention in middle schools, Education and Treatment of Children. 20(3), 295–316.

Skiba, R., Poloni-Staudinger, L., Simmons, A., Feggins-Azziz, L. R., & Chung, C. (2005). Unproven links: Can poverty explain disproportionality in special education? *Journal of Special Education, 39*(3), 130–144.

Sparks, S. (2000). Classroom and curriculum accommodations for Native American students. *Intervention in School and Clinic, 35*(5), 259–264.

Starnes, B. A. (2006). What we don't know can hurt them: White teachers, Indian children. *Phi Delta Kappan, 87*(5), 384–392.

Swisher, K. (1991). *American Indian/Alaskan Native learning styles: Research and practice* (ERIC Document Reproduction Service No. ED335175). Retrieved December 5, 2005, from http://www.ericdigests.org/pre-9220/indian.htm

Townsend, B. (2000). The disproportionate discipline of African American learners: Reducing school suspensions and expulsions. *Exceptional Children, 66*(3), 381–391.

Tucker, C. M., Zaycon, R. A., Herman, K. C., Reinke, W., Trujillo, M., Carraway, K. et al. (2002). Teacher and child variables as predictors of academic engagement among low-income African American children. *Psychology in the Schools, 39*(4), 477–488.

Van Reusen, A. K., Shoho, A. R., & Barker, K. S. (2001). High school teacher attitudes toward inclusion. *High School Journal, 84*(2), 7–14.

Von Secker, C. (2004). Science achievement in social contexts: Analysis from national assessment of educational progress. *Journal of Educational Research, 98*(2), 67–78.

Webb-Johnson, G. (2002). Are schools ready for Joshua? Dimensions of African-American culture among students identified as having behavioral/emotional disorders. *International Journal of Qualitative Studies in Education, 15*(6), 653–671.

Weinstein, C., Curran, M., & Tomlinson-Clarke, S. (2003). Culturally responsive classroom management: Awareness into action. *Theory Into Practice, 42*(4), 269–276.

Wilder, L. K., Jackson, A. P., & Smith, T. B. (2001). Secondary transition of multicultural learners: Lessons from the Navajo Native American experience. *Preventing School Failure, 45*(3), 119–125.

CREATING COMMUNITIES— RELATIONSHIPS AT THE GROUP LEVEL AND CLASSROOM STRUCTURES

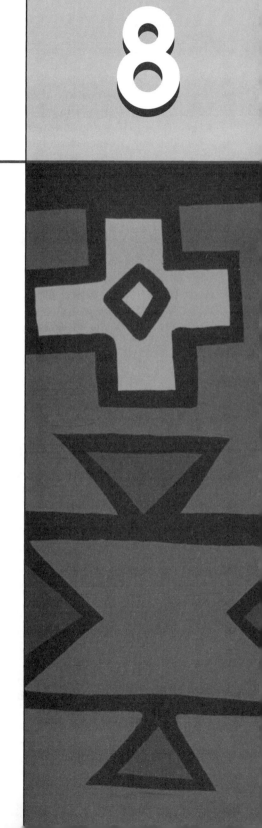

8

So often I have said in the past, when a war is over the statesmen should not go into conference with one another but should turn their attention to the infant rooms, since it is from there that comes peace or war.
Sylvia Ashton-Warner, 1963, p.93

Classrooms and schools are social places where social context and social activity influence the students' thoughts and actions (Mallory & New, 1994). Managing the mayhem that can accompany the social flurry in the classroom can be a challenge to many teachers. Good classroom management involves putting structures into place that capitalize on the social context of the classroom by creating a sense of community and assisting every student in gaining a sense of belonging. Students' behaviors are influenced by membership in and identification with a social group (Ellis & Zarbatany, 2007; Harris, 1995). With a sense of being valued and respected members of the classroom, children and youth will be "ready to learn" and will be more likely to enjoy school. A strong community creates a sense of unity and shared purpose, and children learn to care for each other.

DEVELOPING A STRONG CLASSROOM COMMUNITY

Constructivist teachers seek to develop a community of learners who are responsible for themselves and care for and respect each other. Developing community involves attention to many aspects of classroom life, including social climate, an ethos of caring, classroom discipline, problem solving, expectations, and organizational and instructional structures within the classroom. Each aspect is discussed below.

Social Climate

The social climate of the classroom can greatly influence a student's readiness and enthusiasm for learning. One primary goal of the constructivist teacher is to develop a focus on learning within an environment of security, acceptance, respect, and encouragement. Such an environment needs to be carefully crafted and nourished throughout the year. In a caring classroom community, students feel welcome and a part of the group. Strategies for developing community include traditions, ceremonies, rituals and rites, and allowing students time for celebration, play, and conversation (Howard, 2002; Peterson, 1992). In addition, allowing students time to get to know each other and the opportunity to interact with each other in an environment where respect and appreciation for differences is the expectation and the norm creates a safe, friendly learning environment.

Ceremonies, Rituals, Rites, and Celebrations

Peterson (1992) describes many ways that ceremonies, rituals, rites, and celebrations can influence community in the classroom. In community life, ceremonies bring people together for a shared purpose such as a celebration. They can generate a sense of affiliation with a particular group. Similarly, in the classroom, ceremonies can create a sense of group identity and purpose. They can also signal students to redirect attention from daily life to the classroom and learning. Ceremonies may occur as the day begins, during the day, and at the end of the day. Opening ceremonies might include activities such as a moment of silence, the reading of a poem, a calendar activity, an opportunity to acknowledge and appreciate people at home and in the class, a pledge, and so forth. During the day, ceremonies may include a song or a time to share work. End of the day ceremonies may include sharing something important that happened during the day, reflecting on what was learned, and so forth.

Peterson (1992) describes rituals and rites that provide additional opportunities to connect to the larger community and symbolize time for transitioning from one activity to another. For example, elementary school students may put chairs in a circle for a class meeting and move to a carpeted area when it is storytime. Students of all ages may bring an "author's" chair to the front of the room for students to share a completed work. These rituals allow students to ready themselves for the upcoming activity or experience.

Rites mark the passage of time in the classroom and may include a teacher standing at the threshold of a classroom to welcome his or her students one by one at the beginning of the day in elementary school or the beginning of a class period in middle or high school, having a welcoming committee prepare a desk and materials for a new student, and finding a special way to bring closure to a unit, a term, or the school year. For example, for a rite that brings closure, Peterson (1992) describes Libby Gilmore, a middle school teacher, who during the first days of the school year has her students make a time capsule reflecting their likes, dislikes, interests, and hopes for the future. At the end of the year, the time capsules are opened, providing a time for reflection and acknowledgment of growth and change.

Time for festivity in the classroom allows for group fellowship and can lift the spirit of the classroom community (Peterson, 1992). Celebrations can be for achievement, getting older, special days, or spur of the moment. In one kindergarten classroom, students' birthdays are celebrated when the class forms a circle around a symbol of the sun. The birthday student sits on the sun while the teacher carries a globe around the circle. The globe "orbits the sun" for each year the child has been on earth. As each orbit is made, the teacher and the parents, if they are present, say something about each year in the life of the child.

Conversation and Play

Teachers who are attuned to crafting community in their classroom are also concerned with the thoughts and stories of their students. Allowing time for conversation further strengthens social relationships in the classroom (Gardner, 1991; Habel, Bloom, Ray, & Bacon, 1999). Allowing students to share their stories enables the teacher and the students to get to know each student as a unique individual, to value the students' experiences, and to nurture their dignity (Hutchinson, 1999). Classroom meetings (see Figure 8.1) can provide one vehicle for allowing students to share stories. As students sit in a circle, they can take turns sharing the important events in their lives. Classroom meetings can also provide students with an opportunity to engage in discussion concerning important issues affecting their lives and assist them in understanding and exploring the diverse and varied social worlds of their peers.

The value of sharing stories is illustrated in a classroom meeting in a racially mixed high school resource room for students with behavioral and emotional disorders. One student had expressed concern that a fellow student had hate words, as well as a swastika,

Figure 8.1   Class Meetings

Purposes
Solve problems
Acknowledge and appreciate
Share stories
Plan events
General Guidelines
Elect a chief or student leader
Schedule meetings at least weekly
Sit in a circle
Use student-generated compliments and concerns to develop an agenda.
Pass an object around the circle to indicate whose turn it is to speak.
When addressing problems, focus on solutions rather than blame, consequences, or punishment.
Give everyone an opportunity to speak, but allow individuals to pass if they want.

doodled on his notebook. As students shared their experiences with discrimination, this student made the comment that he hadn't realized how offensive his notebook had been to others. Phelan, Davidson, and Yu (1998) suggest using case studies depicting cultural factors affecting adolescents' relationships with peers in school as a basis for stimulating dialogue relative to community building. These researchers found that using such case studies caused high school juniors to be more aware of their own potential biases in social interactions with others and to show interest in investigating unequal power relationships in their classrooms, school, and society. An excerpt from a case study used by Phelan et al. (1998) follows:

> Mexicans are more crazier than white people. It's like we have like different kinds of thinking I guess; I don't know. Like we want to do everything—it's like they [Whites] take everything slowly, you know. You know, they take everything slow, and I don't know, it's just that they think about the future more and stuff. And us, you know, what happens, happens. And it's just meant to happen. And it's like we do crazy things, and we never think about the consequences that might happen. (p. 242)
>
> ... Right now, it's like if I keep on acting the way I am, I don't know what I'm going to do—end up in the streets, sweeping floors. I don't want to do that, and maybe if I get my act together, I'll go to college, you know. I want to get a degree.

Getting to Know One Another

A positive, caring classroom climate is nurtured when students have the opportunity to get to know each other and connect in some way, while at the same time understanding and appreciating each other's differences. Acknowledging and learning about each other's differences and commonalities is especially important with learners from diverse backgrounds (Banks & Banks, 2004; Bondy, Ross, Gallingane, & Hambacher, 2007; Chamberlain, 2005; Gay, 2000; Ladson-Billings, 1994). For example, Bondy et al. (2007) describe an activity in which students are given a list of questions and sent on an interactive scavenger hunt to find the answers. They talk with each other to find answers to questions such as "Who has more than four pets?" These authors also note the importance of teachers communicating a respect for and appreciation of differences and establishing that teasing, taunting, or laughing at others because of differences will not be tolerated.

Caring

A strong ethos of caring in the classroom can facilitate the development of an effective, nurturing classroom community (Collier, 2006). However, caring, according to Noddings (1992), is an easily neglected concept. Noddings asserts that "the main aim of education should be to produce competent, caring, loving, and lovable people" (p. 45). Kohn (1991) describes the role that schools should play in teaching students to help each other:

> If we had to pick a logical setting in which to guide children toward caring about, empathizing with, and helping other people, it would be a place where they would regularly come into contact with their peers and where some sort of learning is already taking place. The school is such an obvious choice that one wonders how it could be that active encouragement of prosocial values and behavior—apart from occasional exhortations to be polite—plays no part in the vast majority of American classrooms. (p. 499)

Many school rituals only reinforce academic achievement; they do not explicitly foster caring. For students to learn to help others, to contribute to the good of the school, and to care about people other than friends, we must model caring and provide opportunities to develop these values through shared rituals, routines, and discussions (Collier, 2006; Noblit, Rogers, & McCadden, 1995). In a caring classroom or school, learners and teachers operate on the premise of shared responsibility, collaborative achievement, and shared values and goals (Collier, 2006). In caring learning communities, relationships among students and teachers are such that students feel safe to learn, take risks, laugh, and trust one another (Brown, 2004).

Teaching Caring

Teaching and allowing students to demonstrate caring involves reading stories that highlight the importance of caring, having the class discuss specific examples of caring, setting common goals and discussing common values, and being careful to notice times when the students show caring. Children who have been taught to take the feelings of others into account and who have learned to look for ways to show that they care will help make all learners feel included.

Bloom, Perlmutter, and Burrell (1999) recount the story of Dan. Dan had been retained and was placed in special education before coming into Ms. Burrell's classroom.

> Well, when Dan came in with his head down and no smile, our hearts just about broke. He crept to the back of the group and looked scared to death. When the group went through their regular morning activities, we could sense his fear and uncertainty.
>
> After a couple of days of school, the children started playing a math game that requires some reading as well as mental arithmetic. Dan didn't know how to read and he didn't know how to play the game. But I was lucky because my third graders had been in my second grade and we had talked about caring and respect and helping. When they started playing the game, one of them just slid over beside him and watched Dan's card and when it was Dan's turn, he whispered into his ear. Surprisingly, Dan said it out loud.
>
> From then on, Dan played the game. Since the game follows the same basic pattern, gradually Dan got so he could take his turn by himself with some help on reading the numbers. He knew that the words said "I have" and "Who has" and he could do that part by himself. After some time, Dan began to answer the number questions as well as read the repeated phrases. (p. 134)

This teacher had taught her children well by talking about caring, allowing children to share stories about the difficulties in their lives, and by encouraging caring behavior.

Opportunities for Caring

Structured transition times and classroom schedules limit opportunities for students to demonstrate caring and to participate in helping relationships with peers or adults (Bosworth, 1995). When opportunities are available for helping, the academically stronger students are more often afforded those experiences (Bosworth, 1995; McNamara, 1996). However, remarkable results can be obtained when those who are typically helped are put in the role of the helper. When children and youth are seen as competent and contributing, the sense of belonging can only be strengthened. Children and youth who are given responsibilities will learn to be responsible. These individuals are no longer seen only as failures and the attitudes of all involved change. And those changes lead to hope.

In one elementary school, third and fourth grade students with learning disabilities and behavior disorders are tutors for first graders. They listen to the first graders read and read to them. Not only has this activity helped the self-esteem of these children, it also has increased their reading skills, since they now spend time practicing reading the books that they will be reading to their charges.

Curwin (1993) reports on striking, significant changes that difficult youth make in attitudes and behaviors after being given responsibilities as caretakers, tutors, and helpers of people in need. He asserts that, over time, much of the anger that these youth experience can be replaced with caring. Guidelines suggested by Curwin (1993) for developing opportunities for students to experience helping follow:

1. Choose activities that provide sincere and authentic opportunities. Students will recognize when their help is artificial or unnecessary.
2. When choosing opportunities, consider the ability of the student. Ask students to help in a way that they can be successful. These decisions should be made on an individual basis as not all students can be helpful in the same way. Try to use the student's strengths, talents, and interests and involve the student in selecting opportunities for helping or contributing.
3. Opportunities for helping and/or contributing should be optional. Students are not likely to experience a positive effect if forced to provide help.
4. The goal for providing opportunities for generosity and service is to give the student an internal feeling of worth. External reward can deny the experience. Expresss your appreciation privately and avoid providing rewards or incentives. Assist students in focusing on the internal gains that they experience, as well as the effects of their help on the individuals on the receiving end.
5. Do not set up service opportunities as a privilege to be earned. Don't worry about rewarding negative behavior. While some may question giving students who often get in trouble an opportunity to do something that may be fun, the opportunity to help others will not invite students to suddenly behave badly because they want to be helpers. Let all students have the opportunity.
6. Consider having students help others with similar problems. For example, students who fight in the hallway or cafeteria may make good monitors. Students with behavioral disorders are often great tutors for younger special needs students or students with more severe developmental disabilities. They often understand the struggles of other students from a different perspective and may learn to see their own behavior in a different light.
7. Set up reasonable expectations. Students should expect to temporarily lose the opportunity to help if they fight or behave in other unacceptable or inappropriate ways. Expectations should be made clear, but should be reasonable and tailored for the individual. (p. 38)

Opportunities for involving children in caring activities are endless. Suggestions by Curwin (1993) include

- Allow students to do fund raisers and donate the proceeds to charity, to improve the school, or for a relief fund for community families in need.
- Provide opportunities for students to help their classmates or younger children with schoolwork.
- Encourage students to take on a service project for the school, for example, keeping the restrooms clean for a month, planting flowers in the school yard, or cleaning graffiti from school walls.
- Set up a peer mentoring program.
- Visit homes for the elderly. Plan and conduct an afternoon of entertainment for the residents.
- Adopt a school, child, or family in a needy country or neighborhood.

Classroom Discipline

In a constructivist class, management flows from the spirit of community. Children and youth see their acceptable caring behavior as vital to the maintenance of the group because they have a vested interest in the health of the group as a whole. There is an emphasis on students' responsibility for their behavior, self-discipline, and mutual respect. However, students do not automatically know or understand what conduct is appropriate for the classroom community. For many students, learning and refining appropriate classroom behavior is often required.

This involves giving conduct explicit attention throughout the course of the day by taking time to develop codes of conduct, providing explanations for firm but flexible limits, and teaching acceptable behavior. Rather than being governed by the teacher's system of rewards and consequences, the students can be guided in learning appropriate behavior with authoritative leadership in the classroom, classroom mission statements and covenants, and tactics such as coaching and goal setting.

Authoritative Leadership

The leadership style with which a teacher operates the classroom has much to do with how children learn to behave. Constructivist teachers favor an authoritative leadership style. Drawing from research on parenting styles, McCaslin and Good (1992) contrast authoritative styles with laissez-faire and authoritarian styles. Laissez-faire parents provide loose guidelines to which their children may or may not adhere; authoritarian parents maintain strict control over their children without discussing their reasoning; and authoritative parents value behavior that is monitored by self-discipline and self-control, and maintain firm but flexible limits. Children of authoritative parents display more autonomy and independence and have greater confidence and higher self-esteem than children parented under the other two styles. Like authoritative parents, teachers with authoritative leadership in the classroom set firm but flexible limits, take time to explain limits, allow learners to have opportunities for self-regulation, and hold students accountable (Bondy et al., 2007; Brown, 2004; Delpit, 1995). Authoritative teachers also use insistence. According to Bondy et al. (2007), insistence is characterized by straightforward directives given in a firm yet caring and nonhumiliating manner, such as "Put your pencil down" or "Be quiet while I give directions," which are repeated, if necessary, so that students comply.

Authoritative leadership involves planning time during the first days of school and beyond to explain, discuss, role-play, notice, and encourage appropriate behavior. All students need to think about how to act in school and need the security of knowing what is expected. Student investment and interest in following classroom rules and procedures and in engaging in appropriate behavior can be enhanced when students understand the reasons for rules and procedures and are involved in their development. Rules and procedures are purposeful and meaningful to the children and youth who help create them. For example, students can be involved in developing classroom missions and covenants that articulate specific rules and procedures for the classroom.

Mission Statements and Covenants

Mission statements and covenants can provide a code of conduct for members of the classroom community to abide by. A student-generated mission statement gives the class a common cause or unifying theme. In one class, the mission statement posted on the wall reads, "Our mission is to have a community that works together as a group. Our mission is to be courteous to others, to be nice to others, and to help them as much as we can." The process of creating such statements can help learners see the reasons why they should use quiet voices inside the class and teach them skills such as how to get help without disturbing the group. More specific rules and procedures may be generated from the mission statement as classroom community members see the need for them.

In addition to classroom missions, classroom covenants can assist the teacher in encouraging positive appropriate classroom behavior. Classroom covenants are core values represented as the rights, duties, and obligations of community members. Covenants should be deliberated early in the community-building process, put in writing, and posted in the classroom. They may include values such as

> It's okay to make mistakes.
> Everyone learns at his or her own pace.
> It makes sense to ask for help.

Recommendations for maintaining covenants include:

- Communicate them clearly and often.
- Model—Show students that the values help guide the teacher's decisions.
- Ensure that the classroom structure supports the values (e.g., if it is okay for students to help each other in their work, ensure that the desks are arranged to facilitate cooperative work).
- Enforce and commend practices that exemplify core values.
- Express disapproval when practices violate the core values.

In many classrooms, covenants are sufficient to convey expectations for behavior. However, rules generated from classroom covenants can assist students who need norms and expectations to be more explicit.

According to R. Marzano, J. S. Marzano, and Pickering (2003), clear classroom rules can positively influence student behavior. For rules to be most effective, they should be created with students and stated in positive terms (Cangelosi, 2004; Marzano et al., 2003). In addition, explanations and reasons for rules, as well as seeking student input when problems with rules occur, assist students in owning and committing to rules.

When the cultural norms of teacher and student are different, the teacher can make sure that classroom expectations are explicit through the use of specific rules (Gay, 2000). For example, for some students, gaining the floor through assertiveness may be a cultural norm, while for the teacher, waiting for a turn to speak may be the norm. Making explicit the code of conduct for the classroom in a respectful and nonjudgmental manner can alleviate the difficulties that a cultural mismatch can cause. Examples of classroom rules that are positive and specific include

Be on time.
Stay on task.
Keep your hands and feet to yourself.
Listen while others are speaking.

Some students may need more encouragement and explicit instruction than others to learn classroom norms and expectations. Coaching and goal setting may be useful tactics.

Coaching and Goal Setting

Some students, such as those with attention deficit disorder (ADD) or other learning disabilities, may need even more explicit coaching or special cues. For example, in one elementary school class, Tim, a student with ADD, was having difficulty bringing his materials in from his locker. After a class meeting, students decided that someone should remind Tim at the beginning of each day. The students tried this solution without luck. The morning after the meeting, no one was available to remind Tim. After an emergency class meeting, the group decided that others also often forgot their materials and that perhaps a sign posted at the lockers would be a good reminder for everyone. This process helped make the expectations clearer for Tim and gave the class an experience in problem solving.

If one or more students are having difficulties in a particular area, working with those students to develop and monitor personal goals can be helpful. In one class, the teacher helped Stephen, a student with a behavioral disorder, learn appropriate classroom behaviors by assisting him in developing personal goals that related to classroom expectations. These goals were written on a chart and reviewed at the beginning of each day. At the end of each day, Stephen gave himself a rating relative to each goal. This process gave the student and the teacher continued feedback and a positive process for making expectations clear.

Solving Problems in a Classroom Community

As with adult communities, classroom communities will not always run smoothly. Understanding what to do does not always guarantee the best performance, and problems arise regularly in the best of classrooms. Although conflict in the classroom is not likely to be totally eliminated, it can be managed, as well as used to an advantage. Conflicts can provide opportunities for learning appropriate, peaceful problem solving.

Teaching Problem Solving

In traditional classrooms, students are rarely given the opportunity, encouragement, time, or credit for being problem solvers. In a constructivist class, problems are opportunities for individuals to learn and grow. As suggested by the quote at the start of this chapter, gaining these experiences allows students to develop skills for a lifetime of living, working, and getting along with others. In addition, students learn that they can influence what happens to them and that they are capable.

For example, in one elementary school class, a new student, Alex, who happened to have Down syndrome, enrolled in the class. The classroom teacher was fearful of this student because he had been known to run away. This problem was presented to the class, and they were asked to write down their ideas for solutions. Their very thoughtful solutions included, "Let him know that we like him and want him to stay in our room," "When he starts to run away, tell the teacher," "Tell him nicely to go back," "Talk to him more," and "Let him know that we are his friends." Classroom meetings and peer mediation involve using peers to resolve conflicts and are examples of strategies available for allowing students to mediate solutions to predicaments that arise in the school and classrooms.

Class Meetings.   Glasser (1969), an early proponent of class meetings, described them as a way for children to learn to participate in problem solving. He maintained that

> If children learn to participate in a problem-solving group when they enter school and continue to do so with a variety of teachers throughout the six years of elementary school, they learn that the world is not a mysterious and sometimes hostile and frightening place where they have little control over what happens to them. They learn rather that although the world may be difficult and that it may at times appear hostile and mysterious, they can use their brains individually and as a group to solve the problems of living in their school world. (p. 123)

Class meetings provide an opportunity for children to feel safe while learning problem solving without judgments and failure (Nelson, Lott, & Glenn, 1997). Class meetings can help students improve communication skills, develop empathy, and build community (Angell, 1998; Emmet & Monsour, 1996), as well as develop problem-solving, decision-making, and interpersonal skills, and acceptance of responsibility (Sorsdahl & Sanche, 1985).

According to Nelson et al. (2000), the goals of class meetings are as follows:

- Teach mutual respect.
- Develop communication skills.

- Learn about separate realities.
- Solve problems through role-play and brainstorming.
- Recognize the four reasons that people do what they do.
- Give compliments, acknowledgment, and appreciation.
- Generate solutions to classroom predicaments.

The following guidelines can be used to develop class meetings (Nelson et al., 1997):

1. Meetings should be student led. Allow the class to choose a leader and a note taker. These positions can change on a weekly or monthly basis to give many students an opportunity to lead.
2. Hold meetings at least once a week.
3. Establish ground rules. Students should be involved in discussing rules for class meetings, such as "Only one person talks at a time." Passing around a special object, such as an eagle feather or a talking stick, helps bring attention to the one speaking. The focus of the meetings is on acknowledging appreciation and compliments and finding solutions to problems. Blame, ridicule, and punishment are not allowed.
4. All members of the classroom can contribute items for the agenda prior to each meeting. Some classrooms use boxes for compliments and concerns to develop an agenda. Students may add compliments and concerns to the box anytime prior to the meeting.
5. Post sayings in the classroom that support the use of compliments and teach students to be careful not to say things that could hurt the feelings of others. Initially, you may have to remind students about opportunities to write compliments. Teaching students to write concerns in ways that are respectful is helpful.
6. Avoid calling a classroom meeting immediately following a conflict when emotions are high. Allowing time to cool off allows classmates to focus on solutions rather than on the negative emotions present at the time that the problem occurred.
7. Sit in a circle so that all members can see each other.
8. Begin with an opening ceremony for meetings. Some classes recite a classroom pledge, read a classroom mission statement, or don a special T-shirt. An opening ceremony helps students take class meeting time seriously.
9. Follow the opening ceremony with compliments and appreciation. Allow time at the beginning of each meeting for students and the teacher to recognize accomplishments, give thanks for caring acts, and so forth. Teach students how to graciously accept compliments.
10. Read the first concern on the agenda.
11. Pass the concern around at least once. Allow each member to have a chance to say something about the concern and provide a suggestion. Members may pass.
12. Students will become fearful of offering suggestions if they see that some suggestions are considered silly or inappropriate by the teacher or their peers. Hence, all suggestions should be written down as they are stated. Students can be taught to consider and respect all suggestions.

13. Guide students through questioning. If students start blaming each other for problems or become judgmental, use questioning to help them rephrase their concerns or reconsider their position.
14. After each suggestion has been read, ask the student or students involved to choose one that they consider to be the most helpful or, if it is something for the whole class to do, ask them to vote on a solution.
15. Require accountability. Allow time at each meeting for students to report whether solutions from previous meetings have been effective or if new solutions need to be explored.

Give class meetings time. Students may struggle at first and feel awkward, especially if they have not experienced opportunities for problem solving. Class meetings should not be used as an opportunity for the teacher to lecture students or impose his or her rules, rewards, or consequences; instead, such meetings should be a way for students to learn conflict resolution, problem solving, and decision making.

Peer Mediation. In peer mediation, students are taught the skills necessary to resolve conflicts and are empowered to do so within the school or classroom community. As mediation skills are developed, students learn to listen to each other and to consider other viewpoints. They find themselves able to move from anger to a search for solutions. Skills that students learn may include questioning violence as a solution, identifying nonviolent solutions to conflicts, developing empathy for others, identifying sources of conflict, analyzing problems, accepting responsibility, and identifying changes in behavior for preventing future conflicts (Williamson, Warner, Sanders, & Knepper, 1999). Successful results have been reported for peer mediation programs with elementary (Hart & Gunty, 1997; Johnson & Johnson, 1995; Schmitz, 1994), middle (Johnson & Johnson, 1997), and high school students (Tolson, McDonald, & Moriarty, 1992).

"Peacemakers" is one example of a peer mediation program. It involves training students in conflict resolution. Johnson and Johnson (1995) report the results of 5 years of research on conflict resolution training with students from first through ninth grades. Their results indicate that students can learn, retain, and apply conflict resolution in and out of the classroom and, when given the option, engage in problem solving rather than win–lose negotiations. In addition, results indicate that adults perceive the program as helpful and that conflict resolution can be taught in ways that can enhance academic performance. Teaching students to be Peacemakers involves five steps:

1. Create a climate of cooperation. When individuals are in competition, they often strive for a "win" in conflicts instead of finding solutions. A problem-solving approach such as peer mediation requires the members of the community to recognize their long-term interdependence and the need to maintain effective working relationships with each other.
2. Teach students a concrete and specific procedure for negotiating agreements. Teach students who are inexperienced in problem solving by demonstrating and providing practice with the process. Asking students to "be nice," "talk it out," or "solve your problem" is not enough.

- Jointly identify the conflict: Separate the problem actions or behaviors from the person, avoid win–lose thinking, and clarify the goals of both parties.
- Describe wants and feelings, as well as reasons for those feelings (e.g., "I want a turn at the computer and I am frustrated because I haven't had one"). Listen to the other person's proposal and feelings.
- Reverse perspectives: See the situation from the other person's point of view: reverse roles and argue from that perspective.
- Create at least three agreements that allow mutual gain: Brainstorm, focus on goals, and give everyone involved the power to create solutions.
- Reach an integrative agreement: Ensure that the goals of both parties are met. If all else fails, flip a coin, take turns, or ask a third party to mediate.

3. Teach students to use a concrete and specific mediation procedure. See Figure 8.2 for an example mediation procedure. Allow students to practice the procedure until they have developed some expertise. If students are to mediate their classmates' conflicts, they must know how to do so.

Figure 8.2 Peer Mediation Process

Lane and McWhirter (1992, p. 23) recommend the following steps for peer mediation:

1. Mediator introduces him/herself and asks the other parties their name, and whether they want to solve the problem.
2. If they agree to solve the problem, move to an appropriate area for talking.
3. Go over the rules for mediation:
   (a) Agree to find solutions, not blame or punishment.
   (b) Speak respectfully and avoid name-calling or put-downs.
   (c) Be as honest as you can.
   (d) Do not interrupt while another person is speaking.
4. Ask each person to agree to the rules.
5. Ensure the confidentiality of anything that is discussed.
6. Take turns, and ask both persons for their side, restate what they say, and ask the other party how it made him or her feel.
7. Ask each person what they want and repeat it.
8. Ask each person what he or she can do to solve the problem and repeat it.
9. Consider each solution for fairness, balance, and feasibility.
10. Ask each person if he or she agrees to the solution. Ask if the problem is solved.
11. Ask each person what he or she could do differently if the problem were to arise again.
12. Explain that sharing with their friends that the problem has been solved can prevent rumors. Ask each to share.
13. Acknowledge and appreciate their hard work in peaceably finding solutions.

4. Implement the peer mediation program. Working in pairs at first, a mediator is made available to help schoolmates negotiate more effectively. The mediator's role is then rotated so that each student can be a mediator.

5. Continue the training in negotiation and mediation procedures throughout 1st through 12th grades to monitor, refine, and upgrade students' skills. To become competent in resolving conflicts takes years and years. Any thought that a few hours of training is enough to ensure constructive conflict management is terribly misguided.

Reprinted with permission from Johnson and Johnson (1995). Retrieved on Oct. 8, 2007, from http://www.co-operation.org/pages/peace.html

Class meetings and peer mediation can be very similar. A teacher may prefer one or the other, or both. Class meetings are typically scheduled on a daily or weekly basis, while peer mediation occurs at the time that a problem arises. In addition, class meetings are held for more than just problem solving, as seen in Figure 8.1, but both involve peers in the act of conflict resolution and are designed to teach valuable problem-solving skills.

CLASSROOM ATTITUDES AND STRUCTURES THAT SUPPORT COMMUNITY

Various classroom attitudes and structures support the constructivist classroom community. Developing a climate of faith; introducing attitudes, instructional approaches, and structures that allow a focus on learning in an atmosphere that is supportive of mistakes and risk taking; and developing structures can assist in maintaining the successful functioning of the classroom community.

Expectations

Creating a climate of faith in students' abilities and high expectations for their work and behavior is a vital step in constructive classroom management and successful inclusion. Building and maintaining a sense of competence for each individual and allowing all children to see the possibilities for success are important goals. A climate of faith can be developed by appropriate use of encouragement, by helping students identify the strengths and talents within themselves and each other, and by assisting students in appreciating the many sources of talent.

Encouragement
Providing ample encouragement for students strengthens confidence, enhances performance, and supports a healthy connection with the teacher. Faith in students' ability to work hard, achieve their goals, and behave appropriately can be communicated through praise and high expectations. These are described in detail in Chapter 10.

Identifying Strengths and Talents
All children have special talents and skills. Finding and recognizing those talents and skills is well worth the effort. In a classroom previously mentioned and described by

Bloom et al. (1999), Dan had particularly low self-confidence. Dan's teacher and her assistant looked for ways to highlight the strengths that Dan had. Dan's teacher commented, "As we watched him, the thing that we could find to build on is that he liked to draw. He had drawn a beautiful picture of a dog, [in his own] style. We took it to the front and shared it and talked about what a great little artist he was going to be. Although many of the other children could have drawn it better according to our standards, they all accepted that he was a terrific artist. Everybody began looking up to Dan as the great artist in the room. His self-confidence started going up. He started talking to the other children more, interacting with them, playing with them." (p. 135)

Teachers can also help students think about and find their own strengths and talents. In a Peacekeeper's classroom, students are taught about strength words that are posted around the room such as "caring" and "neat." These words are introduced to help children in writing compliments for the compliments and concerns box. At the end of some classroom meetings, students are asked to share a strength word that applies to them. Students respond with comments such as "I am helpful," "I am a good friend," and so forth.

Jack, a special education student identified as behaviorally disordered, began the year with very low self-esteem. He hardly spoke to his classmates and, like Dan in the previous class, he walked around with his head down. At an early Peacekeeper meeting, the teacher asked the students to share strength words that applied to Jack. Each student described Jack with at least one positive word. At the end of the meeting, Jack quietly said, "Gee, maybe you all do like me." By the fourth month of school, Jack applied for and was elected chief. Although he needed a lot of support from his classmates in this role, he was very successful.

Multiple Intelligences

According to Gardner (1993), humans all have different combinations of intelligences. If we recognize and nurture all of them, "not only will people feel better about themselves and more competent; it is even possible that they will also feel more engaged and better able to join the rest of the world community in working for the broader good" (Gardner, 1993, p. 12). Teachers can use Gardner's multiple intelligences to encourage students to understand their strengths and talents and those of others. For example, after discussing multiple intelligences with her elementary school students, Kathy Norris, a special education teacher in an inclusive classroom, has students concoct a recipe for themselves (see Figure 8.3). For high school students, they may construct a pie chart using the multiple intelligences (Armstrong, 2000). These activities assist students in recognizing that we are all intelligent in different ways and encourages them to recognize those talents in themselves and others.

Instructional and Organizational Structures

Providing a classroom structure that enhances a climate of community and a healthy student–teacher relationship is an important consideration in classroom management. Appropriate instructional structures are conducive to academic success for all students in the learning community. Emphasizing a learning orientation, open-ended assignments,

Figure 8.3   Recipe for Multiple Intelligences

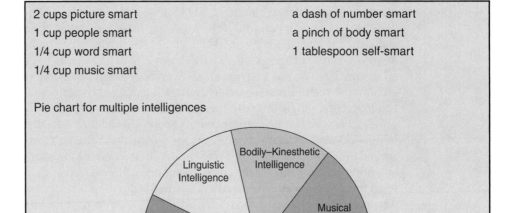

2 cups picture smart   a dash of number smart
1 cup people smart   a pinch of body smart
1/4 cup word smart   1 tablespoon self-smart
1/4 cup music smart

Pie chart for multiple intelligences

and encouraging risk taking, help learners focus on cooperation and learning for under-standing, and enhance student confidence. A differentiated curriculum allows the teacher to plan for the diverse characteristics of learners. Active learning allows students to im-merse themselves in learning in ways that capture their attention and enthusiasm. Choices allow students a sense of ownership and investment in their learning and their classroom.

Organizational structures that are conducive to a smoothly operating community include attending to a classroom schedule, chores and responsibilities, and choices. A well-developed schedule allows for predictability during the day, while chores, responsi-bilities, and choices reinforce a sense of affiliation with and commitment to the classroom community.

INSTRUCTION

Management and instruction are interrelated. For example, McCaslin and Good (1992) maintain that classroom management involving behavior modification and/or empha-sizing obedience through the use of rewards and punishment is compatible with a curriculum of basic skills acquisition. Both involve identification, sequencing, and reinforcement of discrete skills, even though current beliefs support a curriculum with a problem-solving orientation. "We cannot expect that students will profit from the incongruous message we send when we manage for obedience and teach for exploration and risk taking" (McCaslin & Good, 1992, p. 12).

Constructivist classroom management can provide students with opportunities to think and understand, utilizing peer communication and social exchange to enhance the curriculum and allow the teacher to adapt for a diverse range of student interests and abilities. Maintaining a learning orientation, risk taking, open-ended assignments, a differentiated curriculum, and active learning allow opportunities for students to engage in challenging work and problem solving, and for individuals to contribute and perform tasks appropriate to their skill level while engaging in work similar to that of their peers.

Maintaining a Learning Orientation

Maintaining a schedule with a learning orientation, as opposed to work completion, can enhance the classroom climate. A learning orientation means that the focus in the classroom is on learning for meaning and making progress toward learning goals, while a work orientation means that the focus is on completing a predetermined number of assignments for the sake of a grade. Marshall (1988) compared classrooms with a learning orientation and those with a work orientation. She found that classrooms with a learning orientation displayed a learning purpose, peer helping, self-evaluation, supportiveness of errors, fewer negative management situations, and teachers' beliefs in the students' ability to learn. Consequently, the environment in these classrooms encouraged students to engage in academic work reflectively and collaboratively. In classrooms oriented toward work completion, the teacher spoke primarily in terms of completing tasks, stressed competition over cooperation, gave correct answers as opposed to using mistakes as learning opportunities, and inadvertently created a threatening environment for students who were unable to meet task demands.

Allowing time in the daily schedule to review learning goals and progress toward those goals, and allowing for students to engage in self-evaluation, reflection, and problem solving if goals are not being met, can assist the teacher in maintaining a learning orientation. Examples of evaluation and reflection activities that may be part of the daily routine include individual and small-group conferences with students to review learning goals, recapping what was learned at the end of a lesson or at the end of the day, allowing time for students to share their work with each other, and allowing time for students to write in a reflective journal.

Mistakes and Risk Taking

Along with clear and shared expectations of behavior, students need to feel comfortable enough in the classroom to take risks. Children and youth with disabilities may have experienced failure and may develop an attitude of "I can't." The teacher must help children feel competent, but also all children need to learn that mistakes are okay and that everyone, even teachers, make mistakes. Instead of being devastated by mistakes, children need to learn that "mistakes are stepping stones to learning." This message is liberating to the overachieving child and to the child with special needs who struggles academically. Allowing, and even encouraging, mistakes allows children to take risks and to learn from their mistakes.

Open-Ended Assignments

Coupled with permission to try and mess up, open-ended assignments can allow learners to explore multiple ways of knowing because they can be completed in a variety of ways and at a variety of levels. For example, instead of being given one graph to interpret, learners can plan and carry out surveys and display their results. The subjects of the surveys may vary and the skill with which the assignment is completed will vary. When there are many ways to successfully complete an assignment, then all children can feel successful.

Differentiated Curriculum

The concept of differentiated curriculum refers to tailoring the curriculum of the classroom to meet the diverse needs of the students. Teachers can adopt classroom strategies that allow students to acquire knowledge, develop understanding of essential course content, and demonstrate their ability according to individual skills, interests, and talents. According to Tomlinson (1999), essential elements of differentiated instruction include the following:

- The teacher identifies key content for each lesson or unit so that struggling learners focus on essential understanding and skills. Advanced learners spend their time grappling with important complexities instead of repeating work on what they already know.
- Assessment and instruction are inseparable. Assessment has more to do with identifying entry points for instruction and helping students grow than with cataloging their mistakes.
- The teacher modifies content, process, and products based on individual needs.
- All students participate in work that is interesting, important, and engaging.
- The teacher and the students collaborate in learning. The teacher and the students may hold a conference develop learning contracts, identify needed accommodations and modifications, and so forth.

Differentiated instruction can take many forms. For example, in one classroom, all students study presidents Lincoln and Washington. However, the reading materials, assignments, and projects are assigned according to ability. During weekly spelling tests, some students may have a list of 15 words, while others have 10 words. The teacher confers with the students individually in making decisions about curriculum and assignment modifications. In addition, this teacher varies her groups throughout the day. Some groups are based on ability, some are based on interests and talents, some are randomly assigned, and, at times, students choose their own groups. Because the students are grouped in various ways throughout the day, modifications are routinely made for all students who need them, and because students are studying the same content at different levels, low achievers are not identified.

For another example of differentiated instruction, one middle school English teacher reports that students write a project proposal for a final product that will demonstrate knowledge of essential content area skills (Wehrmann, 2000). In this way, students are given flexibility in using different interests and talents to demonstrate learning. Examples include an animated movie or comic strip, or a fairy tale to demonstrate knowledge of mythology.

Tomlinson (1999) describes how a teacher in a 12th-grade government class uses the concept of differentiated instruction. In this class, students are assigned into groups based on readiness skills for a unit on the Bill of Rights. The goal of the unit is to understand how the Bill of Rights has expanded over time and its impact on various groups in society. Even though the assignment for each group has common elements, some research groups will investigate societal groups that are more familiar to them, where the issues are more clearly defined and information written on a basic reading level is available. Other groups examine unfamiliar societal groups, where the issues are less clearly defined and the resources for finding information are more complex.

Active Learning and Transformative Learning

A classroom equipped for active learning, full of centers and real materials for students to explore, is vital to the success of all learners. A classroom where learners can move, where they interact with peers, and where multiple materials are available can develop all the intelligences that students bring with them to school. A student who finds it hard to concentrate on too much seat work may need to use his or her whole body to solve problems in math. Requiring students to write out plans for the use of classroom materials provides a real purpose for reading and writing in which students will eagerly engage. In extensive interviews with high school students, Phelan et al. (1998) found that students dislike reading texts and answering the questions at the end of the chapters. They described their classes as boring and indicated a strong preference for active learning or "transaction rather than transmission" (Phelan et al., 1998, p. 198).

Gardner (1991) contrasts "mimetic" learning with "transformative" learning. In mimetic learning, the task for the student simply is the precise mastery of information or the exact duplication, or mimicry, of a performance or behavior that has been demonstrated by the teacher. Rote tasks and drill and practice are dominant. In contrast, in what has been termed "transformative" learning (Cross & Steadman, 1996), the learning is not merely additive—the accumulation of facts and routines; instead, the teacher arranges the conditions of learning for the purpose of transforming what already exists in the mind of the learner to lead to deeper understanding and greater appreciation. The teacher is not simply a model, but a facilitator or a coach, trying to evoke certain qualities or understanding in students. Teaching occurs through posing problems, creating challenges, placing students in certain situations, and encouraging students to work out their own ideas.

Choice

Providing students with choices within the classroom is another hallmark of constructivist classrooms. Choice and decision making encourage independence, dignity, and self-worth. They are also key to nurturing internal motivation (Deci & Ryan, 1985). According to Deci and Ryan, individuals who are self-determined act out of choice rather than obligation or coercion and are more likely to strive to realize their potential. Examples of ways to provide choices in the classroom follow:

- Use class meetings to allow students to decide on and plan events such as field trips, special projects, and so forth.
- Have "givens" regarding what students must learn, but provide choices about assignments and class projects.
- Allow times when students can choose who they want to work with. Working alone may also be an option at times.

ORGANIZATIONAL STRUCTURES

There is more time for focused learning in a classroom that is organized in both time and materials. Because, in a constructivist classroom, learners are important stakeholders, they can be involved in organizing, scheduling, and maintaining the classroom. Organizational structures include scheduling and chores and responsibilities.

Scheduling

Developing a schedule that fosters learning and supports the learning community involves several considerations. Obviously, it involves consideration of the students' age, cultures, attention spans, levels of ability, special activity scheduling, and the number of students in the classroom. In any classroom with students from diverse cultural backgrounds and educational needs, there should be multiple and differentiated pedagogical approaches included in the daily schedule so that it is ensured that all students, at some time during the day, have the opportunity to work from their strengths (Pugach & Seidl, 1995). A schedule that fosters learning and enhances the classroom climate should include plans to (a) alternate small-group and large-group activities, (b) alternate quiet and active activities, (c) provide adequate transition time, and (d) schedule difficult lessons when students are most alert (Murdick & Petch-Hogan, 1996). Scheduling that involves students' strengths and interests can be done within an ethos of collaboration. For example, classroom meetings can be used to discuss students' ideas about the daily schedule, their interests, and their preferences for incorporation in planning.

Planning for smooth transitions between activities is one key to an orderly classroom. As with classroom expectations and limits, often many students are more comfortable when they know what to expect during the day. While a schedule can be kept flexible, posting a schedule with the anticipated course of events of the day or week can be helpful to both the students and the teacher in maintaining a focus on learning. In addition, posting and/or advising students of upcoming changes in routines and schedules can prevent the chaos in the classroom that often accompanies not knowing what will come next. Giving verbal cues and reminders before it is time to change activities, organizing materials, and establishing routines for storing and retrieving materials between activities can further facilitate transitions.

Chores and Responsibilities

For the peaceful and orderly existence of the community, each member must contribute to its maintenance. In the classroom community, this means that each learner must share in the responsibility of maintaining the room. Students should be given the opportunity to undertake chores such as cleaning the chalkboard, sharpening pencils at the beginning of the day, greeting visitors, taking care of the class pet, running errands, and so forth.

Chores should be divvied and rotated periodically so that each student has an opportunity to contribute to the maintenance of the classroom in some way. Students can help determine what chores are needed and how they should be assigned. In some classrooms, students must complete an application for classroom responsibilities such as pet keeper, treasurer, and board eraser. The application can contain questions about qualifications, experience, and so forth. In cooperation with the teacher, a committee of students can review the applications to select the classroom member for the job. Classroom elections may be held for positions such as chief and vice chief, or president and secretary.

BOX 8.1
Peacekeepers

In one classroom on a nearby Cherokee reservation, elementary school students are involved weekly in a council of peers aptly named "Peacekeepers." The structure of Peacekeepers represents the local tribal council. A box is placed in the room, and children, as well as teachers, put "compliments" and "concerns" in the box throughout the week. Each week, when it is time for the meeting, the children get out their Peacekeeper T-shirts, which are stored in the room and worn during Peacekeeper meetings. After donning their T-shirts, students move their seats into a circle. The meeting is called to order by the chief and begins with all members (students, teachers, and assistants) reciting the Peacekeepers' Pledge: "We the Peacekeepers promise to be truthful, respectful, and caring to all." The first part ("We the Peacekeepers") is recited in both Cherokee and English.

The chief conducts the meeting. The assistant chief helps by passing concern and compliment cards to the chief. The recorder takes notes. These positions rotate monthly. Students apply for each position by filling out an application. They are then elected by the class.

An eagle feather, which is a sacred symbol for the Cherokee, is passed around at each meeting. The holder of the feather is the only one with permission to speak. The chief reads each compliment and the receiver is applauded by the group. Concerns then provide an opportunity to engage in problem solving and conflict resolution. Concerns may be for individual students or for the class. Each concern is read and all parties involved are given an opportunity to tell their stories. Each member of the council is given a chance to give a solution. Members are reminded that the purpose of discussing the concerns is not to blame or punish, but to solve problems. Each solution is recorded and then the group decides which suggestions would be the best to try. At follow-up meetings, the group decides whether the problem has been solved or whether further action is needed.

For example, one week a student had taken money from a jar that was being used to collect donations for an orphanage in South America. The teacher dealt with the student individually and allowed him to talk to his classmates about making restitution. The next week, a concern placed in the concern box queried, "How can we keep our jar safe?" The student's name was never mentioned during the meeting and the class focused soley on solutions to the problem.

After addressing classroom concerns, the chief may decide to either end the meeting or have a "go-around." The chief picks the topic for the go-around. "Tell what you did over the weekend" and "Tell about anything you want" are popular go-arounds. The go-arounds give the students, as well as the adults, a chance to share something about themselves.

After a go-around, the chief asks each adult in the room if he or she has anything to add. Finally, the meeting is brought to a close when all members lock arms and recite the Peacekeepers' Pledge.

The Peacekeepers take their job very seriously. Excerpts from transcripts of Peacekeepers' meetings (Scalone, 1997), which provide specific examples of concerns and solutions that the children have generated, follow.

The student-generated suggestions focus on helping and teaching instead of punishing. When the message is problem solving instead of blame, the entire community grows stronger and mistakes become learning opportunities.

The Peacekeepers also keep a Basket of Acceptance. This basket is placed in the center of the council and is filled with something from each member of the classroom. Each member brings in a small object that tells something about him/herself and places it in the basket together with objects from other members of the community. Items have included shells that one child collected on a special trip, a small token given to another child by his grandfather, and so forth. This type of ritual gives every child a chance to participate and symbolizes togetherness. In all, Peacekeepers provides for strong group cohesiveness and identity.

Here are some excerpts from Peacekeepers' meetings (Scalone, 1997):

- The chief reads: "A concern card for Jamie as he never gets his work done on time." Solutions generated by the students are "Move Jamie to another table." "Allow the teacher to talk with his parents and have a student Peacekeeper present at the meeting to share with (Jamie's) parents that the entire classroom community is concerned that (Jamie) is not completing his work." "Allow Jamie to talk with the counselor if he would like to, and seat Jamie near a student role model."

- The chief reads: "A concern card for Todd as he is often put in time-out during music class." The students respond: "Remind him of the Peacekeepers' Pledge." "Sit him near someone who he will not try to play with." "Let him apologize to the music teacher."

- The chief reads: "A concern card for the entire class as the students are not getting their work finished on time." The Peacekeepers generated the following ideas: "Work more quietly during free time in order to get more work finished." "Help other table members with their work." "Do not disturb students who are working." "If you get stuck, skip it and go on, then ask for help."

- The chief reads: "A concern card for Bob as he is not staying in the class line." The students suggest: "Pat Bob on the shoulder to remind him when he gets out of line." "Place Bob in front or behind a line monitor." "Gently show Bob with your hands not to talk or get out of line."

SUMMARY

Constructivist teachers capitalize on the social context of the classroom by creating a sense of community and assisting every student in gaining a sense of belonging. They involve students in all operations of the classroom, including developing classroom mission statements and convenants, problem solving, and deciding how they want their classroom to be. The voices of the students are sought and respected. The emphasis is on student responsibility instead of teacher control. Active learning prevails and teachers maintain and communicate high expectations for all students. The curriculum goes beyond academics to include teaching students to care for each other, to take care of the classroom, and to be responsible members of the community. The strategies in this chapter will allow all students to negotiate the social world of the classroom, develop strong affiliations with their peers and the classroom community, and be ready for learning.

REFERENCES

Angell, A.V. (1998). Practicing democracy at school: A qualitative analysis of an elementary class council. *Theory and Research in Social Education, 26*(2), 149–172.

Armstrong, T. (2000). *Multiple intelligences in the classroom.* Alexandria, VA: Association for Curriculum and Development.

Ashton-Warner, S. (1963). *Teacher.* New York: Simon and Schuster.

Banks, J. A., & Banks, C. A. M. (Eds.). (2004). *Handbook of research on multicultural education* (2nd ed.). San Francisco: Jossey–Bass.

Bloom, L. A., Perlmutter, J., & Burrell, L. (1999). The general educator: Applying constructivism to inclusive classrooms. *Intervention in School and Clinic, 34*(3), 132–137.

Bondy, E. D., Ross, D. D., Gallingane, C., & Hambacher, E. (2007). Creating environments of success and resilience: Culturally responsive classroom management and more. *Urban Education, 42*(4), 326–348.

Bosworth K. (1995). Caring for others and being cared for. *Phi Delta Kappan, 76*(9), 686–694.

Brown, D. F. (2004). Urban teachers' professed classroom management strategies. *Urban Education, 39*(3), 266–289.

Cangelosi, J. S. (2004). *Classroom management strategies: Gaining and maintaining students' cooperation* (5th ed.). Hoboken, NJ: Wiley.

Chamberlain, S. P. (2005). Recognizing and responding to cultural differences in the education of culturally and linguistically diverse learners. *Intervention in School and Clinic, 40*(4), 195–211.

Collier, M. D. (2006). A structure for caring in schools. *Journal of Human Behavior in the Social Environment, 13*(4), 73–83.

Cross, K. P., & Steadman, M. H. (1996). *Classroom research: Implementing the scholarship of teaching.* San Francisco: Jossey–Bass.

Curwin, R. L. (1993). The healing power of altruism. *Educational Leadership, 51*(3), 36–39.

Deci, E. L., & Ryan, R. M. (1985). *Intrinsic motivation and self-determination in human behavior.* New York: Plenum.

Delpit, L. (1995). *Other people's children: Cultural conflict in the classroom.* New York: New Press.

Ellis, W. E., & Zarbatany, L. (2007). Peer group status as a moderator of group influence on children's deviant, aggressive, and prosocial behavior. *Child Development, 78*(4), 1240–1254.

Emmett, J., & Monsour, F. (1996). Open classroom meetings: Promoting peaceful schools. *Elementary School Guidance and Counseling, 31*(1), 3–11.

Gardner, H. (1991). *The unschooled mind: How children think and how schools should teach.* New York: Basic Books.

Gardner, H. (1993). *Frames of mind: The theory of multiple intelligences.* New York: Basic Books.

Gay, G. (2000). *Culturally responsive teaching: Theory, research, and practice.* New York: Teachers College Press.

Glasser, W. (1969). *Schools without failure.* New York: Harper & Row.

Glasser, W. (1986). *Control theory in the classroom.* New York: Harper Collins.

Habel, J., Bloom, L. A., Ray, M. S., & Bacon, E. (1999). Consumer reports: What students with behavior disorders say about school. *Remedial and Special Education, 20*(2), 93–105.

Harris J. R. (1995). Where is the child's environment? A group socialization theory of development. *Pschyological Review, 102*(3), 458–489.

Hart, J., & Gunty, M. (1997). The impact of a peer mediation program on an elementary school environment. *Peace and Change, 22*(1), 76–92.

Howard, T. C. (2002). Hearing footsteps in the dark: African American students' descriptions of effective teachers. *Journal of Education for Students Placed at Risk, 7*(4), 425–444.

Hutchinson, J. (1999). *Students on the Margins: Education, stories, dignity.* albany, New York: State University of New York Press.

Johnson, D., & Johnson, R. (1997). The impact of conflict resolution training on middle school students. *Journal of Social Psychology, 137*(1), 11–22.

Johnson, D. W., & Johnson, R. (1995). *Teaching students to be peacemakers* (3rd ed.). Edina, MN: Interaction Book Company.

Kohn, A. (1991). Caring kids: The role of the schools. *Phi Delta Kappan, 72*(7), 496–506.

Ladson-Billings, G. (1994). *The dreamkeepers: Successful teachers of African American children.* San Francisco: Jossey–Bass.

Lane, P. S., & McWhirter, J. J. (1992). A peer mediation model: Conflict resolution for elementary and middle school children. *Elementary School Guidance and Counseling, 27*(1), 15–24.

Mallory, B. L., & New, R. S. (1994). Social constructivist theory and principles of inclusion: Challenges for early childhood special education. *The Journal of Special Education, 28*(3), 322–333.

Marshall, H. H. (1988). Work or learning: Implications of classroom metaphors. *Educational Researcher, 17*(9), 9–16.

Marzano, R., Marzano, J. S., & Pickering, D. J. (2003). *Classroom management that works.* Alexandria, VA: Association for Supervision and Curriculum Development (ASCD).

McCaslin, M., & Good, T. L. (1992). Compliant cognition: The misalliance of management and instructional goals in current school reform. *Educational Researcher, 21*(3), 4–17.

McNamara, K. (1996). Bonding to school and the development of responsibility. *Reclaiming Children and Youth, 4*(4), 33–55.

Murdick, N. L., & Petch-Hogan, B. (1996). Inclusive classroom management: Using preintervention strategies. *Intervention in School and Clinic, 13*(3), 172–196.

Nelson, J., Lott, L., & Glenn, H. (1997). *Positive discipline in the classroom* (3rd ed.). Rocklin, CA: Prima.

Noblit, G. W., Rogers, D. L., & McCadden, B. M. (1995). In the meantime: The possibilities of caring. *Phi Delta Kappan, 76*(9), 680–685.

Noddings, N. (1992). *The challenge to care in schools.* New York: Teachers College Press.

Peterson, R. (1992). *Life in a crowded place: Making a learning community.* Portsmouth, NH: Heinemann.

Phelan, P., Davidson, A. L., & Yu, H. C. (1998). *Adolescents' worlds: Negotiating family, peers, and school.* New York: Teachers College Press.

Pugach, M., & Seidl, B. (1995). From exclusion to inclusion in urban schools: A new case for teacher education reform. *Education and Urban Society, 27*(4), 379–395.

Scalone, L. (1997). *The Peacekeepers: A qualitative study of an intervention program for children who are at risk for school failure.* Unpublished master's thesis, Western Carolina University, Cullowhee, NC.

Schmitz, R. (1994). Teaching students to manage their conflicts. *Social Work in Education, 16*(2), 125–129.

Sorsdahl, S.N., Sanche, R.P. (1985). The Effects of Classroom Meetings on Self Concept and Behavior. Elementary School Guidance and Counseling 20 (1) 49–56.

Tolson, E. R., McDonald, S., & Moriarty, A.R. (1992). Peer mediation among high school students: A test of effectiveness. *Social Work in Education, 14*(2), 86–93.

Tomlinson, C. (1999). *The differentiated classroom: Responding to the needs of all learners.* Alexandria, VA: ASCD.

Wehrmann, K. S. (2000). Baby steps: A beginner's guide. *Educational Leadership, 58*(1), 20–23.

Williamson, D., Warner, D. E., Sanders, P., & Knepper, P. (1999). We can work it out: Teaching conflict management through peer mediation. *Social Work in Education, 21*(2), 89–96.

RELATIONSHIPS AND STRUCTURES

STUDENT–TEACHER RELATIONSHIPS

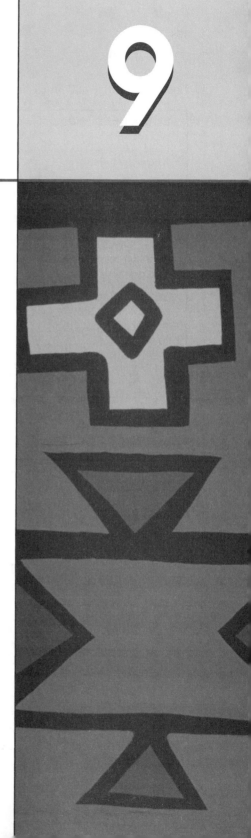

9

Teaching is thoroughly relational, and many of its goods are relational: the feeling of safety in a thoughtful teacher's classroom, a growing intellectual enthusiasm in both teacher and student, the challenge and satisfaction shared by both in engaging new material, the awakening sense (for both) that teaching and life are never-ending moral quests.
Noddings (2003, p. 249)

Schools should become places in which teachers and students live together, talk to each other, reason together, take delight in each other's company.
Noddings (1991, p. 169).

Although multiple factors contribute to school performance, teachers play an important role in determining students' success or failure. As both quotes at the beginning of this chapter suggest, teaching, to a large extent, is about relationships. Developing a positive productive relationship between the teacher and the learner can help students realize their full potential academically and socially in the classroom. On the other hand, certain attitudes and behaviors can devalue students, deter relationships, and contribute to failure.

The nature and influence of student–teacher relationships have been studied from many perspectives and approaches. Davis (2003) provides a synthesis of research to date from attachment, motivation, and sociocultural perspectives. Although each perspective differs in its approach and findings, each informs our understanding of the nature and influence of student–teacher relationships. Looking across perspectives, Davis (2003) identifies three common aspects of positive student–teacher relationships: relatedness and involvement, competence, and autonomy. These aspects are also in line with a constructivist perspective and are

Figure 9.1   Circle of Courage and Relationships

RELATEDNESS AND INVOLVEMENT	COMPETENCE	AUTONOMY	GENEROSITY
• Knowing students • Appreciating students for who they are • Listening to students • Using language that communicates respect and dignity • When conflicts occur, expressing disdain for the behavior, not the individual	• Using reliable sources in order to have appropriate expectations for students • Changing expectations based on student performance • Looking at changes in instruction when students do not meet expectations • Communicating high expectations • Using words of encouragement, praise and appreciation	• Gaining and understanding students' perspectives • Understanding sources of bias • Construing students as multifaceted individuals • Engaging in problem solving	• Caring—The overarching theme for positive student–teacher relationships • Demonstrating and modeling caring for students by taking time to know, interact with, encourage, and appreciate each student as an individual

strikingly similar to belonging, autonomy, and competence from the Circle of Courage. The fourth area of the Circle of Courage—generosity—for the sake of discussions of student–teacher relationships, can be referred to as care, or the nurturing and support modeled and offered by a teacher to his or her students. Figure 9.1 illustrates the four areas of the Circle of Courage as they relate to student–teacher relationships.

Caring is an overarching theme of the other aspects of student–teacher relationships identified by Davis (2003). In fact, caring seems to be the resonating factor identified as key to positive relationships throughout professional research and literature on education. Nurturance of relatedness and involvement, competence, and autonomy are the means for establishing a caring relationship. Hence, teachers build relationships by caring for their students, making personal connections with their students, conveying high expectations for their students, and treating their students with respect and justice. Effective communication conveys caring and can build and preserve relationships, while some communication patterns can deter and deteriorate relationships.

Some students come to school wary of adults who seek to establish relationships. Previous negative school experiences, as well as circumstances of culture, disability, and economic disadvantage, can contribute to barriers in building relationships. Even well-intentioned teachers can contribute to student failure simply because they are often unaware of those circumstances and, consequently, alienate students. This chapter is devoted to appropriate practices for cultivating relationships with even the most relationship-reluctant student. First, as the overarching theme of positive relationships, the concept of caring will be discussed, followed by relatedness and involvement, competence, and autonomy. Finally, strategies for developing relationships with wary students will be presented.

CARING

Research suggests that warmth, caring, and acceptance are necessary qualities for successful teachers (Birch & Ladd, 1997; Perry, Donohue, & Weinstein, 2007; Poplin and Weeres, 1992; Murray and Pianta, 2007). Students need to know that their teachers want the best for them and care about their well-being and appreciate who they are as individuals. Students can readily identify teacher actions that communicate caring.

Benefits of Caring

A caring student–teacher relationship has a positive impact on academic achievement for children of all grade levels (Arroyo & Rhoad, 1999; Birch & Ladd, 1997; Crosnoe, Johnson, & Elder, 2004; Shann, 1999) and especially for culturally diverse students and students with disabilities (Crowley, 1993; Fránquiz & del Carmen Salazar, 2004; Freed & Smith, 2004; Howard, 2002). In addition to academic achievement, a caring teacher can have a positive effect on prosocial behavior and can find classroom management to be a much easier task. For example, Wentzel (1994) found that young adolescents' pursuit of the goals to behave prosocially and responsibly were related to perceived support and caring from teachers. In more recent studies of perceived support from teachers, parents, and peers, Wentzel (1998, 2002) found that perceived support from teachers was a significant and positive predictor of students' pursuit of the goal to adhere to classroom rules and norms.

What Learners Say About Caring Teachers

Although many teachers recognize the importance of establishing a caring relationship with students, knowing how to convey caring in ways that students interpret as nurturing can be more complicated. In a study by Wentzel (1997), middle school students were asked to describe the characteristics of teachers who care and those who do not. Students described caring teachers as those who demonstrated democratic and egalitarian communication styles designed to elicit student participation and input, who developed appropriate expectations for student behavior based on individual differences and abilities, who modeled a "caring" attitude and interest in their instruction and interpersonal dealings with students, and who provided constructive instead of harsh and critical feedback. In contrast, teachers who do not care are described most often as demonstrating maladaptive communication styles (e.g., yelling, interrupting) and communicating low expectations by not providing explanations or individual help.

In a study by Bloom and Habel (1999), students asked about their best teacher often told of caring teachers. In reference to his best teacher, one student remarked, "She helps me more than other teachers. She understands me. She knows I'm not as smart as other kids, but she knows I'm not stupid either. She knows [that] with help, I can accomplish a lot." (p. 5)

Students in the same study also reported on uncaring teachers:

I'm not a great speller. She put me in a kindergarten or a first-grade spelling book, and everybody started laughing at me. She knew everybody would laugh at me, and that's why she put me in it.

You go up to a teacher to say something really important, right? When you go up to a teacher and do that, they just look at you as if you're not important, as if they don't see you.

Not very many people around here know what I want. . . . Nobody really takes time to notice.

Well, at school, when I come back [from suspension], the teacher says . . . "There goes the troublemaker." Or a teacher tells a friend of mine who never gets in trouble that they had better stay away from me or they'll get in trouble.

You can't just ask her a question in class. You have to raise your hand and wait and wait. That makes kids not want to ask questions. You want to ask it right when you think of it, like when she's writing on the board and stuff. I don't know. I don't think she really cares that much because everybody else in the county is in algebra in the eighth [grade], and we're doing seventh-grade math.

In his study of the perceptions of African American students regarding effective teaching, Howard (2002) found that culturally connected caring was identified as one of the three key characteristics of effective teachers. Howard describes culturally connected caring as a display of caring that is similar to caring in the student's culture—a style of caring students are familiar with. For African American students in his study, Howard describes culturally connected caring as being demonstrated by encouraging students with warm pats on the back, expressing high expectations, and directly telling students about their academic potential.

According to these studies, as well as in other professional literature (e.g., Gay, 2000; Noddings, 1992; Poplin and Weeres, 1992; Sherman, 2004), caring is more than a word or a feeling; rather, caring requires responsiveness, action, and intentionality.

RELATEDNESS AND INVOLVEMENT

Caring teachers intentionally seek to find out about the lives of their students, hear their voices, gain their perspectives, understand their experiences, and remain diligent with regard to communication that is respectful as well as authentic.

Knowing Students

Involvement and closeness with students and being responsive to their unique needs requires knowing the students and understanding their circumstances and conceptions (Sherman, 2004). It involves gathering information, through personal interactions, conversations, and encounters, as well as through observation, and using that information to be reflective about responses to students. Sherman (2004) describes the process as follows:

Such intentionality requires the teacher to capture the essence of each student's personal learning space, recognize the uniqueness of that space, and enter it with respect and understanding. The teacher seeks to become part of that space to advance students' learning. To accomplish this, the teacher learns about the student in a multitude of ways. These include intellectual strengths, personal dispositions, and special interests, as well as family background and prior learning experiences. (p. 119)

Teachers can use many strategies to get to know students. An Internet search offers a plethora of sources for a wide variety of "getting to know you" activities. While these activities offer fun and engaging ideas to start out a new term or to start with a new group of students, they cannot replace the ongoing diligence of a caring teacher in knowing his or her students. Hutchinson (1999) cautions that "making biographical or chronological lists describing the self at the beginning of the year does little to reveal the meaning or sense that students make in their lives" (p. 77). She suggests that opportunities to respond verbally or in writing to more open-ended interesting questions may offer greater insight about the lives of students. She describes the tactic that one teacher uses, where students create a cover of *Time* magazine with themselves as the "Person of the Year" and then write one page on why they received this honor. In addition to such planned activities, Hutchinson suggests that opportunities for learning about students come in other, less-planned situations, such as recess and lunch. Teachers can look for these opportunities for a glimpse into the lives of their students through conversation. Some of the best tactics for getting to know students include

- spending time with each student individually through periodic learning conferences;
- creating dialogue journals in which students write about their experiences, concerns, reactions, and so forth, and the teacher responds;
- playing with students at recess;
- eating lunch with students;
- attending extracurricular activities;
- greeting students as they enter the classroom;
- talking with students as they work through problems in order to gain information about thinking processes, and so forth;
- having informal conversations with students; and
- being willing to offer appropriate self-disclosure. When teachers allow students to know them as human beings—their triumphs, disappointments, interests, and so forth—students are more willing to share of themselves.

In addition to these strategies, the functional assessment described in Chapter 12 provides a vehicle for understanding students who exhibit more serious learning, behavioral, or emotional issues. A functional assessment allows a teacher to gain knowledge of a student through a variety of sources and from multiple perspectives.

Listening

One of the most powerful means of establishing effective communication, learning about students, and building trusting relationships with students is through active listening. Gordon (n.d.) describes active listening as empathetic listening that allows the speaker to know that his or her message has been heard and understood. When students know that they can talk and that the teacher will listen, the need for using inappropriate behavior to communicate needs and desires lessens. Letting students know that they have been heard can involve gestures and words that indicate attention, (e.g., a nod; comments such as "I hear what you are saying," "Go on," "I see"; invitations to continue ["Tell me more"]; and rephrasing what the students have said to assure them that they were heard accurately). In addition, the active listener avoids phrases such as "It can't be all that bad" that discount what the student is saying. According to Gordon (2003), many undesirable messages, such as unacceptance, inadequacy or fault, or denial of a problem, can be communicated to students. Gordon considers these types of messages to be roadblocks to communication that can unintentionally slow down or completely stop productive communication. Gordon's roadblocks to communication are summarized in Table 9.1.

Respectful Dialogue

In addition to knowing and listening to students, positive student–teacher relationships are built through respectful communication on the part of the teacher. As the following quote from Haim Ginott (1972), a pioneer in classroom management, illustrates, the words of a teacher have the power to humiliate or heal, encourage or discourage children:

> I have come to a frightening conclusion.
> I am the decisive element in the classroom.
> It is my personal approach that creates the climate.
> It is my daily mood that makes the weather.
> As a teacher, I possess tremendous power to make a child's life miserable or joyous.
> I can be a tool of torture or an instrument of inspiration.
> I can humiliate or humor, hurt or heal.
> In all situations, it is my response that decides whether a crisis will be escalated or de-escalated, and a child humanized or de-humanized. (p. 13)

Between Teacher and Child

Ginott asserted that children's self-esteem and self-concept are shaped by adult communication patterns. Thoughtful comments and questions such as, "Thank you for taking such care with our classroom materials" and "How is the new baby at your house?" can let students know that they are appreciated, that the teacher is interested in their lives.

While a teacher may not condone certain behaviors or actions, conveying disappointment, dissatisfaction, or disapproval of a student's actions can be done in ways that preserve student dignity and the student–teacher relationship. Ginott recommended that teachers strive to use congruent communication or communication that is harmonious with and accepting of a student's feelings about a situation, that is authentic or genuine, and that addresses the situation, and not character or personality. Ginott contended that this type of communication aids the teacher in avoiding authoritarian behavior.

Table 9.1 Gordon's Roadblocks to Communication

Unacceptance

1. Ordering, commanding, directing.

    Example: "Stop complaining and just get your work done."

2. Warning, threatening.

    Example: "You had better get your act together if you expect to have recess."

3. Moralizing, preaching, giving "shoulds" and "oughts."

    Example: "You should leave your personal problems at home, they don't belong in here."

4. Advising, offering solutions or suggestions.

    Example: "I think you need to get a daily planner so that you can organize your time better to get your homework finished."

5. Teaching, lecturing, giving logical arguments.

    Example: "Remember, if you wait until the last minute, you'll never get your project done."

Inadequacies and Faults

6. Judging, criticizing, disagreeing, blaming.

    Example: "You are so sloppy. You'll never go far with those kinds of habits."

7. Name-calling, stereotyping, labeling.

    Example: "Act your age. You are not a kindergartner."

8. Interpreting, analyzing, diagnosing.

    Example: "If you had paid attention to the directions instead of talking, you wouldn't be avoiding this assignment."

Denial of a Problem

9. Praising, agreeing, giving positive evaluations.

    Example: "You are such a bright kid. You can figure out a way to finish this assignment."

10. Reassuring, sympathizing, consoling, supporting.

    Example: "I know exactly how you are feeling. If you just begin, it won't seem so bad."

Solving the problem for the student

11. Questioning, probing, interrogating, cross-examining.

    Example: "Why did you wait so long to ask for help? What was so hard about these problems? Why didn't you come to me sooner?"

Diverting or Avoiding the student

12. Withdrawing, distracting, being sarcastic, humoring, diverting.

    Example: "I bet you forgot to eat your Wheaties today."

Ginott recommended the use of "sane" messages or messages that avoid judgment of a student's character while addressing misbehavior (e.g., "I would like to finish helping Joey" as opposed to "You are rude to interrupt Joey's lesson"). Ginott strongly admonished against the use of name-calling and labeling, such as "You are just being lazy," as well as sarcasm or ridicule, such as "Yeah right, you really tried your hardest on that one" or "Miss Susie thinks that she is the teacher today."

Ginott also recommended the use of language that is accepting instead of critical, such as "You seem upset about missing recess, it's too bad that it's raining," as opposed to "Consider yourself lucky to get recess at all." Critical and sarcastic messages can degrade, humiliate, and alienate students from teachers.

As an alternative to sarcasm and ridicule, Gordon (n.d.), building on the work of Ginott, recommends "I-messages." Similar to Ginott's "sane messages," I-messages communicate three things: the problem behavior, what the teacher is feeling about the behavior, and why the behavior is causing a problem. For example, comments such as "I am concerned," "I feel frustrated when," and "I feel angry," as opposed to You-messages (e.g., "You always interrupt," "You never finish your work," "You are lazy. . . "), can communicate disdain for an action without humiliating, degrading, or judging the student. Likewise, appreciative or affirmative comments that begin with "I agree" or "I appreciate" may build relationships better than "You" comments (e.g., "You always do such a nice job," "You have good handwriting"); the latter may sound less sincere and/or condescending. The following are examples of I-messages:

> I am concerned that if you don't finish your math work, we won't have time to complete our project.
> I am concerned that since you are coming late to class, you are missing the chance to talk with your peers about your project.
> When everyone is talking all at once, I can't hear what anyone is saying.
> When materials aren't put away, I have to take a lot of time to do it myself.
> When you don't complete an assignment, I'm afraid that you won't learn.
> I appreciate when you work problems out among each other; it helps keep our community focused on learning.
> I'm happy that you made a good choice about where to sit today, it looks like this spot helped you stay focused on your work.

In summary, knowing students, listening to students, and using respectful dialogue can assist teachers in making personal connections with students. Students who sense that a teacher respects them, knows who they are, and values them will be eager and ready to engage in the learning process.

COMPETENCE

Actions and words that express high expectations and faith in the students' ability to meet those expectations are another way that teachers demonstrate caring and build relationships (Diero, 1996). Maintaining and communicating appropriate expectations and words of encouragement take intentional action and reflection.

Teacher Expectations

Teacher expectations can be defined as the teacher-held beliefs about the ability or lack of ability that a student brings to school, as well as what the student will be capable of achieving in the future (Cotton, 1989). Although research is not clear regarding the extent of the effect, it is clear that teacher expectations indeed have an effect on student achievement (Cotton, 1989; Good & Nichols, 2001).

Sources of Expectations

Many teachers form expectations for students based on relatively reliable data, including data from student records and evaluations. In addition, effective teachers monitor student progress frequently and let student progress inform expectations. That is, as a student's progress shows improved performance, an effective teacher raises expectations accordingly. These teachers also know that effective teaching that is responsive to student needs has the power to improve student performance. On the other hand, some teachers base expectations on preconceived notions of the learner based on irrelevant characteristics such as gender, race, and ethnicity. These teachers may also believe that a student's ability is fixed and, therefore, they may lower their standards and/or treat a student with a perceived lower ability differently from a student with a perceived higher capability. Furthermore, teachers who have low expectations for students have less confidence in their own ability to teach (Gay, 2000). Table 9.2 indicates unreliable and often subconscious sources of teacher expectations for students.

Table 9.2 Unreliable Sources of Expectations

Gender: Girls are often subject to lower expectations, especially in the areas of math and science.

Socioeconomic status (SES): Some teachers hold lower expectations for students from lower SES backgrounds.

Race/ethnicity: Some teachers may perceive students from ethnic and minority groups as less capable than Anglo students.

Type of school: Students from inner city or rural schools are viewed as less capable than students from suburban schools.

Appearance: Teachers' expectations can be influenced by students' style of dress and hygiene.

Oral language: Teachers may view students who speak nonstandard English as less capable.

Messiness/disorganization: Students who lack organizational skills, present messy assignments, and have disorganized desks may be viewed as less capable.

Source: Information adapted from Cotton, 1989

Effects of Low Expectations

Low expectations can result in differential treatment of perceived high achievers and low achievers. In addition, communicating low expectations to students can have a detrimental effect on a student's perception of available teacher support, willingness to be an active participant in the learning process, and effort (Good & Nichols, 2001). In fact, research indicates that low expectations can have an even greater effect on limiting student performance than communicating high expectations has on raising performance (Cotton, 1989; Good & Brophy, 2003).

Whether consciously or subconsciously, intentionally or unintentionally, low expectations can be communicated to students in many ways and can be interpreted by students as an indication that a teacher doesn't care about a student's achievement or doesn't think that a student is capable of achieving. Some ways that teachers can directly or indirectly communicate their beliefs about a child's low level of ability are by providing students with answers instead of encouraging them to find answers on their own (Cotton, 1989), interacting less frequently with perceived low achievers (Bamburg, 1994), providing less challenging or less interesting assignments to perceived low achievers (Good & Nichols, 2001), engaging perceived low achievers in instruction less frequently or for shorter periods of time than other students (Clark, 2002), emphasizing drill and practice rather than higher level thinking tasks, giving less eye contact and a less positive response to low achievers, calling on low achievers less frequently, and asking less challenging questions and giving less feedback to low achievers (Good & Brophy, 2003).

Appropriate Expectations

Holding appropriate expectations for students involves knowing where students are academically through reliable sources of information, as well as changing expectations based on student performance. Research on teacher expectations (See Clark, 2002; Cotton, 1989; Good & Brophy, 2003) provides many concrete suggestions for avoiding the communication of low expectations to students by knowing and valuing all students, providing adequate learning opportunities for all students, and encouraging all students. Table 9.3 summarizes these suggestions.

Communicating High Expectations

Diero (1996) completed a qualitative study of teachers who had been identified as being excellent, as well as nurturing, teachers. She found that having high expectations of students while conveying a belief in their capabilities requires two distinct behaviors on the teacher's part: First, teachers must hold high academic standards for their students. Second, teachers need to believe that students can meet these high standards. This belief is conveyed by working from the assumption that students will accomplish whatever is expected of them. When students fall short of the expectations, teachers with high expectations assume that something is blocking the students from using their abilities, and they solve problems from this perspective. In this way, teachers convey a belief in students' capabilities and academic strengths, and focus on solutions instead of expressing discouragement and disappointment about their students' academic deficiencies.

Table 9.3   Communicating High Expectations

Knowing and valuing all students

- Use varied and authentic assessments that provide opportunities to validate student areas of strength, not just areas of need.
- Recognize the unique strengths and talents of each individual.
- Incorporate the ideas of all students into class projects and activities.
- Give students feedback that emphasizes progress relative to previous levels of performance, instead of just a comparison with peers.

Creating a community that values all learners

- Avoid classroom competitions that allow students to compare their academic progress.
- Use heterogeneous groupings

Providing adequate learning opportunities for all learners

- Build lessons around students' strengths and interests.
- Encourage critical thinking in all children.
- Think in terms of stretching students and stimulating them, as opposed to protecting them from failure.
- Engage students in tasks that have no particular correct answer.

Encouraging all learners

- Let children know that their work is important, acknowledge their efforts, and praise their accomplishments.
- Provide authentic praise for student accomplishments, as opposed to random, gratuitous, or insincere praise.
- Provide supports or scaffolding and the time needed for students to solve problems and arrive at answers.
- Set goals for individuals and the classroom that are minimally acceptable standards, not ceilings.
- Let students know that they can meet those standards.

Encouragement

Providing ample encouragement for students supports a healthy connection with the teacher. Teachers can use words to inspire confidence, as well as praise and appreciate student efforts. One third-grade general education teacher describes several of her children this way:

> First and most important, they have an attitude that they can't. They think they can't do anything. To cover up that they can't read, or do math, they do other things, like make quacking sounds with their mouths, fiddle with things, and play instead of doing what they are supposed to do. These things are devices to protect themselves. (Bloom, Perlmutter, & Burrell, 1999).

The same teacher goes on to tell about the approach she uses to inspire confidence:

> I look them straight in the eye and say I expect you to do this. I see no reason why you can't. I stress to the whole group that we are all different. We wear different size shoes; we are different heights and weights, and we read differently and we do math differently. There is not a thing wrong with that, and if you happen to be in here and you've not started reading yet, that's just great because that's where we start learning. You don't have to be a reader yet. (p. 134)

This teacher realizes that confidence grows with encouragement.

In addition to inspiring confidence, appropriate use of praise can provide a source of encouragement for students. According to Brophy (1981), praise that is contingent, specific, accurate, and authentic can be reinforcing to students, while praise used incorrectly can be a source of embarrassment and discouragement. In examining the classrooms of more effective and less effective teachers, Bohn, Roehrig, and Pressley (2004) found that while all the teachers used praise, more effective teachers were likely to give praise that was authentic and specific, as opposed to generic praise (e.g., "Good job"). Furthermore, Good and Brophy (2003) caution that in studies of teachers' use of praise, teacher praise is not always provided equitably across children. Teachers may be more credible and spontaneous when praising students whom they like and may praise low achievers even for poor responses. Good and Brophy (2003) and Brophy (1981) provide the following guideline for the appropriate use of praise to encourage students:

- Give praise contingent on genuine accomplishment (e.g., "Nice work on your math assignment") instead of randomly or haphazardly.
- Give praise as appreciation for specific accomplishments, such as answering a question correctly or completing a homework assignment accurately, rather than as a judgment of the character of the student (e.g., "Thank you for listening and following the directions for this assignment so carefully," as opposed to "What a great student you are").
- Give praise sincerely and indicate appreciation of the student's efforts or actions (e.g., "You turned in an excellent project, I appreciate the effort that went into completing it," as opposed to "Aren't you the best little student").
- Vary the words used to give praise. Overused words will start to sound insincere.
- Praise in straightforward declarative sentences, as opposed to dramatic exclamations. The latter may sound condescending and may cause embarrassment.

In summary, inspiring competence involves having and communicating appropriate expectations, as well as using genuine and sincere words of encouragement.

AUTONOMY

Adults who engage learners in finding solutions to concerns and predicaments communicate faith in the students' abilities to solve problems, make decisions, and be responsible and autonomous. On the other hand, adults who solve problems for students and then punish students for failure to conform to those solutions deny students the opportunity for autonomy and may further alienate them. The use of the sane messages and I-messages discussed earlier sets the stage for the possibility of democratic and judicial problem solving. In addition to providing respectful communication, wise teachers are willing to step back from difficult situations and consider the students', as well as their own, perspective and biases. By doing so, teacher and learner can engage in mutual problem solving and ensure sound opportunities for responsibility and autonomy.

Gaining Perspective

In their discussion of using dialogue to build caring relationships, Dollard and Christensen (1996) recommend a willingness to understand students' perspectives and an awareness of how biases and values color the way the teacher perceives the student, as well as a conscious choice to view the student as a multifaceted individual. While gaining the student perspective is discussed in Chapter 4, it should be noted here that establishing care and trust involves two-way dialogue that elicits and accepts the student's experiences and perspectives with issues and concerns.

As a caring teacher engages in dialogue, he is also mindful of how his biases and values may affect his perspective of a student and consequently the way he interacts with that student. Dollard and Christensen (1996) contend that an awareness of biases can assist the teacher in choosing how to look at or construe a student. The teacher can identify an aggravating or aggressive student as one with a behavior problem or as a multifaceted person who has difficulty controlling activity or aggression. By taking the latter perspective, more productive, multifaceted dialogue can ensue. Hence, free from value judgments, control, or coercion, a student can feel safe in expressing himself, and mutual problem solving and shared understandings become the focus of dialogue. This type of communication does not mean that the teacher must agree with or condone the actions or perceptions of the student; instead, the teacher can develop an understanding of the student's experiences and actions. Problems can be viewed as opportunities to learn and the student–teacher relationship can be preserved.

Noddings (1992) suggests the following five features of positive interpersonal reasoning and problem solving:

1. **An attitude of caring and solicitude.** When a caring relationship has been nurtured, dialogue within the relationship will ensue. Students will feel safe to express perceptions and needs without fear of coercion or manipulation.
2. **Flexibility.** When problem solving, outcomes are not planned; instead, the participants explore multiple possibilities as they arise within the dialogue.
3. **Attention.** Both teacher and students are committed to listening to and understanding the other party. Some students may need instruction in listening skills, but this instruction should not occur within the context of a problem-solving dialogue.
4. **Efforts are aimed at cultivating the relationship.** The teacher works at building the confidence and self-esteem of the student, conveying faith in the possibility of mutual problem solving.
5. **A search for an appropriate response.** This is the mutual identification and analysis of a range of possibilities that would address the situation or problem being discussed.

Learners may resent adults who use punishment and coercion to deal with issues and concerns in the classroom. Teachers who can engage learners in solution-oriented dialogue invite autonomy and mutually respectful relationships.

RELATIONSHIP-RELUCTANT STUDENTS

For a variety of reasons, many students are at a disadvantage; these students may have experienced more negative interactions, as well as rejection, from previous teachers or other adults in their lives and consequently may resist positive relationships. The reasons may be due to disability, cultural factors, or economic disadvantages. For example, students with behavior disorders tend to experience rejection and low tolerance and higher rates of negative interactions than their nondisabled peers (Habel, Bloom, Ray, & Bacon, 1999). Gunter and Jack (1994) found that negative interactions between teachers and students with behavior disorders occurred 22% of the time in the classroom, while positive interactions occurred only 3% of the time. With regard to low-income students, many also experience more frequent negative interactions. In a study by Brantlinger (1991), low-income adolescents reported a greater number and variety of penalties that seemed both disproportionate to the offenses and humiliating in nature. Brantlinger suggests that inequitable school conditions and disciplinary practices for low-income students influence their behaviors and contribute to anger and alienation. Finally, dissonance between school and culture may put some students at a disadvantage (Gay, 2000; Ladson-Billings, 1994). With regard to cultural factors, when teachers interpret and respond to students' behaviors from the perspective of the mainstream cultural norms, they actually discriminate against students from racial and ethnic minority groups (Weinstein, Curran, & Tomlinson-Clarke, 2003). Such teachers fail to recognize that behavior is culturally influenced and may devalue, censure, and punish the behaviors of the nonmainstream group. These practices alienate and marginalize many students.

Weinstein et. al. (2003) recommend culturally responsive classroom management strategies, but with regard to student–teacher relationships, teachers who are culturally responsive are knowledgeable about the cultures of their students, understand how culture may affect classroom behavior, and do not devalue cultural practices that are different from the mainstream cultural group. In addition, they are willing to consider how their biases and values may inadvertently affect their treatment of students who are culturally different.

While understanding the influence of culture, disability, and economic status can assist teachers in guarding against biased practices, youth who have been at a disadvantage may become wary of teachers who try to make connections with them. Seita and Brendtro (1996) describe many strategies for relating to students who have been alienated from the school or classroom community. These strategies include the following:

1. **Use problem situations as windows of opportunity for learning.** When students make mistakes and must experience negative consequences, use the opportunity for learning and growth. For example, when a bully harasses a victim while others stand by, use the opportunity to teach the bully about appropriate leadership skills, the victim about assertiveness, and the onlookers about responsible citizenship in a community.

2. **Provide opportunities for fail-safe relationships.** In citing Bronfenbrenner, these authors suggest that every child needs to know that there is an adult who is crazy about him. Guarded children should have a "fan club" of adults who will provide support and advocacy. In addition, students need opportunities to be friends to others. Engaging students in ways to be friends and give to others can help build relationships.

3. **Increase nurturance.** Guarded youth will not assume that you care about them without concrete evidence. Time is one of the best pieces of evidence—time to listen, time to help with academic work, time to notice what the student is doing, and time to express genuine interest in the student or concern for their welfare. In addition, while public displays of affection may be threatening to some students, other indications of positive regard, such as humorous interactions, high fives, or other spontaneous gestures of friendliness, can break relational barriers.

4. **Find a key to the back door.** Direct attempts at building relationships with wary students can backfire. But often, when a teacher can meet another need, such as one for safety or competence, the student may be more open to establishing a relationship.

5. **Avoid coming on too strong.** Sometimes, smaller doses over time with reluctant students leave a far more lasting impression than aggressive frontal efforts to establish a relationship.

6. **Wait for seeds to grow.** Do not expect relationship-reluctant students to respond immediately to positive attempts to make connections. Diligence, endurance, and ever-open invitations will eventually pay off. (p. 144)

In summary, many learners can be suspicious of adults who try to connect with them. Opening the door for positive student–teacher relationships entails careful, consistent, and enduring actions that communicate caring and respect.

RELATIONSHIPS FROM A BEHAVIORIST PERSPECTIVE

From a behaviorist perspective, student–teacher relationships are seldom addressed directly; they are more often discussed as the relationship between student behavior and teacher behavior. Even so, contingent use of teacher praise and attention is a highly relevant topic for student–teacher relationships. While the use of praise and encouragement were discussed, it was done in the context of fostering competence.

From the behaviorist perspective, contingent teacher attention and praise is a very powerful reinforcer in the classroom. (See Chapter 2 for a discussion of how positive reinforcement can be applied in the classroom.) In a rather extensive review of research, Beaman and Wheldall (2000) illustrate how contingent use of praise can improve the academic and social behaviors of students. Despite the proven advantage of praise, this review also indicates that teachers tend to use disapproval of inappropriate behavior at a much higher rate than approval or praise of appropriate behavior. Furthermore, approval tends to be reserved for praise of academic responses, while appropriate social behavior tends to remain unnoticed. These authors argue that in many classrooms, if students are desirous of teacher attention, they may be more successful in acquiring it through inappropriate behavior. Although the attention may be in the form of a reprimand, it may still serve as a reinforcer, with the function of increasing the likelihood of a behavior. Hence, teachers may inadvertently promote inappropriate behavior, giving teachers more opportunities for reprimands and less for praise.

In fact, according to the research reviewed by Beaman and Wheldall (2000), higher rates of on-task and disruptive behavior are correlated with higher rates of teacher disapproval. This cycle may be especially true for students with "problem behaviors." Beaman and Wheldall's review includes several studies which showed that teachers give even less praise and attention to children who are less well behaved—those who need positive attention the most. They also found that in some cases, teachers' approval and praise may be nefarious or inadvertently given for inappropriate behavior.

The implications of this research for student–teacher relationships are apparent. Teachers who wish to encourage appropriate social and academic behaviors need to be intentional and consistent with their use of praise and attention. The following are specific guidelines:

- Teacher attention and approval in terms of specific praise should be contingent on appropriate academic and social behaviors. In order to use praise in ways that are genuine to students, see the guidelines for encouragement given earlier in this chapter.
- Care should be taken to ensure that the rate of praise and approval for appropriate behavior is higher than the rate of disapproval for inappropriate behavior.
- Care should be taken to give attention and praise to all students and even more so to students with higher rates of inappropriate behavior.
- For some students, especially adolescents, praise from the teacher in front of peers may be embarrassing. Teachers must be sensitive to those students. In such cases, praise can be delivered privately and quietly, or in the form of a note handed discreetly to the student.

SUMMARY

Building positive, caring student–teacher relationships is an integral part of constructive classroom management. Many teachers may believe that relationships develop naturally during the course of the school year and that feeling a sense of caring for the students may be enough. However, truly positive, productive relationships require intentional actions and words on the part of the teacher—actions and words that foster involvement and relatedness, competence, and autonomy. Some students may be resistant to a teacher's attempts to make a connection. Such circumstances require even greater action, persistence, and reflection. From a behaviorist perspective, teachers need to be cognizant of the use of attention and approval—a powerful tool for classroom management.

REFERENCES

Arroyo, A. A., & Rhoad, R. (1999). Meeting diverse student needs in urban schools: Research-based recommendations for school personnel. *Preventing School Failure, 43*(4), 145–154.

Bamburg, J. (1994). *Raising expectations to improve student learning*. Oak Brook, IL: North Central Regional Educational Laboratory. (ERIC Document Reproduction Service No. ED378290).

Beaman, R., & Wheldall, K. (2000). Teachers' use of approval and disapproval in the classroom. *Educational Psychology, 20*(4), 431–447.

Birch, S. H., & Ladd, G. W. (1997). The teacher–child relationship and children's early school adjustment. *Journal of School Psychology, 35*(1), 61–79.

Bloom, L., & Habel, J. (1999). "Interviewing students with behavioral disorders: Theoretical and practical considerations." Paper presented at the American Educational Research Association, April 21, 1999, Montreal, Canada.

Bloom, L. A., Perlmutter, J., & Burrell, L. (1999). The general educator: Applying constructivism to the inclusive classroom. *Intervention in School and Clinic, 34*(3), 132–137.

Bohn, C. M., Roehrig, A. D., & Pressley, M. (2004). The first days of school in the classrooms of two more effective and two less effective primary-grade teachers. *Elementary School Journal, 104*(4), 269–287.

Brantlinger, E. (1991). Social class distinctions in adolescents' reports of problems and punishment in school. *Behavioral Disorders, 17*(1), 36–46.

Brophy, J. E. (1981). Teacher praise: A functional analysis. *Review of Educational Research, 51*(1), 5–32.

Clark, R. (2002). *In-school and out-of-school factors that build student achievement: Research-based implications for school instructional policy*. Retrieved September 12, 2004, from North Central Regional Educational Library Web site: http://www.ncrel.org/gap/clark/factors.htm

Cotton, K. (1989). *Expectations and student outcomes* (SIRS Close-up No. 7). Portland, OR: Northwest Regional Educational Library.

Crosnoe, R., Johnson, M. K., & Elder, G. H. (2004, January). Intergenerational bonding in school: The behavioral and contextual correlates of student–teacher relationships. *Sociology of Education, 77*(4), 60–81.

Crowley, P. E. (1993). A qualitative analysis of a mainstreamed behaviorally disordered aggressive adolescents' perceptions of helpful and unhelpful teacher attitudes and behaviors. *Exceptionality, 4* (3), 131–151.

Davis, H. A. (2003). Conceptualizing the role and influence of student–teacher relationships on children's social and cognitive development. *Educational Psychologist, 38*(4), 207–234.

Dollard, N., & Christensen, L. (1996). Constructive classroom management. *Focus on Exceptional Children, 29*(2), 1–12.

Diero, J. (1996). Teaching with heart: Making healthy connections with students. Thousand Oaks, CA: Crowin Press.

Flowerday, T., & Schraw, G. (2000, December). Teacher beliefs about instructional choice: A phenomenological study. *Journal of Educational Psychology, 92*(4), 634–645.

Fránquiz, M. E., & del Carmen Salazar, M. (2004). The transformative potential of humanizing pedagogy: Addressing the diverse needs of Chicano/Mexicano students. *High School Journal, 87*(4), 36–54.

Freed, C., & Smith, K. (2004). American Indian children's voices from prison: School days remembered. *American Secondary Education, 32*(3), 16–34.

Gay, G. (2000). *Culturally responsive teaching: Theory, research, and practice*. New York: Teachers College Press.

Ginott, H. (1972). *Between teacher and child*. New York: Macmillan.

Good, T. L., & Brophy, J. E. (2003). *Looking in classrooms*. Boston: Allyn and Bacon.

Good, T. L., & Nichols, S. L. (2001). Expectancy effects in the classroom: A special focus on improving the reading performance of minority student in first-grade classrooms. *Educational Psychologist, 36*(2), 113–126.

Gordon, T. (2003). Teacher effectiveness training: The program proven to help teachers bring out the best in students of all ages three rivers press: Three Rivers, CA.

Gordon, T. (n.d.). The case against disciplining children at home or in school. Retrieved October 7, 2004, from http://eqi.org/tgordon2.htm

Gunter, P. L., & Jack, S. L. (1994). Effects of challenging behaviors of students with EBD on teacher instructional behavior. *Preventing School Failure, 38*(3), 35–40.

Habel, J., Bloom, L. A., Ray, M. S., & Bacon, E. (1999). Consumer reports. What students with behaviour disorders say about school. *Remedial and Special Education, 20*(2), 93–105.

Howard, T. (2002). Hearing footsteps in the dark: African American students' descriptions of effective teachers. *Journal of Education for Students Placed at Risk, 7*(4), 425–444.

Hutchinson, J. N. (1999). *Students on the margins: Education, stories, dignity.* Albany: State University of New York Press.

Ladson-Billings, G. (1994). *The dreamkeepers: Successful teachers of African American students.* San Francisco: Jossey–Bass.

Marzano, R. J., Pickering, D. J., & Pollock, J. E. (2001). *Classroom instruction that works.* Alexandria, VA: Association for Supervision and Curriculum Development.

Murray, C. Pianta, R. (2007). The Importance of Teacher-Student Relationships for Adolescents with High Incidence Disabilities. By: Murray, Christopher; Pianta, Robert C.. Theory Into Practice, 46(2) 105–112.

Noddings, N. (1992). *The challenge to care in schools: An alternative approach to education.* New York: Teachers College Press.

Noddings, N. (2003). Is teaching a practice. *Journal of Philosophy of Education, 37*(2), 241–252.

Perry, K., Donohue, K., & Weinstein, R. (2007). Teaching practices and the promotion of achievement and adjustment in the first grade. *Journal of School Psychology, 45*(3), 269–292.

Poplin, M., & Weeres, J. (1992). *Voices from the inside.* Claremont, CA: The Institute for Education in Transformation at The Claremont Graduate School.

Seita, J. R., & Brendtro, L. K. (2002). *Kids who outwit adults: Your toolkit for working with challenging youth and at-risk youth.* West Longmont, CO: Sopris.

Shann, M. H. (1999). Academics and a culture of caring: The relationship between school achievement and prosocial and antisocial behaviors in four urban middle schools. *School Effectiveness and School Improvement, 10*(4), 390–413.

Sherman, S. (2004, Winter). Responsiveness in teaching: Responsibility in its most particular sense. *Educational Forum, 68*(2), 115–124.

Tomlinson, C. A., & McTighe, J. (2006). *Integrating differentiated instruction and understanding design.* Alexandria, VA: ASCD.

Weinstein, C., Curran, M., & Tomlinson-Clarke, S. (2003). Culturally responsive classroom management: Awareness into action. *Theory Into Practice, 42*(4), 269–276.

Wentzel, K. R. (1994). Relations of social goal pursuit to social acceptance, classroom behavior, and perceived social support. *Journal of Educational Psychology, 86*(2), 173–183.

Wentzel, K. R. (1997). Student motivation in middle school: The role of perceived pedagogical caring. *Journal of Educational Psychology, 89*(3), 411–419.

Wentzel, K. R. (1998). Social relationships and motivation in middle school: The role of parents, teachers, and peers. *Journal of Educational Psychology, 90*(2), 202–209.

Wentzel, K. R. (2002). Are effective teachers like good parents? Teaching styles and student adjustment in early adolescence. *Child Development, 1*(73), 287–302.

Wentzel, K. R. (2003). Motivating students to behave in socially competent ways. *Theory Into Practice, 42*(4), 319–327.

MOTIVATION AND ENGAGEMENT

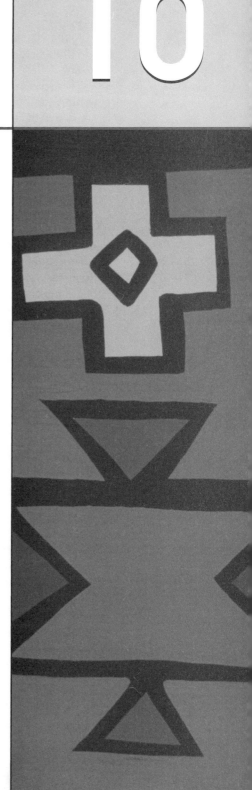

If you want to build a ship, don't drum up the men to gather wood, divide the work, and give orders. Instead, teach them to yearn for the vast and endless sea.
Antoine de Saint Exupéry, 1900–1944

N eal had always performed well and earned good grades, especially in math. He was very enthusiastic about math and saw it as his best subject. In sixth grade, his math grades were high the first weeks of school. However, by the end of the first term, his grades were beginning to fall, as was his confidence in math. He began claiming that he just stunk at math. He became careless on his math homework and on school assignments. In addition, the class as a whole was reportedly becoming unruly. More and more students were being sent to the office or assigned silent lunch each week. At report card time, Neal received an 85% on his report card. While this was not a failing grade, it was much lower than what he had been earning in math. By the end of the year, he was barely passing. Many other students actually received failing grades. What changes had occurred to cause the drop in motivation and effort?

Compare Neal's story with that of his brother, Todd. Todd hated to write; he had difficulty with handwriting from the very beginning. His hand got very tired when he tried to write neatly. Writing even two sentences seemed tortuous. While he aced every spelling test, his spelling in writing assignments was atrocious. He rarely wrote a complete sentence and his grammar left much to be desired. He was extremely anxious about writing going into fourth grade. He wrote the following poem about the writing test he knew he would face at the end of fourth grade.

The writing test is really cheap
When it comes up, it gives me the creeps

When it comes up, I go down
The whole world stops spinning around.

However, by the end of the first quarter of fourth grade, things were looking up. His writing was improving and he even looked forward to some writing assignments. By the end of fourth grade, Todd was actually heard to say that he liked to write and that it was one of his best subjects.

Motivation and engagement were at issue in each of these stories. In Neal's case, they took a turn for the worse, while in Todd's case, they took a turn for the better. In Neal's case, even the motivation and engagement of the whole class waned, and hence, behavior deteriorated. An examination of classroom management and teaching practices sheds light on contributing factors.

Neal's math teacher took a very tough stance with regard to math and her expectations for the work her students would do. She assigned silent lunch and very low homework grades for students who forgot to show their calculations on their math homework. Neal was assigned silent lunch when he tried to help another student who had a question about the math they were doing in class. The teacher told the class as a whole that they were irresponsible and that she couldn't teach math the way she would like because of their immaturity. Much of the math grade was made up of completion of homework and in-class assignments, following the directions given in class. Each exam was to be signed by a parent; if the exam was not signed or was signed in the wrong place, points were deducted. On one day, Neal received a 20% on his homework because even though he had solved the problems correctly, he had not followed directions. While this real-life example is extreme, it is easy to see how the motivation of students who had previously excelled at math easily declined and how that decline could influence their desire to follow classroom rules.

In Todd's room, encouragement for writing was abundant. Mr. Watson told his students not to worry about the writing test. Their goal was to learn to write and he was going to help them achieve it. He communicated high expectations for writing, but gave the students interesting writing assignments. Many of the assignments were directly related to what students were reading and learning in other areas. They had an opportunity to edit and refine their work, they had choices on the assignments, and they produced a newsletter that went out to parents. The teacher did not accept Todd's excuses for not wanting to write. He offered Todd the use of the computer instead. He communicated an expectation that Todd would improve his writing skills and gave Todd and his peers plenty of feedback. He pointed out Todd's progress on a regular basis so that Todd could see that his writing really was improving.

The central mission and focus of activity in a classroom is learning. Students who are willing learners and who are active participants in the learning process have little desire or time to misbehave. Hence, motivation and engagement are important classroom management goals. Academic engagement and motivation, two closely related concepts for the classroom, make for both teachers and students who are happy to be in school and eager to learn. However, creating classroom contexts that promote engagement and foster positive dispositions for learning take the concerted effort of the teacher. In the examples above, teachers took two different approaches to motivation with contrasting results.

Theories of motivation and engagement from psychology and education inform us about classroom structures and teacher behaviors that enhance motivation and engagement. These theories complement the basic tenets of the Circle of Courage. In this chapter, I will synthesize those theories and subsequent recommendations for classroom practice. In addition, I address recommended practices for students who come to the classroom with low motivation and poor attitudes toward learning.

THEORIES OF ENGAGMENT AND MOTIVATION
Engagement

Active academic engagement is necessary for learning and success in school. Students who are disengaged are at increased risk for academic failure and dropping out (Caraway, Tucker, Reinke, & Hall, 2003; National Research Council & Institute of Medicine, 2004). Students who are disengaged may be bored, distracted, and apathetic about the subject matter, as well as the learning goals, and/or have a fear of failure. Although teachers have little or no control over some factors that contribute to disengagement, such as lack of family support, and economic and social marginalization of families and communities, many school and classroom factors can influence active engagement (Connell, Halpern-Felsher, Clifford, Crichlow, & Usinger, 1995; National Research Council & Institute of Medicine, 2004).

Engagement is a multifaceted construct that includes behavioral, emotional, and cognitive engagement (Fredricks, Blumenfield, & Paris, 2004). Behavioral engagement refers to participation in academic and social activities, including extracurricular activities. It is related to student conduct and on-task behavior. Emotional engagement refers to positive and negative reactions to teachers, peers, school, and academic subjects. It is related to student interest, attitudes, and values. Finally, cognitive engagement encompasses the idea of investment or willingness to exert effort and is related to motivational goals. Hence, learners who are actively engaged display behaviors, attitudes, efforts, and goals conducive to learning.

Motivation

Motivation is also a complex construct that researchers are just beginning to understand. Typically, with regard to educational practices, two types of motivation are identified: extrinsic and intrinsic. Extrinsic motivation refers to a learner's desire to complete a task or master a skill for the sake of an external reward, whether tangible (e.g., a sticker, a prize) or intangible (e.g., praise, a high grade). Intrinsic motivation refers to the drive to accomplish a task or master a skill for reasons internal to the learner–the sense of accomplishment, the love of learning, curiosity, and so forth.

Several theories of motivation are prominent in the psychological and educational research and literature, including goal theory, expectancy–value theory, self-determination

Figure 10.1   Prominent Motivational Theories

MOTIVATIONAL THEORY	BRIEF DESCRIPTION	CLASSROOM IMPLICATION
Goal Theory	Learners adopt learning goals or performance goals. Learning goals are associated with positive academic behaviors.	Create a learning orientation in the classroom by emphasizing learning and attaining knowledge and skills.
Self-efficacy Theory	Motivation is related to the learner's sense of self-efficacy. High self-efficacy is important to motivation.	Provide structures that facilitate successful learning experiences. Learners, as well as teachers, adopt high self-efficacy beliefs. Promote effort.
Expectancy–Value Theory	Motivation is a product of the learner's belief in his or her ability to achieve a task and its perceived value.	Structure activities so that students can experience success, but challenge the students. Create interest, relevance, and real-world connections for learning activities.
Attribution Theory	Attribution of success to effort and/or ability and attribution of failure to lack of effort or factors other than lack of ability enhance motivation.	Promote the connection between effort and achievement.
Self-determination Theory	Competence, relatedness, and autonomy promote intrinsic motivation.	Structure the classroom for learner success. Use practices that allow for socialization and positive student–teacher relationships. Provide a structure of autonomy by providing meaningful choices.
Behavioral Theory	Learners will more likely repeat academic responses that result in positive consequences.	Help learners experience success and reward correct academic responses. Be cautious with the use of rewards to avoid undermining intrinsic motivation.

theory, and behavioral theory. Each theory and subsequent research has much to tell about classroom structures that promote motivation and engagement. While a thorough exploration of each theory is beyond the scope of this chapter, a brief explanation of each can be found below and is summarized in Figure 10.1.

Goal Theory

Goal theory tells us that the behavior, motivation, and engagement of a learner are influenced by the types of goals that he or she adopts in the learning process (Ames, 1992). There are basically two types of goal orientation: learning goal (mastery) orientation and performance goal orientation. Students with a learning goal orientation seek to acquire new skills and knowledge and develop competence. Students with a learning goal orientation tend to have higher motivation, persist in the face of difficulty, and seek challenge. Learning goals focus students' attention on strategies and processes that help them acquire the knowledge and skills (Schunk, 1996). As students achieve a learning goal, self-efficacy is enhanced and motivation is sustained (Schunk, 1996, 2003). An orientation toward mastery goals may be optimal for academic engagement.

On the other hand, students with a performance goal orientation tend to complete tasks for the sake of task completion and seek a sense of competence by seeking favorable judgments (e.g., grades, teacher praise, rewards) and avoiding negative judgments. Performance goals can lead students to compare their performance with their peers. These social comparisons can lead to a sense of failure or incompetence that adversely affects motivation. Researchers further suggest that those with a performance orientation tend to be task approachers or task avoiders. Task approachers seek to complete a task so that favorable judgment will occur, while task avoiders tend to avoid academic work and the chance of appearing incompetent. Students with a performance orientation tend to give only the amount of effort required to seek a good grade, or a favorable judgment on a task.

Expectancy–Value Theory

Expectancy–value theory tells us that learner motivation is a product of the value that learners place on an activity, as well as their expectation of or lack of expectation of success (Eccles, Wigfield, & Schiefele, 1998). Activities that have high value or interest for learners and in which learners have a high expectation that they can be successful optimize engagement. Furthermore, a learner's value or disposition for different subjects is positively correlated with the amount of success they have experienced in those subjects (Green, 2002). On the other hand, if the learner feels as though a task is out of his reach or sees little value in a task, he will put little effort into the task. If a learner sees high value in a task, but has a low expectation of success, he may avoid the task to avoid looking like a failure, or cheat to accomplish the task to maintain the appearance of competence. If a learner has little interest in a task, but regards the task as easy, he may put minimal effort into its completion. By showing Todd his progress, Todd's teacher was able to help Todd expect success in writing. Neal, on the other hand, began to have low expectancy, "No matter what I do, I can't be successful."

Self-Efficacy Theory

Self-efficacy theory suggests motivation is mediated by one's sense of efficacy (Bandura, 1997). That is, learners have beliefs about their competence, and those beliefs determine the amount of effort that a learner will extend. Individuals with high self-efficacy tend to persist even in the face of difficulty in a task that they believe is within their ability.

They tend to avoid, and give up easily on, tasks that they believe exceed their abilities. Bandura (1997) differentiates between outcome expectations and efficacy expectations. Outcome expectations are expectations that a task is doable, while efficacy expectations are the belief that one is capable of completing a task. In other words, a learner might believe that a task is doable (outcome expectations), especially for some of his classmates, but may not believe in his own ability to accomplish the task. Learners with high outcome expectations and high self-efficacy are more confident and persist at a challenge because they believe that it is possible and that they have the ability to do it. High self-efficacy is associated with higher goals and greater commitment, while low self-efficacy is associated with lower levels of frustration tolerance and individuals who are easily discouraged by failure.

Bandura posits that self-efficacy beliefs are influenced by experiences of success that the learner believes are due to effort and/or ability, as opposed to a task for which the answer was given or was deemed to be too easy. On the other hand, an individual who starts with a high outcome expectancy and high self-efficacy, but who then meets with failure and negative feedback, may begin to lower her self-efficacy belief and begin to extend less energy. A strong sense of self-efficacy produces greater efforts to overcome challenges.

Attribution Theory

Attribution theory suggests that individual motivation is affected by how the learner attributes successes and failures (Weiner, 1986). Learners who attribute success to effort and ability and attribute failure to lack of effort and/or factors other than lack of ability will more likely persist on subsequent tasks. Learners who attribute their failures to a lack of ability are not driven to continue their efforts. Expending effort and succeeding brings a sense of accomplishment. However, expending a great deal of effort to succeed in comparison to peers may lower a student's perception of his ability. If a learner does not believe that he has the ability, he may extend little or no effort, because failing would make low ability public knowledge.

Self-Determination Theory

According to self-determination theory, learners are most motivated when the basic psychological needs of belonging, competence, and autonomy are met (Ryan & Deci, 2000; Skinner & Belmont, 1993). When these basic needs are met, intrinsic motivation results. This theory links very closely with the Circle of Courage, addressing three of its basic tenets: belonging, independence, and mastery.

Behavioral Theory

According to behavioral theory, the probability of correct academic responses and appropriate learning behaviors can be increased through the use of positive consequences (e.g., reinforcement via praise, extrinsic rewards) and decreased through negative consequences (e.g., ignoring, punishment). With regard to motivation, behavioral theory is generally applied in the classroom via the use of incentive systems (e.g., stickers, tangible rewards, etc.) for academic work.

SYNTHESIS OF MOTIVATIONAL AND ENGAGEMENT THEORY

Taken together, these theories of engagement and motivation are generally complementary rather than contradictory and speak to the numerous complex factors that contribute to student engagement or disengagement, or enthusiasm or apathy, and that can inform classroom practice. Learners' beliefs in their own competence, as well as their beliefs regarding the value of learning and effort, seem to permeate the classroom.

One point of disagreement with regard to motivational research and theory, however, is the role of extrinsic motivation. From a behaviorist perspective, rewards or extrinsic motivation can be used to maximize learning in the classroom. Others argue that rewards are coercive in nature and can undermine intrinsic motivation (Kohn, 1999). While theorists do not agree on the exact effect of extrinsic rewards on intrinsic motivation, most do agree that the ultimate goal is for learners to become intrinsically motivated and to enjoy learning for learning's sake. Hence, rewards can be used with caution and in ways that reportedly enhance intrinsic motivation (Covington & Müeller, 2001; Witzel & Mercer, 2003).

Applying Theories of Engagement and Motivation

Goal theory, self-efficacy theory, expectancy–value theory, attribution theory, and self-determination theory can complement each other and inform constructivist classroom management practices (Palmer, 2005). Practices that enhance engagement and motivation include maintaining a learning orientation; fostering competence, relatedness, and autonomy; attending to student interest in and value of learning goals; and promoting effort. A well-managed classroom combines these practices for attaining the goal. The following are guidelines and practical examples for applying each.

Learning Goal Orientation

Mastery or learning goal orientation can influence students' achievement-related behaviors on academic tasks (Covington, 2000; Roeser, Midgley, & Urdan, 1996; Schunk, 1996; Wolters, 2004). In classrooms with learning goal orientations, effort and outcome are related: greater efforts produce greater outcomes. In addition, failures allow for feedback and are viewed as learning opportunities. Teachers can attend to the classroom variables that are necessary so that children orient themselves toward a learning goal versus a performance goal. These variables include teacher beliefs about self-efficacy and intelligence, their cues and instructions regarding mastery goals and the role of effort, the types of learning goals that they promote, and classroom structures that deter competition and comparisons of individuals with their peers.

Teacher Beliefs

Citing relevant research, Deemer (2004) explains that the teacher's own sense of efficacy with regard to his or her ability to help students learn, as well as the teacher's belief regarding the malleability of intelligence, influence the goals that he or she promotes in the classroom. That is, teachers with a low sense of efficacy tend to extend little effort in planning lessons and finding resources, show little persistence with students having difficulties, and use little variety in their teaching methods. Conversely, teachers with a high sense of efficacy employ greater variety, are more persistent with students having difficulties, extend greater effort in finding resources, and develop more challenging lessons. In Neal's classroom, the teacher conveyed the view that efforts in teaching another way would be fruitless because of the students' immaturity; in this way, she communicated her doubts about her own efficacy. Todd's teacher was willing to accommodate Todd's difficulty with handwriting so that he could help Todd progress toward his learning goal.

Teachers who believe that intelligence is malleable are likely to explain success and failures in terms of effort expenditure and promote learning goals, while teachers who believe that intelligence is fixed are likely to explain success and failure as due to ability or lack of it, and are more likely to adopt a performance goal orientation. Given the influence of teacher beliefs, teachers can examine their own beliefs regarding their own self-efficacy and theory of intelligence and challenge those beliefs that paint the teacher as unable to influence student performance due to lack of efficacy and/or a view of intelligence as a stable factor.

Cues About Learning Goals

In Todd's example, students were well informed about their progress in writing. Their mission was to improve their writing skills, not to just complete assignments. With regular feedback and encouragement, they were able to see the way to this goal. In Neal's classroom, the emphasis was on completing work and following directions. The goal of learning math was lost on the students. According to Deemer (2004), teachers establish goal orientations in the classroom by providing cues through their instructional practices about goals held for their students. The following strategies can be incorporated into the classroom to orient students toward learning goals:

- Develop learning goals with students in conjunction with school curricular requirements. While the school, county, or state may prescribe curriculum, teachers can review those goals with students and work with students to put goals in words that are meaningful to the student. Goals that are important to the learner can be incorporated.
- Engage students in developing learning goals by completing a Know, Want, Learn (KWL) chart (see Figure 10.2). This type of chart allows students to indicate what they Know about a topic; set goals specifying what they Want to learn; and after reading or completing classroom activities or projects, students discuss what they have Learned.
- Tie assignments that are posted on the board to the predetermined goals.
- Hold individual learning conferences with students on a regular basis to review individual progress toward learning goals.
- Ask students what they learned when reviewing the day or the lesson.
- Tie assignments to the learning goal. Avoid an emphasis on work or assignments that need to be completed; keep the focus on the goal for learning. Figure 10.3 includes examples of task completion goals and learning goals.

Figure 10.2   Know, Want, Learn Chart

What I know	What I want to know	What I learned
A KWL chart can assist students in identifying the background knowledge that they bring to a project or learning activity, and can engage students in identifying learning goals and evaluating what they have learned.		

Types of Learning Goals

In addition to maintaining a focus on learning goals, Schunk (2003) describes three important properties of goals that can influence their effect on motivation, specificity, proximity, and difficulty. Goals that are specific are more likely to enhance learning and motivation

Figure 10.3   Examples of Task Completion Goals and Learning Goals

High school

Task Completion Goal

Write a paper that compares concentration camps in Germany with Japanese internment camps in the United States.

Learning Goal

Describe and compare German concentration camps and Japenese internment camps in the United States.

Middle school

Task Completion Goal

Complete Chapter 4 in math text.

Learning Goal

Understand how to solve algebraic equations for *n*.

Elementary school

Task Completion Goal

Write spelling words in sentences each week.

Learning Goal

Be able to use spelling words in writing projects.

than goals such as "Do your best work." Specific performance standards, such as learning to use descriptive adjectives in a paragraph, allow students to evaluate their progress. Short-term goals in which the end is in sight result in greater motivation and higher self-efficacy than goals in the distant future. This is especially true for young children who respond well to goals that can be achieved in a few minutes. Finally, difficulty is an important factor in goal setting. Students will work harder toward more difficult goals than towards easy goals as long as they perceive that the difficult goals are within their grasp.

In addition to these three properties of goals, Schunk also contends that motivation and self-efficacy are enhanced when learners receive goal progress feedback. Feedback with regard to student progress toward their learning goals can enhance motivation when this feedback conveys that the learner is competent and can continue to improve by working diligently.

Structures That Deter Competition and Peer Comparisons

To maximize learning goal orientations, teachers should be wary of incentive systems that allow students to compare themselves with their peers (Deemer, 2004; Palmer, 2005). In her review of motivational research, Covington (2000) describes how classrooms that promote competition tend to encourage peer comparisons and foster a performance orientation. In competitive classrooms, conditions for both performance approach and performance avoidance are set. For example, in classrooms where competition is encouraged and rewards are given to a few, students who have a high sense of self-efficacy are likely to adopt a performance orientation and work diligently to earn the reward to show off their competence. But under such competitive goals, individuals are likely to continue striving only as long as they are winners. For many students, in competitive classrooms where there is a scarcity of rewards, many learners are likely to adopt a performance avoidance goal as a protective device to avoid appearing incompetent in the likely event that they do not win the prize. They are likely to give up and disengage to avoid unfavorable comparisons with peers.

As an alternative to competitive classrooms where there are few "winners," Covington (2000) argues for creating "motivational equity." To create motivational equity, Covington suggests "yardsticks" that are open to all and that recognize individual progress and a student's efforts at self-improvement. According to Covington's review of the research, allowing students to set individual learning goals and compare their progress to their own starting points has many benefits, including an increased willingness to take risks, less task anxiety, greater metacognitive self-regulation, thoughtfulness in approaching problems, and greater interest in the subject matter.

Interest and Value

Motivation and engagement can be at their peak when student interest in and value of the subject matter is considered and orchestrated. In Todd's class, writing a newsletter for parents incurred benefits in the act of writing. Whether it be science and math, or reading and language arts, research continually shows that student interest in and value of the subject matter are strong forces in engagement and achievement (Guthrie & Wigfield, 2000; Singh, Granville, & Dika, 2002).

Figure 10.4   Sample Questions for Student Interests or Preferences Inventory

When I have free time at home, I like to _____

My favorite subject at school is _____

I like to read books about _____

After school I like to _____

My favorite movie is_____

My favorite TV show is _____

If I could change something at school, it would be _____

The things that I like about school are _____

Teachers can learn about student interest in various ways. They can use an interest inventory or an interview/conference, or ask students to respond to an open-ended questionnaire with key questions about their learning preferences (depending on the age group). Many curriculum guides contain an informal interest inventory or teachers can create their own. Figure 10.4 includes an example of interest inventory items for elementary, middle, and secondary school students.

In addition to identifying student interests, creating value in the subject matter can assist with motivation (Pintrich, 2003). Learners need to know how academic activities relate to their world, how they are useful in the present, and how they relate to distant goals (e.g., job skills, career goals). Boekaerts (2002) provides the following suggestions for increasing student interest and value in learning goals

- Make tasks and activities meaningful by reminding students of the intrinsic value of the tasks and their potential application to other subjects and life activities outside of school.
- Find out about students, current interests and future career aspirations, and relate the content to those interests.
- Show videos or bring in newspaper clippings that highlight the importance or relevance of a skill.
- Ask students who are motivated in a particular area to explain the value of a skill to others.
- Have students interview parents and others in the community to find out how they use the skill.
- Use a variety of activities—even the most exciting activity can lose its appeal if it is used too often.

Adopting teaching pedagogies, such as project-based learning, can help teachers capitalize on student interests (Helm, 2004; Jurow, 2005; Langhout, 2004). In project-based learning, students choose a problem or project based on their interests, research the topic, and choose a way to present the information to the class or other audience.

Schraw, Flowerday, & Lehman (2001) suggest that teachers must generate situational interest in subject matter for which students have no prior personal interest.

Situational interest is environmentally activated and often precedes personal interest. These authors suggest that to generate situational interest, teachers can select interesting texts, provide the background knowledge needed to understand a topic, and give students meaningful choices.

Interesting Texts

Schraw et al. (2001) suggest that since teachers often rely on texts, their selection should be given careful consideration. They suggest three criteria for selecting texts: coherence, relevance, and vividness. With regard to coherence, texts should require little inference and be well organized. Texts that contain features that connect information to readers' lives can increase interest and learning. Finally, texts that are vivid may include an element of suspense, as well as vivid, engaging segments.

Background Knowledge

Schraw et al. (2001) also suggest that interest is enhanced when students have some background knowledge of the material. Teachers can provide students with background knowledge by using texts that have material which is somewhat familiar, but not too familiar, and by holding small-group discussions so that students can bring their prior knowledge to light. A KWL chart (Figure 10.2) can help teachers determine students' prior knowledge.

Meaningful Choices

Choice can increase student interest because it gives students a sense of control and provides students with an opportunity to be creative. Choice is further discussed with regard to autonomy structures.

Competence

In his review of research on motivation, Pintrich (2003) clearly indicates that students who believe that they are capable and that they can succeed are much more motivated with regard to effort, persistence, and behavior than students who lack this type of confidence. This research translates into classroom practices, including providing opportunities for success, giving accurate feedback, using language that fosters competence, providing a structure for support, and reducing performance anxiety.

Opportunities for Success

Teachers can design learning activities and lessons that offer opportunities for success, but that also challenge students. Teachers can use differentiation of assignments so that students receive the appropriate level of challenge. For example, trade books at various reading levels are available on the same topics.

Accurate Feedback

Teachers can give students clear and accurate feedback regarding competence and self-efficacy, focusing on the development of competence, expertise, and skill. Teachers can let students know their progress toward accomplishing learning goals, as opposed to judgment regarding perceived ability. For example, teachers can use comments such as "Your reading has improved this far since the beginning of the year," as opposed to "You are still in the lowest level of readers in this class."

Language That Communicates Competence

Teachers can use language that fosters a sense of competence in the face of frustration (Green, 2002). For example, teachers may be tempted to say, "Jose, come on, this isn't hard for you; you are such a bright boy." A comment such as this one may lead Jose to think that since a task isn't hard, he must not be so bright. Instead, Green (2002) recommends statements that convey confidence, such as "I think that if you keep trying, you will get it"; or convey challenge, such as "This is much harder than the last one you solved." Green also suggests using statements that confirm that students have met or exceeded expectations, such as "It was a difficult assignment, but everyone was able to complete it successfully!" In addition, students should be given regular feedback on their work, and praise should be given for improvements instead of grades (Xiang, McBride, & Solmon, 2003). Comments that provide social comparisons of performance (e.g., "That was the best grade in the class," or "You are way behind your classmates") should be avoided (Deemer, 2004).

Structure to Encourage Success

In addition to the preceding practices, according to Skinner and Belmont (1993), competence can be fostered by having structure in the classroom. According to these authors, structure refers to having adequate information about how to achieve desired outcomes, clear communication of expectations, and teacher responses that are consistent and predictable. Structure also includes offering instrumental help and support, and adjusting teaching strategies to the level of the learner so that success is attainable. Students can become easily frustrated when they do not know what is expected or they do not how to get help when they need it. Putting these structures in place can foster competence.

Reduction of Performance Anxiety

Learners are more likely to feel motivated and focus on learning goals when the atmosphere in the classroom is relaxed and anxiety is minimized. Good and Brophy (2003) suggest that performance anxiety can be minimized when most instructional activities are structured as learning experiences rather than tests, and when the teacher communicates that mistakes are opportunities for learning. Students may become anxious when they are evaluated on every assignment so that each mistake counts against their grade. In Neal's classroom, described at the beginning of the chapter, the teacher's often unexpected punitive responses to math work took their toll on morale in the classroom.

Autonomy

Teachers can support autonomy by allowing freedom within the classroom structure. Teachers can give children latitude in their learning activities, offer meaningful choices, and avoid coercive strategies such as external controls, rewards, and pressures. Research indicates that providing meaningful choices increases student interest and engagement (Flowerday & Schraw, 2000; Pintrich, 2003), but too many choices may not be wise, as some students may always choose the path of least resistance. Consider the following example:

One teacher in an elementary school, Jonnie Walkingstick, allows students to decide how they will complete their work. If a child proposes a choice, such as "Can I do my math problems on the board?" the teacher responds, "I don't know, we haven't made that choice before, let's see if it will work." The teacher and the students then can decide if a choice helped them learn and would be wise to make another time.

On the other hand, some choices interfere with learning, for example, in the same classroom, two students sitting next to each other to complete an assignment are distracting each other. The teacher tells them that their seating choice isn't working and they will need to make a different choice for now. This teacher provides support for autonomy by allowing students to make decisions about learning, within limits. There is a requirement that those decisions must be ones that support learning.

Teachers can offer choices in many ways, including the following:

- Choice of topic for a report;
- Choice of book to read;
- Choice of project;
- Choice of where to sit during independent work;
- Choice of assignment—Tic-Tac-Toe described by Tomlinson (2001) provides one strategy for offering students choices on assignments. Figures 10.5 and 10.6 provide examples.

Figure 10.5   Tic-Tac-Toe Board for Studying Spelling Words

Choose three squares diagonally, horizontally, or vertically so that you have tic-tac-toe.		
Ask a classmate to ask you your spelling words.	Write your spelling words in alphabetical order.	Write a story using as many of your spelling words as you can.
Draw a picture of your spelling words.	Take a practice spelling test.	Pick three challenging words to add to your word list, look them up in the dictionary, and practice spelling them.
Use your spelling words in sentences.	Make a word pyramid for each spelling word.	Write a synonym and an antonym for each spelling word.

For this tic-tac-toe board, students can choose three different ways to learn their spelling words. Students might come up with different ideas. This grid can be easily adapted to many other content areas or units.

Figure 10.6   Tic-Tac-Toe Board for a Social Studies Unit on Australia

With your group, choose three squares diagonally, horizontally, or vertically so that you have tic-tac-toe.		
Using information from at least three different sources, create a presentation depicting the physical geography, customs, and issue facing Australia. Share with the class.	Using at least three different sources, study a famous individual in history from Australia and write a personal diary or journal as if written by that individual. Share with the class.	Using the textbook and at least three other sources, compare and contrast the government of Australia with that of the United States. Prepare your results in the form of a poster to share with the class. You may want to include a Venn diagram.
Complete the Australia crossword puzzle.	Take the unit quiz on Australia.	Create a climagraph for a capital city in Australia.
Create a diagram to show how a geologic feature was formed.	Prepare a tourist brochure for Australia that includes climate, geography, sites to see, transportation, and popular culture.	Using your textbook and at least three different sources, create a time line of important events in the history of Australia.

For this tic-tac-toe board, students are assigned to groups of three to complete their choice of three squares that make tic-tac-toe.

Relatedness

A sense of belonging or relatedness can be a powerful motivator in the classroom. Students who like and are liked by their teachers and peers are happier at school and have more fun learning. A sense of relatedness has a positive effect on student confidence, work habits, coping skills, and academic perfomance (Furrer & Skinner, 2003). Creating a classroom climate of community, where everyone belongs and all children are valued (see Chapter 8), and encouraging a positive student–teacher relationship (see in Chapter 9) by being attuned to, enjoying, and dedicating resources of time and energy to students contribute to a sense of relatedness.

In addition, teaching strategies that allow children to work together and learn from each other help children achieve social goals, as well as academic goals. Practices that foster relatedness include peer tutoring and cooperative learning. Not only do cooperative learning and peer tutoring assist with relatedness in the classroom, but they can increase motivation by increasing self-esteem, as well as increasing positive attitudes toward the subject area (d'Arripe-Longueville, Gernigon, Huet, Cadopi, & Winnykamen, 2002; Topping, Campbell, Douglas, & Smith, 2003).

PROMOTING EFFORT AND STRATEGY USE

In summarizing the research on effort, Marazano, Pickering, and Pollock (2001) indicate that learners tend to attribute success and failure to either ability, effort, other people, or luck. With regard to motivation in the classroom, belief in effort, including the effort involved in using good learning strategies, is the most useful. While not all students believe in the importance of effort, teachers can help them change their beliefs by teaching and exemplifying the connection between effort and achievement. Teachers can share personal examples of times when effort and persistence paid off despite initial failure. They can also have students read about famous individuals who, because of their persistence, succeeded despite great obstacles.

Boekaerts (2002) suggests that students be asked to predict the effort required for a task and reflect on it after task completion. In this way, learners begin to understand the link between effort and achievement, and begin to self-regulate effort. When students can attribute successes to effort and the use of good strategies, they are more likely to persist when tasks appear to be difficult.

Teachers who are conscious of applying research on motivation are cognizant of the beliefs that learners bring to the classroom regarding goals, competence, reasons for successes and failures, and the value of learning. Teachers can use instructional cues and practices that help learners adopt learning goals and shape beliefs about competence and the importance of effort. In addition, teachers can use practices that build on student interests and support competence and autonomy.

Reluctant Learners

Learners come to the classroom with varying levels of motivation and differing motivational beliefs. Enthusiasm for learning, as well as motivational beliefs, can vary with the subject matter, as well as with time and learner characteristics. Students may have high motivation in one area, such as reading, but low motivation and efficacy beliefs in another area, such as math and science. As with the example of Neal, students may begin the school year with high levels of self-efficacy and/or value, and depending on experiences, those beliefs can change. In addition, students can begin their schooling as youngsters with positive motivational beliefs, but for many students, those beliefs begin to change and motivation wanes during the middle school years. Students who are at a disadvantage due to a history of school failure, family or cultural factors, or disabilities such as learning and behavioral disorders may have poor attitudes toward learning and low self-efficacy. Teachers can attend to the motivation of reluctant learners in several ways, including being cognizant of the reciprocal effect of engagement, changing learner beliefs, and cautiously using rewards.

Reciprocal Effect of Engagement

Student engagement and teacher behavior can have a reciprocal effect in that learners who are enthusiastic and eager to learn elicit more enthusiasm on the part of the teacher. On the other hand, learners who demonstrate negative dispositions to learning may elicit teacher behaviors that undermine motivation (Skinner & Belmont, 1993). Teachers may steer away from those learners and focus more effort on students who appear to appreciate learning. A conscious effort is needed to break this pattern. The wise teacher can look at student anxiety or boredom as a cue that the children may need even greater support for success, more interesting materials and activities, or more latitude in the classroom.

Changing Beliefs

Learners' beliefs about motivational goals, self-efficacy, and attributions of success and failure are influenced by experiences, parents, teachers, and peers (Altermatt & Pomerantz, 2003; Boekaerts, 2002; Eccles et al., 1998). Students with a history of academic failure or with overly critical parents, or those who compare themselves with their peers, may develop beliefs that are counterproductive to learning. Learners with particularly low self-efficacy may benefit from attribution retraining in which they are taught to change their beliefs about their successes and failures.

Craven, Marsh, and Debus (1991) suggest explicitly teaching students with low self-efficacy to examine both success and failures in terms of effort, use of appropriate task-specific strategies, and perseverance, while confirming that the student has the ability to complete the task. In addition to attribution retraining, these learners can be encouraged to look at their learning in terms of where they started and the progress they are making, and they should be discouraged from making peer comparisons.

Rewards

While generally classroom management and motivation research do not favor a reliance on the use of rewards (Evertson & Weinstein, 2006), students who are less engaged may be enticed into the world of learning through the use of rewards. If rewards are used with caution to avoid the adoption of performance goals and a reliance on extrinsic rewards, their effect on intrinsic motivation can be minimal. According to Reeve (2006), rewards may have a paradoxical effect of enhancing competence, but decreasing autonomy, depending on how they are used. When rewards are used to give information about performance, they may enhance a student's sense of competence. However, although a reward given in a way that indicates control of behavior—if you do this, then you will get this— may enhance competence, it undermines the student's need for autonomy and hence discourages intrinsic motivation. Reeves indicates that rewards can be either contingent or noncontingent, and expected or unexpected.

> Task contingent—A reward is given for the completion of a task, such as a worksheet.
> Task noncontingent—A reward is given irrespective of a task (e.g., just showing up).
> Engagement contingent—A reward is given for merely engaging in a task.
> Performance contingent—A reward is given for a good performance.
> Expected—A reward is revealed ahead of time.
> Unexpected—A reward is not announced ahead of time and is given after the desired behavior or performance.

Reeve (2006) indicates the importance of identifying the purpose of a reward. If the purpose of a reward is solely to provide feedback regarding performance, it may not be damaging to intrinsic motivation. In order to avoid the use of rewards to control behavior, Reeve suggests that the rewards which are least detrimental and perceived as less controlling are nontangible, unexpected, and performance contingent. For example, when Mary has shown improvement in spelling performance, she is rewarded with praise, "Look at how much you have improved since the beginning of the year!" This compliment gives Mary competence information, but is not administered in a way that is controlling.

Witzel and Mercer (2003) provide the following guidelines for the use of rewards:

- Avoid using rewards for activities that students are already motivated to complete or that are easy for the student.
- Give rewards only after the value of the activity has been established.
- Pair rewards with praise and encouragement regarding student effort, the use of appropriate strategies, and the value of the task.
- Avoid reward structures in which students compete for rewards.
- If students are reluctant to perform certain tasks, reflect on the value and purpose of the task and change it to be more intrinsically rewarding, if possible, before offering a tangible reward.
- Use intangible rewards over tangible rewards.

For one example of the use of rewards, Self-Brown and Mathews (2003) found that a contingency contract system, where students contracted individually with the teacher, had advantages over a token economy system, where goals and rewards were uniform across the classroom. Students who were engaged in contingency contracts adopted more learning goals than those in the token economy. The researchers suggest that if reward systems are kept on an individual basis, students are less likely to compare their progress with that of their peers, more likely to be successful, and more likely to feel a greater sense of accomplishment for their work.

THE CIRCLE OF COURAGE

It is evident from a review of motivation literature that practices that foster motivation support the basic tenets of the Circle of Courage, especially with regard to mastery. Students who feel competent are likely to be willing learners. In addition, motivation is enhanced when students have a sense of belonging or relatedness. Practices that allow students to work together, as well as maintaining a sense of community and positive student–teacher relationships, have been shown to increase motivation. Furthermore, structures that promote autonomy or independence relate well to self-determination theory. Students have a greater investment in learning activities when they have helped to develop learning goals and have meaningful choices about how to achieve them. The only tenet of the Circle of Courage not readily apparent in motivational research is generosity. However, the caring relationships between teachers and students, and students and their peers promote both competence and belonging. Students who are allowed to be in the role of a tutor and provide academic support to others may experience enhanced self-efficacy and belonging.

SUMMARY

Engagement and motivation are best maximized in classrooms with an emphasis on learning goals, as opposed to an emphasis on task completion, that promote competence (self-efficacy), relatedness, and autonomy; and that maximize student effort, interest in, and value for academic activities.

In classrooms that promote academic engagement, teachers provide prominent learning goals; real-world connections to those goals; meaningful choices about what, when, and how to learn; and interesting activities and materials that are familiar, vivid, important, and relevant. Likewise, teachers in classrooms with high academic engagement further attend to the motivation of students by engaging students in setting learning goals, promoting effort, scaffolding instruction for success, and providing meaningful choices. For reluctant learners, even greater effort is required to intentionally change learners' motivational beliefs and entice them into the learning process. The tenets of the Circle of Courage relate well to these theories of motivation and constructive classroom management.

REFERENCES

Ames, C. (1992). Classrooms: Goals, structures, and student motivation. *Journal of Educational Psychology, 84* (3), 261–271.

Altermatt, E. R, & Pomerantz, E. M. (2003). The development of competency-related and motivational beliefs: An investigation of similarity and influence among friends. *Journal of Educational Psychology, 95*(1), 111–123.

Bandura, A. (1997). *Self-efficacy: The exercise of control.* New York: W. H. Freeman.

Boekaerts, M. (2002). *Motivation to learn.* Retrieved on January 5, 2005, from International Academy of Education & International Bureau of Education Web site: http://www.ibe.unesco.org/publications/Practices.htm

Caraway, K., Tucker, C. M., Reinke, W. M., & Hall, C. (2003). Self-efficacy, goal orientation, and fear of failure as predictors of school engagement in high school students. *Psychology in the Schools, 40*(4), 417–427.

Connell, J. P., Halpern-Felsher, B. L., Clifford, E., Crichlow, W., & Usinger, P. (1995). Hanging in there: Behavioral, psychological, and contextual factors affecting whether African American adolescents stay in high school. *Journal of Adolescent Research, 10*(1), 41–63.

Covington, M. V. (2000). Goal theory, motivation, and school achievement: An integrative review. *Annual Review of Psychology, 51*(1), 171–200.

Covington, M. V., & Müeller, K. J. (2001). Intrinsic versus extrinsic motivation: An approach/-avoidance reformulation. *Educational Psychology Review, 13*(2), 157–177.

Craven, R. G., Marsh, H. W., & Debus, R. L. (1991). Effects of internally focused feedback and attributional feedback on the enhancement of academic self-concept. *Journal of Educational Psychology, 83*(1), 17–27.

d'Arripe-Longueville, F., Gernigon, C., Huet, M. L, Cadopi, M., & Winnykamen, F. (2002). Peer tutoring in a physical education setting: Influence of tutor skill level on novice learners' motivation and performance. *Journal of Teaching in Physical Education, 22*(1), 105–124.

Deemer, S. A. (2004). Classroom goal orientation in high school classrooms: Revealing links between teacher beliefs and classroom environments. *Educational Research, 46*(1), 73–90.

Eccles , J. S., Wigfield, A., & Schiefele, U. (1998). Motivation to succeed. In W. Damon (Series Ed.) & N. Eisenberg, (Vol. Ed.), *Handbook of child psychology: Social, emotional, and personality development* (5th ed., pp. 1017–1095). New York: Wiley.

Evertson, C. M., & Weinstein, C. S. (Eds.). (2006). *Handbook of classroom management: Research, practice, and contemporary issues.* New York: Lawrence Erlbaum.

Flowerday, T. and Schraw, G. (2000). Teacher Beliefs About Instructional Choice: A Phenomenological Study. *Journal of Educational Psychology, 92*(4), 634–645.

Fredricks, J. A., Blumenfield, P. C., & Paris, A. H. (2004). School engagement: Potential for the concept and state of the evidence. *Review of Educational Research, 74*(1), 59–110.

Furrer, C., & Skinner, E. (2003). Sense of relatedness as a factor in children's academic engagement and performance. *Journal of Educational Psychology, 95*(1), 148–162.

Good, T. L., & Brophy, J. E. (2003). Looking in classrooms (9th ed.). Boston: Allyn and Bacon.

Green, S. K. (2002). Using an expectancy–value approach to examine teachers' motivational strategies. *Teaching and Teacher Education, 18*(8), 989–1005.

Greene, B., & Miller, R. (1996). Influences on achievement: Goals, perceived ability, and cognitive engagement. *Contemporary Educational Psychology, 21*(2), 181–192.

Guthrie, J. T., & Wigfield, A. (2000). Engagement and motivation in reading. In M. L. Kamil, P. B. Mosenthal, P. D. Pearson, & R. Barr (Eds.), *Handbook of reading research: Volume III* (pp. 403–422). New York: Lawrence Erlbaum.

Helm, J. H. (2004). Projects that power young minds. *Educational Leadership, 62*(1), 58–63.

Jurow, A. S. (2005). Shifting engagements in figured worlds: Middle school mathematics students' participation in an architectural design project. *Journal of Learning Sciences, 14*(1), 35–68.

Kohn, A. (1999). *Punished by rewards: The trouble with gold stars, incentive plans, A's, praise, and other bribes.* Boston: Houghton Mifflin.

Langhout, R. D. (2004). Facilitators and inhibitors of positive school feelings: An exploratory study. *American Journal of Community Psychology, 34*(1), 111–127.

Marzano, R. J., Pickering, D. J., & Pollock, J. E. (2001). Classroom Instruction that Works. Alexandria, Virginia:ASCD.

National Research Council & Institute of Medicine. (2004). Engaging schools: Fostering high school students' motivation to learn. Washington, DC: National Academy Press.

Palmer, D. (2005). A motivational view of constructivist-informed teaching. *International Journal of Science Education, 27*(15), 1853–1881.

Pintrich, R. P. (2003). A motivational science perspective on the role of student motivation in learning and teaching contexts. *Journal of Educational Psychology, 95*(4), 667–686.

Reeve, J. (2006). Extrinsic rewards and internal motivation. In C. M. Evertson, & C. S. Weinstein (Eds.), *Handbook of classroom management: Research, practice, and contemporary issues.* New York: Lawrence Erlbaum.

Roeser, R. W., Midgley, C., & Urdan, T. C. (1996). Perceptions of the school psychological environment and early adolescents' psychological and behavioral functioning in school: The mediating role of goals and belonging. *Journal of Educational Psychology, 88*(3), 408–422.

Ryan, R. M., & Deci, E. L. (2000). Self-determination theory and the facilitation of intrinsic motivation, social development, and well-being. *American Psychologist, 55*(1), 68–78.

Schraw, G., Flowerday, T., & Lehman, S. (2001). Increasing situational interest in the classroom. *Educational Psychology Review, 13*(3), 211–224.

Schunk, D. H. (1996). Goals and self-evaluative influences during children's cognitive skill learning. *American Educational Research Journal, 33*(2), 359–382.

Schunk, D. H. (2003). Self-efficacy for reading and writing: Influence of modeling, goal setting, and self-evaluation. *Reading and Writing Quarterly, 19*(2), 159–172.

Self-Brown, S. R., & Mathews, L. (2003). Effects of classroom structure on student achievement goal orientation. *Journal of Educational Research, 97*(2), 106–112.

Singh, K., Granville, M., & Dika, S. (2002). Mathematics and science achievement: Effects of motivation, interest, and academic engagement. *The Journal of Educational Research, 95*(6), 323–333.

Skinner, E. A., & Belmont, M. J. (1993). Motivation in the classroom: Reciprocal effects of teacher behavior and student engagement across the school year. *Journal of Educational Psychology, 85*(4), 571–581.

Tomlinson, C. A. (2001). How to differentiate instruction in mixed-ability classrooms. (2nd Ed.) Alexandria, VA: ASCD.

Topping , K. J., Campbell, J., Douglas, W., & Smith, A. (2003). Cross-age peer tutoring in mathematics with seven- and 11-year-olds: Influence on mathematical vocabulary, strategic dialogue, and self-concept. *Educational Research, 45*(3), 287–308.

Weiner, B. (1986). *An attributional theory of motivation and emotion.* New York: Springer–Verlag.

Witzel, B. S., & Mercer, C. D. (2003). Using rewards to teach students with disabilities. *Remedial and Special Education, 24*(2), 88–97.

Wolters, C. A. (2004). Advancing achievement goal theory: Using goal structures and goal orientations to predict students' motivation, cognition, and achievement. *Journal of Educational Psychology, 96*(2), 236–250.

Xiang, P., McBride, R., & Solmon, M. A. (2003). Motivational climates in ten teachers' elementary physical education classes: An achievement goal theory approach. *The Elementary School Journal, 104*(1), 71–92.

DISCIPLINE, DISRUPTION, AND VIOLENCE

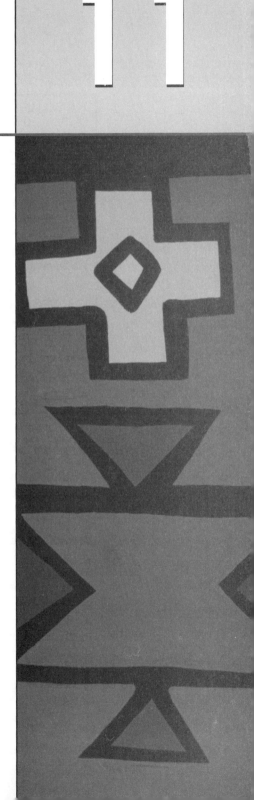

Misbehavior and punishment are not opposites that cancel each other; on the contrary, they breed and reinforce each other.
Haim Ginott

Despite their best efforts at developing community, actively engaging students in meaningful learning activities, and utilizing strategies for preventing discipline problems, teachers may face behaviors from their students that interfere with learning in the classroom and in the school. The purpose of this chapter is to explore the range of discipline challenges and to present appropriate practices for dealing with such issues.

DISCIPLINARY TRENDS

In today's schools, teachers may face a range of disciplinary issues—from minor disruptions, distractions, and disrespectfulness to more serious infractions such as bullying, aggression, and violence. For example, in a poll of teachers' attitudes about school issues, the percentage of teachers who reported dealing with frequent disciplinary issues is high (Langdon, 1997), as shown in Table 11.1.

Among the more serious but less frequent issues that teachers reported encountering were stealing money or personal property belonging to other students, teachers, or staff; vandalizing school property; using or selling drugs at school; theft of school property; racially provoked fights; and the carrying of knives, firearms, or other weapons at school. More recent surveys of schools indicate that these same issues continue to affect school climate, and student and teacher attitudes (National Center for Education Statistics, 2007).

In a survey of more than 700 teachers, Kimberling and Wantland (2002) asked respondents to describe changes in disciplinary issues

Table 11.1   Frequency of Disciplinary Issues Reported by Elementary and High School
Teachers (percentage of teachers reporting that the problem occurs most
of the time or fairly often)

PROBLEM REPORTED AS DISPLAYED MOST OF THE TIME OR FAIRLY OFTEN	ALL TEACHERS	ELEMENTARY SCHOOL TEACHERS	HIGH SCHOOL TEACHERS
Schoolwork/Homework assignments are not completed	71	68	78
Behavior that disrupts class	58	65	45
Talking back to, disobeying teachers	50	54	43
Truancy/Being absent from school	41	35	57

Source: Information taken from Langdon, 1997

over the last 10 years. Teachers reported the following trends: students were less respectful; assumed less personal responsibility; were more impatient, impulsive, noncompliant, oppositional, and defiant; had negative attitudes; had difficulty paying
attention; were more aggressive; wanted instant gratification; and used more inappropriate language.

Of course, possibly the most serious of all school disciplinary issues may be aggression and violence. Although recent statistics indicate that school violence is on the decline (National Center for Education Statistics, 2007) school violence and its prevention
have certainly received increased attention from administrators, teachers, parents, and
the public in recent years. While the chances of serious injury or death from violence in
school may be low, related bullying-type behaviors such as nonfatal aggression, verbal
taunting and teasing, and name-calling occur frequently.

According to a recent survey of more than 15,000 teenagers, more than one third of
the students (39% of middle schoolers and 36% of high schoolers) say that they don't
feel safe at school (Josephson Institute of Ethics, 2001). This report also indicates that
students perceive violence as an acceptable solution to their problems. For example,
43% of high school and 37% of middle school boys believe that it is acceptable to hit or
threaten a person who makes them angry. Nearly one in five girls (19%) agree. Seventy-
five percent of the boys and more than 60% of the girls surveyed said that they had hit
someone in the past 12 months because they had been angry. In a national study of bullying, 13% of sixth graders reported being a victim of bullying at least once a week, and
10% reported being responsible for bullying someone (Nansel et al., 2001).

Precursors of more serious behavioral problems are often seen in the early grades (Loeber, Green, Lahey, Frick, & McBurnett, 2000; Stouthammer-Loeber & Loeber, 2002). If dealt with effectively in the classroom, oftentimes more serious behavioral issues can be averted (Forness & Kavale, 2001) and placement in special education avoided (Kennedy et al., 2001). Whether dealing with minor distractions and disruptions or more serious issues related to discipline, the constructivist teacher is mindful of solutions that address issues *and* preserve the dignity of students in the classroom, as well as the student–teacher relationship. The rest of this chapter is devoted to such solutions and practices. I start with minor classroom disruptions, identifying ways to address unique student needs, and then move to dealing with more serious problems.

MINOR DISRUPTIONS TO CLASSROOM LEARNING
Preferred Strategies

In studying classroom management, Kounin (1970) defined the characteristic of "withitness" as a teacher's ability to know what is going on in the classroom and to stop inappropriate behavior with minimal disruption to learning. Withitness requires the ability to monitor the goings-on in the entire classroom, even during small-group or individual instruction. Withitness is one key to being able to respond appropriately to minor disruptions in the classroom. When students know that teachers are continually monitoring the goings-on in the room, they are less likely to engage in behavior that would gain the teacher's disapproval. In addition, the "withit" teacher can determine if a response is necessary and can notice and respond to inappropriate behavior before it has a chance to escalate.

Although a teacher monitors the classroom continually, responding to every action that occurs in the room can be disruptive in itself. Fleeting minor distractions, including drumming a desk with a pencil, students momentarily whispering to each other, students muttering to themselves, and so forth, can be ignored (Good & Brophy, 2000). Intervening in these types of behaviors could actually result in more disruption to academic engagement.

Other behaviors lend themselves to delayed action. These behaviors include failure to put away equipment, clean up materials, or finish an assignment. The teacher may address these behaviors with a student after a lesson in order to avoid disrupting learning activities. However, when minor disruptive behavior continues, intensifies, or becomes contagious, intervention by the teacher is necessary.

Good and Brophy (2000) identify the following strategies for stopping sustained minor misbehavior:

- Eye contact—When students know that a teacher is watching, they may desist from engaging in the inappropriate behavior.
- Touch and gestures—A tap on the shoulder or a signal with which the student is familiar, such as a finger in the air, can cue a student to desist inappropriate behavior and return to a task.

- Asking for responses—The teacher can ask an inattentive student a question to call him or her back to attention. However, care should be taken not to use this strategy to "catch" a student and embarrass him or her by asking a question that the student can't answer. Instead, asking a question that the student is likely to be able to answer, whether or not he or she is listening, will serve the purpose of bringing the student's attention back to the lesson.
- Name-dropping—A teacher may interrupt inappropriate behavior by merely dropping a student's name while giving instructions or information. For example, the teacher may say, "The third thing to remember, Mark, is to . . ."

Redirection is also an appropriate strategy for handling minor classroom disruptions (DuPaul and Weyandt 2006). Redirection involves an instruction by the teacher to change behavior. One elementary school teacher communicates redirection in very positive ways that maintain the dignity of the student. Some comments one might hear in her room include, "I am afraid that sitting next to Martha is not helping you learn. I want you to make another choice today about where to sit so that you will be able to focus on your learning," or "The mechanical pencil is holding your attention, see if this pencil will help you focus on learning." Research by Weyandt and DuPaul (2006) suggests that redirections be delivered in a calm and succinct manner.

When misbehavior is disruptive to learning and/or persists despite a teacher's efforts to redirect a student back to the lesson, a reprimand or direct correction is appropriate (Good & Brophy, 2000). The following are guidelines for correcting student behavior:

- Give corrections in close proximity, with eye contact, and in a quiet voice (Pfiffner, O'Leary, Rosen, & Sanderson, 1985).
- Give corrections immediately following the disruptive behavior (Abramowitz & O'Leary, 1990).
- Give students specific feedback regarding their behavior via an appropriate alternative (Good & Brophy, 2000). For example, instead of pointing out to a student what it is that he or she is doing wrong, indicate the expected behavior. "You need to work quietly," as opposed to "You are being entirely too noisy."
- Corrections should be concise (Abramowitz, O'Leary, & Futtersak, 1988).
- Deliver corrections privately and in a respectful manner to help the student and the teacher maintain dignity. When a reprimanded is given publicly, it may humiliate the student and/or increase the chances of a win–lose situation in which the student may feel inclined to get even with the teacher (Lasley, 2001).
- Corrections can be delivered in a way that reinforces the mission of the classroom instead of being a judgment of the child. One teacher uses statements such as "This seating arrangement isn't helping you learn. Maybe sitting in another seat would help you focus on your work." A correction given in this way, as opposed to "I guess you aren't mature enough to sit next to your friend, you will need to move," keeps the focus on the primary mission—learning—rather than being a judgment of the maturity of the student.
- Students may also be quietly reminded of the classroom covenant and classroom community expectations in a concise statement such as "We must work quietly so others can concentrate on what they are doing."

- According to Good and Brophy (2000), teachers giving direct corrections should avoid making unnecessary threats and displays of authority, and/or dwelling on past misbehavior. Statements such as "Must you always cause a ruckus when it is time for lunch," "Do it or else," and "I thought you learned your lesson last week" undermine the student–teacher relationship.
- During adolescence, students are more concerned about the approval of their peers than approval from teachers. For adolescents, Tierno (1991) cautions that reprimanding adolescents in front of peers may result in open defianace. Instead, Tierno suggests trying proximity first to signal an awareness of the problem. If proximity fails, call on a well-respected peer to answer a question and announce that the answer cannot be heard due to the noise in the room. This approach avoids singling out a student, calls to attention the need to be respectful to peers, and maintains a focus on learning.
- One middle school teacher describes how she teaches her students sign language for words such as stop, quiet, sit down, pay attention, and so forth. The students enjoy learning the signs, and the teacher has a quiet way of signaling for the students to desist.

PUNITIVE TECHNIQUES

Many teachers and schools rely on punishment for behavior that is inappropriate or disruptive. However, punitive techniques can bring with them undesirable consequences. While punishment may offer teachers short-term results, an understanding of its negative effects, as well as useful alternatives, is essential.

Mayer (1999) summarizes the disadvantages of punitive approaches:

- When punitive techniques are used to address misbehavior, the school climate tends to become overly negative and teachers rely more and more on such techniques.
- When punishment is applied frequently, it loses its effectiveness and is no longer punishing.
- When the school staff relies on punishment, they tend to become excessively punitive and teachers tend to ignore desired behavior and praise for the academic behaviors of students who misbehave becomes scarce.

In addition to these disadvantages, punitive practices can breed further misbehaviors, as suggested by Haim Ginott's words at the beginning of this chapter. Punishment can increase negative behavior and provoke noncompliance, aggression, and/or escape and avoidance, as well as cause the student–teacher relationship to deteriorate. A student who is punished may seek revenge against the teacher at a later time, or may seek to avoid the punitive teacher or classroom through tardiness and truancy. Shores, Gunter, and Jack (1993) contend that punitive approaches and student noncompliance interact to perpetuate a coercive cycle that actually increases the likelihood of disruptive behavior.

Furthermore, overuse of punishment occurs disproportionately with males, minority students, and students from low-income households (Brantlinger, 1991; Ruck & Wortley, 2002; Sheets & Gay, 1996; Skiba, Peterson, & Williams, 1997). Students with learning disabilities and those who are in foster care or protective custody, are homeless, or are in the free or reduced-fee lunch program are more likely to receive the most severe punishment (Skiba, 2000a). Thus, students with greater needs receive less support and attend school in a climate that is neither reinforcing nor inviting.

Some classroom management systems require teachers to count or document each infraction of a rule in the classroom by turning a card, putting a name or a check mark on the board, or by some other method. These systems offer students one or two warnings, or chances, before rule infractions result in a punishment such as loss of recess, walking laps at recess, a trip to the principal's office, and so forth. Rules are spelled out for students so that they know what behavior will result in a warning or other consequence. Unfortunately, these types of systems have disadvantages, including the following:

- These programs may work best for the children who do not need it and present more negative effects with the others (Maag, 2001). Children who need help or support for their behavioral difficulties often receive consequences over and over. This can lead to peer rejection and a pattern of negative interactions with the teacher.
- Small infractions can add up to a big consequence like a visit to the principal's office, resulting in loss of academic time and/or escape from academic work.
- Teachers can be on the lookout for negative behaviors and forget to acknowledge and encourage appropriate behavior.
- These programs may emphasize power, control, and obedience, and disallow opportunities for students to develop prosocial behaviors (Lake, 2004).

Finally, according to Nelson, Lott, and Glenn (2000), when adults punish children and youth, they do so in order to "discipline" or "teach" children a lesson. The definition of the word "discipline" does indeed include learning. However, using punishment to teach a lesson may lead to unintentional learning. For example, harsh or physical punishment may teach children the following:

Might makes right.
If someone hurts you, hurt them back.
You must feel pain in order to learn from your mistakes.
Aggression is an appropriate way to solve a problem.

Alternatives to Punishment

Teachers may rely on punitive approaches when they believe that students must experience discomfort to learn from their mistakes or when the application of such an approach is inadvertently reinforced. Nelson et al. (2000) amply make the argument that you don't have to hurt to learn from your mistakes. Students who engage in behavior that is more than a minor temporary distraction that can be ignored easily, corrected, or redirected can also learn from their mistakes.

Maag (2001) explains how teachers can experience negative reinforcement for the use of punitive approaches. For example, if a student is avoiding difficult work by causing a ruckus in the classroom, the teacher could demand that the student go to the principal's office. The ruckus then ceases. The irritation to the teacher that was caused by the student has been removed. By definition, removal of an aversive (student ruckus) can increase the likelihood that the teacher will again use the punitive technique of sending the student to the principal's office. Meanwhile, the student has lost valuable instruction time.

If the consequences of inappropriate behavior are handled carefully, students may learn more desirable lessons, such as mistakes are opportunities to learn; you don't have to hurt to learn from your mistakes; when you make a mistake, make it right; and all behavior has consequences. In addition, the time taken from instruction can be minimal.

Mistakes Are Opportunities to Learn

Through class meetings (discussed in Chapter 8) or individual conferences with a student or small group, learners can be guided toward developing a plan or solution regarding the behavior of concern. For example, two students may have gotten in an argument that resulted in a physical fight. The teacher can guide the students in developing a plan for a better way to interact with each other the next time conflict occurs. The plan might include an appropriate way to express feelings to each other, steps for reaching an agreement, and ways to apologize.

Another student may have difficulty with anger management. The teacher or a counselor might work with the student to take the following steps: Stop, take a deep breath, count to 10, think of my options, think of the consequences of each action, and choose the best option. A child who is easily distracted and overly active might generate a solution with a teacher of an appropriate way to ask for a break. Engaging children in solutions can teach children new skills, as well as preserve the student–teacher relationship.

When You Make a Mistake, You Can Make Things Right

Small infractions can be dealt with very matter of factly, with a quick instruction for making it right: "John, you are chewing gum, here is the garbage can." "Alex, you have made a mess with the materials, clean it up." No other punishment or consequence is required. For more serious transgressions, the idea of restitution can give learners an opportunity to make amends for their mistakes. Gossen (2007) describes restitution as a process for students to learn that everyone makes mistakes, that what they did could have been worse, and that they can make an improvement in how they behave. In addition, the teacher and/or counselor can work with a student to determine the best way to make amends. A learner who has damaged school property can make restitution by paying for or fixing the damage. A child who has been disrespectful to another student can write a letter of apology. For restitution to work, students are not to be humiliated or forced into something that is not sincere. Instead, a dialogue with the learner about the effects of the transgression on others and his or her ideas on how to make it right, as well as a plan to improve the way he or she reacts, teaches the learner that when we make a mistake, we should make it right.

All Behavior Has Consequences

When you don't brush your teeth, you get cavities; if you eat too much all at once, you get a bellyache; if you pick on your friends, you lose them. Teachers can help children learn the natural consequences of their behaviors. Children who are reluctant to complete learning tasks in the classroom can learn that if their work is not completed in a timely manner, they may have to use recess time to complete it. In this way, losing recess is presented not as a painful punishment, but as a logical consequence. As another example, Louise Burrel, a third-grade teacher, had a student who was oppositional, resistant to any request. After lunch one day, Carlie had spaghetti on her face. Ms. Burrell asked her to wipe her face off because there was spaghetti sauce on it. Carlie, in her usual mode, responded with a loud "NO!" Ms. Burrell's response was "Okay, but I just want you to know that if the other children laugh at you, it might be because your face looks funny with the spaghetti sauce on it." Carlie then washed her face.

Nelson et al. (2000) recommend the following criteria for using logical consequences and restitution:

- There should be a clear relationship between the behavior and the consequences or restitution: "If you are going to hit students that you sit next to, you need to sit by yourself until we have a good plan so that all children in this room will be safe." "You ripped Joey's art work. Do you think that taking care of his classroom chores today so that Joey has a chance to redo his picture and apologizing to Joey will help make that right?"
- Consequences and restitution should be relayed to students in a respectful and calm manner. Consequences should not be given in anger or in a way that is humiliating to the child. Consequences and restitution should be reasonable. The purpose of the consequence or restitution is for the student to learn from his or her mistake. Being required to overcompensate or perform unreasonable tasks to make things right serves only to cause discomfort and can further alienate the child. For example, if a child has work to complete during recess, as soon as the work is completed, he should go outside. Taking away the entire recess could be considered overcompensation designed to punish the learner.

PERSISTENT PROBLEMS

For any number of reasons, the difficult behavior of one or more students in a classroom may persist. Some individuals may have temporary behavioral difficulties that if handled with care, will subside. Some students, who have experienced academic failure, learn that disruptive behavior is an easy route to avoid academic tasks. Some students may experience stressful life circumstances (e.g., abuse and neglect) that can interfere with learning. Others may have disabilities, including behavioral and emotional disorders, learning disabilities, and attention deficit disorders. These students may present a variety of behavioral difficulties, including impulsiveness, inattentiveness, lack of social skills, and high activity levels. The students who are under these various circumstances may require specific modifications and accommodations to support them in the classroom. These accommodations should be planned and implemented carefully. Positive behavioral support is the process by which accommodations and modifications are made to support students, either individually or within problematic groups, with persistent behavioral difficulties. Positive behavioral support is discussed in detail in Chapter 12.

Bullying, Aggression, and Violence

While violent behavior may occur much less frequently than minor and more persistent behavior that is disruptive to classroom learning, violence and related behaviors such as aggression and bullying are among the more serious behavioral concerns that schools face. Optimal learning conditions cannot be fostered when students and staff do not feel safe. However, if we understand and attend to what leads to violent behavior and implement the types of programs that research has shown are effective in addressing violence, aggression, and bullying, we can make our schools safer and improve the school climate. Many schools have implemented a range of policies and programs regarding violence— from zero tolerance programs to schoolwide programs aimed at prevention. In this section, precursors to bullying, aggression, and violence; zero tolerance policies; and aspects of effective schoolwide and classroom programs are presented.

Recognizing the Precursors to Bullying, Aggression, and Violence

There are a number of indicators that a student may have a propensity toward violence and aggression. Awareness of these signs can assist teachers in identifying students in need of support. In an extensive review of the literature, Dwyer, Osher, and Hoffman (2000) identified early and imminent warning signs for violence and aggression. While early warning signs provide an opportunity for preventive, supportive responses, Dwyer et al. caution that the early warning signs should not be used to label or stigmatize children. The imminent warning signs require immediate referral to a school psychologist or mental health worker for intervention. Imminent signs are summarized below and early warning signs are summarized in Table 11.2.

Table 11.2   Early Warning Signs of Violence and Aggression in Children and Youth

SIGN	DESCRIPTION
Social withdrawal	Withdrawal from social relationships may stem from feelings of depression, persecution, and/or unworthiness.
Excessive feelings of isolation and being alone	In some cases, social isolation and friendlessness are risk factors.
Excessive feelings of rejection	Troubled children may be isolated from their peers. Some may seek out aggressive friends.
Being a victim of violence	Victims, including those who are victims of physical or sexual abuse, are sometimes at risk for violence themselves.

(continued)

Table 11.2 *continued*

SIGN	DESCRIPTION
Feelings of being picked on and persecuted	A child who feels bullied, teased, and ridiculed, and is without support, may vent feelings through aggression.
Low school interest and poor academic performance	Feelings of frustration, denigration, and chastisement can lead to aggressive behavior.
Expression of violence in writings and drawings	Overrepresentation of violent themes in drawings and writings may signal emotional problems.
Uncontrolled anger	Frequent and intense expressions of anger in response to minor annoyances may occur.
Impulsive and chronic hitting, intimidation, and bullying	Mildly aggressive behaviors in the early years, if not addressed, may escalate.
History of discipline problems	Chronic behavioral problems and disciplinary problems suggest a need for support. They may set the stage for future violations of norms and rules.
Past history of violent and aggressive behavior	Without support and counseling, a history of aggressive and violent behavior indicates a risk of future, more serious aggressive behavior.
Intolerance for differences and prejudicial attitudes	Intense prejudice, membership in hate groups, or willingness to victimize individuals with disabilities occurs.
Drug and alcohol use	Drug and alcohol use reduce self-control and expose youth to violence as perpetrators or victims, or both.
Affiliation with gangs	Youth who seek gang affiliation may adopt antisocial values and behaviors, and find reason for violence and aggression.
Serious threat of violence	A detailed and specific threat of violence is one of the most reliable indicators. All threats of violence should be taken seriously.

Source: Information taken from "Creating Responsive Schools: Contextualizing Early Warning, Timely Response," by K. P. Dwyer, D. Osher, and C. C. Hoffman, 2000, *Exceptional Children, 66*(3), 347–365.

- Serious physical aggression or fighting with peers or family members
- Severe destruction of property
- Acute rage with little provocation
- Detailed threats of lethal violence
- Possession and/or use of firearms
- Self-injurious behavior or talk of suicide

Bullying is one precursor or warning sign that is often ignored. Victims of bullying may be afraid to tell about incidents or may attempt to report bullying to their teachers only to be asked to "work it out" with their classmate. Bullying can have devastating effects on both the victim and the perpetrator. Victims may feel vengefulness, anger, and self-pity (Borg, 1998). Left untreated, these feelings can lead to more serious emotional distress, such as depression and even suicide (Rigby, 2003). In addition, many students who have been involved in school violence have often reported being the victim of bullying. As for the perpetrator, left unchecked, bullying behavior may lead to increased aggression and violence (Rigby, 2003).

In addition to early behavioral and emotional warning signs, it is important for teachers to understand the relationship between disruptive behavior and academic performance. Scott, Nelson, and Liaupsin (2001), in an analysis of research, contend that there is a strong relationship between academic failure and school discipline problems; students who experience academic failure often engage in disruptive behavior and vice versa.

Scott et al. reveal three especially strong relationships in this regard. First, the onset, frequency, persistence, and seriousness of disruptive behavior are linked to poor academic performance. Second, attention problems and cognitive deficits are associated with poor academic performance and delinquency. Third, providing interventions that assist students in improving academic performance is associated with a reduction in the prevalence of delinquency. Unfortunately, students with disruptive behavior or academic deficits are more likely to experience aversive interactions with teachers and less time engaged in instruction. Furthermore, students who experience academic failure are likely to avoid academic tasks, leading to further negative interactions with the teacher, thus perpetuating the cycle of poor achievement, negative behavior, and disenfranchisement from school. Because of this relationship, the constructivist teacher is mindful of academic instruction that fosters a sense of mastery and competence, and is sure to engage all students in meaningful instruction geared to success.

Zero Tolerance Policies

Many schools have responded to issues of school violence with "Zero Tolerance" approaches to school discipline. Zero tolerance policies represent "get tough" policies that require automatic suspension or expulsion for threatening behavior and/or bringing weapons to school. These policies began during the Reagan Administration's war on drugs, but gained popularity and widespread use with the 1999 Columbine shootings, although at this time, school violence was on the decline.

Unfortunately, zero tolerance polices have yielded less than favorable results. As schools implementing their zero tolerance policies have broadened their definitions of weapons and threatening acts, suspensions have increased dramatically (Fuentes, 2003).

According to Skiba (2000a, 2000b), these increases have occurred with considerable racial disparity. While African American students represent 17% of the entire school population, they account for 34% of all out-of-school suspensions and 30% of expulsions. In contrast, White students, representing 62% of the school population, account for 48% of out-of-school suspensions and 49% of expulsions.

Research indicates that suspension and expulsion, instead of improving school outcomes, may increase the likelihood of student alienation from school, dropping out, and delinquency (Skiba et al., 1997). These disciplinary practices neither improve outcomes or the behavior of the receiver, nor necessarily improve the education of the students who remain in school (Noguera, 2003). Consequently, many schools have sought more effective and comprehensive programs for creating safe schools.

Effective Programs

Being aware of the precursors to bullying, aggression, and violence is key to developing successful programs for preventing and reducing their occurrence. In addition, experts agree that effective programs are organized and systemic, and involve students, parents, the community, and the school.

Key Components

Peterson and Skiba (2000) identify the key components of successful programs:

- **Conflict resolution/social instruction.** Students need instruction in appropriate alternatives to violence for resolving conflict with their peers and teachers. While conflict resolution and social instruction may not be enough for students who have already engaged in aggressive behavior, they can help establish a climate of nonviolence. Class meetings, peer mediation, and teaching social behavior are addressed in Chapter 5.
- **Classroom strategies for disruptive behavior.** Handling minor misbehavior appropriately can keep it from escalating into a crisis. Positive behavioral support can be employed to prevent and reduce disruptive behavior.
- **Parental involvement.** Family instability, unsupportive parents, and lack of family resources are often blamed for contributing to behavioral issues in schools. Research indicates that effective disciplinary practices require strong partnerships among schools, families, and the community.
- **Early warning signs and screening.** Using early warning signs as an opportunity to provide positive behavioral support for students with social and behavioral needs can help prevent the development of more serious behavioral patterns.
- **School and district data systems.** Record keeping with regard to office referrals, disciplinary actions, suspensions, and expulsions can assist schools in evaluating disciplinary processes, as well as identifying risk factors.
- **Schoolwide disciplinary policies.** Teams should be in place that address the development, evaluation, and implementation of schoolwide disciplinary policies, rules, and procedures. Schoolwide teams can provide consistency, cohesiveness, awareness, and communication so that all students and staff understand schoolwide expectations, policies, and procedures.

- **Positive behavioral support teams.** Behavioral support teams can fulfill the functional assessment mandate of the Individuals with Disabilities Education Act (IDEA), as well as assist in planning, implementing, and evaluating positive behavioral support.
- **Crisis and security planning.** Schools should have effective plans in place and school security available to handle crises should the need arise.

Research also indicates that programs need to be tailored to the individual school. Needs assessments and violence prevention teams can gear widely used programs to fit the unique circumstances, population, and needs of a particular school.

Bullying Prevention

According to Peterson and Skiba (2002), awareness and adult involvement are key to creating a climate that discourages bullying and aggression. Research indicates that anti-bullying programs that focus solely on peer involvement (Cowie & Olafsson, 2000) or short-term indoctrination, such as exposing students to a video about bullying (Boulton & Flemington, 1996), are not effective.

Parents and professionals must become aware of the extent of bullying and commit to reducing or eliminating it. Successful bullying prevention programs include a prevention committee at the school level and a coordinator of prevention activities and curricula. An assessment of the extent of the problem is conducted by administering an anonymous student questionnaire. The committee can use this data for planning and implementation of a program designed to meet the needs of the school.

The Center for the Study and Prevention of Violence (2002) identified several successful "BluePrint" programs for violence intervention and prevention. These programs provide a blueprint for schools seeking to develop violence prevention programs. Each program had to meet strict criteria with regard to effective research-based practices in order to qualify. One example, the Bullying Prevention Program (Center for the Study and Prevention of Violence, 2002) is a schoolwide program designed to reduce and prevent bullying. The program is implemented at the school, class, and individual level. This program targets all students, but provides additional interventions for perpetrators and victims. Schoolwide components include the following:

- Administration of an anonymous questionnaire to assess the nature and prevalence of bullying at the school
- A conference day to discuss bullying at the school and to plan interventions
- Formation of a bullying prevention committee
- Increased supervision in areas of the school that are conducive to bullying

Classroom components include classroom rules against bullying and regular classroom meetings. (Classroom rules and classroom meetings are discussed in Chapter 5.) Individual components include interventions with the children identified as perpetrators and victims, discussions with the parents of the involved students, and the involvement of counselors and school-based mental health professionals.

R. A. Heydenberk, W. R. Heydenberk, and Tzenova (2006) describe a bullying prevention program that was successful in decreasing bullying and increasing a sense of safety in one elementary school. This program involved awareness activities and the sustained engagement of the students in developing prosocial behaviors and conflict resolution skills. This program is summarized in Figure 11.1.

Whether it be minor distractions and disruptions or more serious and persistent issues, the constructivist teacher seeks to assist students in ways that promote dignity, learning, responsibility, and empathy. When disruptions and distractions to learning are dealt with in ways that preserve the dignity of the student, the student can learn from his or her mistakes and still maintain a sense of belonging. However, punishment and humiliation can alienate students and deteriorate the student–teacher relationship. When students are engaged in finding solutions to classroom predicaments, learning self-regulation, and learning from their mistakes, their self-efficacy and sense of autonomy are enhanced. On the other hand, practices that rely on teacher control and power send students the message that they are not capable of regulating themselves or making wise decisions. Students can also learn empathy so that they can understand and appreciate each others' uniqueness and circumstances, and contribute to a peaceful environment. Ignoring these differences can contribute to bullying, aggression, and violence. Mindful practices and/or the Circle of Courage can assist teachers in dealing with discipline problems and promote a safe school climate. Examples of practices for dealing with discipline, disruption, and violence that align with the Circle of Courage are provided in Figure 11.2.

SUMMARY

The predicaments that teachers encounter with regard to discipline are varied and complex. As illustrated in the quote by Haim Ginnot at the beginning of the chapter, the way that disciplinary issues are handled can humiliate or heal, can make the difference between a child learning or tuning out, or a situation being escalated or de-escalated. A constructivist teacher avoids approaches that alienate the student and/or detract from the primary mission of the classroom: learning. She allows learners the opportunity to learn from their mistakes, solve problems, and make things right.

The more serious issues of bullying, aggression, and violence contribute to an uninviting school climate where students and teachers do not feel safe to conduct the business of learning. Simply "getting tough" with students does little to improve circumstances for the school, the community, or the perpetrators. Research has provided strategies for reducing and preventing violence and aggression. These issues must be tended to systematically, and various levels of support for the students and the school must be provided.

Figure 11.1   A Successful Bullying and Conflict Resolution Program

Program Components

Check-in

- At the beginning of the day, students are allowed to share stories of important events in their lives.
- Students are taught to use I-messages (see Chapter 8) during Check-in, as well as affective vocabulary (feeling words).

Check-in allowed students to develop an understanding, appreciation, and empathy regarding the lives of their classmates.

Peaceful Being

Students created life-size silhouettes that were called Peaceful Beings. After brainstorming negative social behaviors (e.g., insults, name-calling, pushing, and shoving), students thought of peaceful alternatives that they wrote on their silhouettes. The alternatives included phrases such as "Give a compliment," and "Say something kind." The silhouettes were hung around the classroom to serve as reminders of peaceful and appropriate ways to interact with peers and others. Peaceful Beings were also reviewed regularly with peers and teachers as reminders of prosocial behaviors.

The Emotional Cup

Classroom activities, such as the Emotional Cup, were incorporated throughout the year. The Emotional Cup activity engaged students in creating an origami cup. Students put the feeling words generated by the Check-in activity in the cup. Students were led in a discussion of how just as cups can overflow, feelings can be overwhelming.

The STAR Activity

The STAR activity provided students with a metacognitive, self-regulation strategy to use in times of anger, frustration, or other overwhelming emotions. The STAR activity provided students with a helpful mnemonic for engaging the steps of Stop, Think, Act, and Review.

Community- and Team-Building Activities

Community- and team-building activities engaged students in complimenting each other, empathy building, and discussion of conflict resolution. For example, students tossed a ball of yarn around; as the yarn unraveled and a web between students was built, the student who tossed the ball gave a compliment to the one who caught it. This activity is called the Web of Life activity.

Results: Students in the treatment group scored significantly higher than their peers in the nontreatment groups on the "student attitudes about conflict" test. Teachers and students reported a decrease in bullying and an increase in the use of prosocial behaviors and conflict resolution. Teachers reported spending less time on conflict, while students reported feeling safer in school.

Source: Information taken from Heydenberk, Heydenberk, and Tzenova (2006)

Figure 11.2   Handling Discipline in Ways that Promote the Circle of Courage

	BELONGING	GENEROSITY	COMPETENCE	INDEPENDENCE
Disruption	Preserve the dignity of the student by giving quiet and private reprimands. Avoid zero tolerance policies that do not allow for cultural and individual considerations.	Allow opportunities for restitution.	Assist children in learning the natural consequences of behavior. Teach children that mistakes are opportunities to learn. Avoid approaches that disrupt instruction or cause learners to miss learning activities.	Engage learners in finding solutions to classroom disciplinary problems.
Violence and Bullying Prevention	Engage students in community-building activities such as Check-in. Provide opportunities for students to acknowledge their peers with compliments through class meetings, the Web of Life activity, and so forth.	Engage students in empathy-building activities.	Teach prosocial behaviors and successful ways of communicating, such as I-statements, Peaceful Beings, and so forth.	Teach self-regulation skills such as STAR.

REFERENCES

Abramowitz, A. J., & O'Leary, S. G. (1990). The effectiveness of delayed punishment in applied settings. *Behavior Therapy, 21*(2), 231–239.

Abramowitz, A. J., O'Leary, S. G., & Futtersak, M. W. (1988). The relative impact of long and short reprimands on children's off-task behavior in the classroom. *Behavioral Therapy, 19*(2), 243–247.

Borg, M. G. (1998). The emotional reactions of school bullies and their victims. *Educational Psychology, 18*(4), 433–444.

Boulton, M. J., & Flemington, I. (1996). The effects of a short video intervention on secondary school pupils' involvement in definitions of and attitudes towards bullying. *School Psychology International, 17*(4), 331–345.

Brantlinger, E. (1991). Social class distinctions in adolescents' reports of problems and punishment in school. *Behavior Disorders, 17*(1), 36–46.

Center for the Study and Prevention of Violence. (2002). Blueprints for violence prevention. In *Book Nine: Bullying Prevention Program*. Boulder, CO: University of Colorado Press.

Cowie, H., & Olafsson, R. (2000). The role of peer support in helping the victims of bullying in a school with high levels of aggression. *School Psychology International, 21*(1), 79–95.

DuPaul, G. J., & Weyandt, L. L. (2006). School-based interventions for children and adolescents with attention-deficit/hyperactivity disorder: Enhancing academic and behavioral outcomes. *Education and Treatment of Children, 29*, 341–358.

Dwyer, K. P., Osher, D., & Hoffman, C. C. (2000). Creating responsive schools: Contextualizing early warning, timely response. *Exceptional Children, 66*(3), 347–365.

Forness, R., & Kavale, K. (2001). Reflections of the future of prevention. *Preventing School Failure, 45*(2), 75–82.

Fuentes, A. (2003). Discipline and punish. *Nation, 277*(20), 17–21.

Good, T., & Brophy, J. (2000). *Looking in classrooms* (8th ed.). New York: Longman.

Gossen, D. (2007) Student Behavior. *International Journal of Reality Therapy, 27*(1), 17–20.

Heydenberk, R. A., Heydenberk, W. R., & Tzenova, V. (2006). Conflict resolution and bully prevention: Skills for school success. *Conflict Resolution Quarterly, 24*(1), 55–69.

Jolivette, K., Stichter-Peek, J., & McCormick, K. M. (2002). Making choices—improving behavior—engaging in learning. *Teaching Exceptional Children, 34*(3), 24–30.

Josephson Institute of Ethics. (2001). *2000 Report card: Report #1: The ethics of American youth: Violence and substance abuse, data & commentary*. Author. http://www.josephsoninstitute.org/survey2000/violence2000-commentary.htm

Kennedy, C. H., Long, T., Jolivette, K., Cox, J., Jung-Chang, T., & Thompson, T. (2001). Facilitating general education participation for students with behavior problems by linking positive behavior supports and person-centered planning. *Journal of Emotional and Behavioral Disorders, 9*(3), 161–172.

Kimberling, S., & Wantland, C. B. (2002). *Guides to creating safer schools, guide 3: Implementing ongoing staff development to enhance safe schools*. Portland, OR: Northwest Regional Educational Laboratory.

Kounin, J. S. Discipline and Group Management in Classrooms. Holt, Reinhardt and Winston, NY, NY. 1970.

Lake, V. (2004). Ante up: Reconsidering classroom management philosophies so every child is a winner. *Early Child Development and Care, 174*(6), 565–574.

Langdon, C. A. (1997). The fourth Phi Delta Kappan pool of teachers' attitudes toward public schools. *Phi Delta Kappan, 79*(3), 212–221.

Lasley, T. (2001). Fostering non-aggression in the classroom: An anthropological perspective. *Theory Into Practice, 24*(4), 247–255.

Loeber, R., Green, S. M., Lahey, B. B., Frick, P. J., & McBurnett, K. (2000). Findings on disruptive behavior disorders from the first decade of the developmental trends study. *Clinical Child and Family Psychology Review, 3*(1), 37–59.

Maag, J. (2001). Rewarded by punishment: Reflections on the disuse of positive reinforcement in the schools. *Exceptional Children, 67*(2), 173–186.

Mayer, G. R. (1999). Constructive discipline for school personnel. *Education and Treatment of Children, 22*(1), 36–39.

Nansel, T. R., Overpeck, M., Pilla, R. S., Ruan, W. J., Simons-Morton, B., & Scheidt, P. (2001). Bullying behaviors among U.S. youth—Prevalence and association with psychosocial adjustment. *Journal of the American Medical Association, 285*(16), 2094–2100.

National Center for Education Statistics. (2007). *Indicators of school crime and safety.* Washington, DC: Author.

Nelson, J., Lott, L., & Glenn, S. (2000). *Positive discipline in the classroom: Developing mutual respect, cooperation, and responsibility in your classroom* (Rev. 3rd ed.). New York: Random House.

Noguera, P. A. (2003). Schools, prisons, and the social implications of punishment: Rethinking disciplinary practices. *Theory Into Practice, 42*(4), 341–351.

Peterson, R. and Skiba, R. (2001). Creating School Climates That Prevent School Violence: *Social Studies,* 92(4) 167–176.

Pfiffner, L. J., O'Leary, S. G., Rosen, L. A., & Sanderson, W. C. (1985). A comparison of the effects of continuous and intermittent response-costs and reprimands in the classroom. *Journal of Clinical Child Psychology, 14*(4), 348–353.

Rigby, K. (2003). Consequences of bullying in schools. *Canadian Journal of Psychiatry, 48*(9), 583–590.

Ruck, M., Wortley, S. (2002). Racial and ethnic minority high school students' perceptions of school disciplinary practices: A look at some Canadian findings. *Journal of Youth and Adolescence, 31*(3), 185–195.

Scott, T. M., Nelson, C. M., & Liaupsin, C. J. (2001). Effective instruction: The forgotten component in preventing school violence. *Education and Treatment of Children, 24*(3), 309–322.

Sheets, R. H., & Gay, G. (1996). Student perceptions of disciplinary conflict in ethnically diverse classrooms. *NASSP Bulletin, 80*(580), 84–94.

Shores, R. E., Gunter, P. L., & Jack, S. L. (1993). Classroom management strategies: Are they setting events for coercion? *Behavioral Disorders, 18*(2), 92–102.

Skiba, R. J. (2000a). *Zero tolerance, zero evidence: An analysis of school disciplinary practice.* Bloomington: Indiana University Education Policy Center.

Skiba, R. J. (2000b). When is disproportionality discrimination? The overrepresentation of Black students in school suspension. In W. Ayers, B. Dohrn, & R. Ayers (Eds.), *Zero tolerance: Resisting the drive for punishment in our schools* (p. 23). New York: The New Press.

Skiba, R. J., Peterson, R. L., & Williams, T. (1997). Office referrals and suspension: Disciplinary intervention in middle schools. *Education and Treatment of Children, 20*(3), 295–316.

Stouthammer-Loeber, M., & Loeber, R. (2002). Lost opportunities for intervention: Undetected markers for the development of serious juvenile delinquency. *Criminal Behavior and Mental Health, 12*(1), 69–82.

Tierno, M. J. (1991). Responding to the socially motivated behaviors of early adolescents: Recommendations for classroom management. *Adolescence, 26*(103), 569–578.

POSITIVE BEHAVIORAL SUPPORT

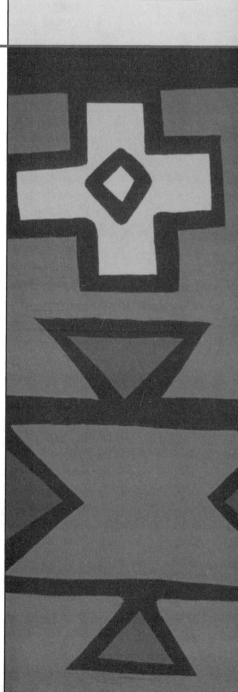

All of us, at some time or another, need help. Whether we're giving or receiving help, each one of us has something valuable to bring to this world. That's one of the things that connects us as neighbors—In our own way, each one of us is a giver and a receiver.
Mister Rogers (Rogers, F., 2003, p.136),

Some learners, for whatever reason, have difficulty living up to classroom expectations. At the level of the individual, positive behavioral support offers teachers a systematic way of identifying needs and developing help and support for individuals who experience difficulty. In classrooms with a strong sense of community, learners understand that everyone needs help and support at times and are willing partners in the positive behavioral support process.

While the roots of positive behavioral support lie in behaviorist philosophy, positive behavioral support transcends traditional behavior management, where the focus is on changing the behavior of the student through the use of rewards and consequences. For example, positive behavioral support requires teachers to examine perceived problems, such as noncompliance on the part of the child, from many perspectives, including looking at what the child is being asked to comply with. Positive behavioral support recognizes that the context of the behavior is as important a consideration as the behavior itself in developing a plan to intervene. Furthermore, the focus of a plan may be a change in the environment instead of direct attempts at modifying the behavior of the child or group of children.

Constructivist principles can easily be applied to positive behavioral support as well, and they extend the focus of the support to the needs and contributions of the community. While traditional behavior management considers quick fixes, positive behavioral support and constructivist ideas look to long-term solutions

Figure 12.1 Comparison of Traditional Positive Behavioral Support and Constructivist
Perspectives

TRADITIONAL BEHAVIOR MANAGEMENT*	POSITIVE BEHAVIORAL SUPPORT*	CONSTRUCTIVIST PERSPECTIVE
Deficit model, the individual is "the problem"	Systems, settings, or skill deficiencies of the individual may be "the problem"	Views problems as opportunities for everyone to grow & recognizes that everyone needs help at different times
Attempts to "fix' the individual	Attempts to "fix" systems, settings, or teach skills to the individual	Finds solutions that build community and relationships Utilizes students strengths
Extinguishes or changes behavior	Creates new contacts, experiences, relationships, and skills	Focuses on developing supportive relationships and building belonging, independence, mastery, and generosity as opposed to "fixing" a child
Uses aversives	Favors positive approaches	Sanctions getting help from others in the community
Takes days or weeks to "fix" a single behavior	Takes years to create responsive systems, personalized settings, and appropriate/empowering skills	Takes continuous care, support and time to develop community and an appreciation of diversity
Implemented by a behavioral specialist often outside the general classroom	Implemented by a collaborative team using a student-centered, approach in an inclusive classroom	Implemented by the classroom community where everyone has a voice & solutions are the focus
Often relied upon when systems are inflexible	Flourishes when systems are flexible	Flourishes when the focus remains on building community

*First two columns adapted from Lombardo (1997)

for supporting individuals within the community. See Figure 12.1 for a comparison of traditional behavior management, positive behavioral support, and the extension of positive behavioral support to include constructivist principles. Consider the following example of a positive behavioral support plan based on constructivist principles from a community perspective:

Brian was having difficulty completing "morning work" in his first-grade classroom. The classroom teacher's first strategy was to implement a reward system where students earned tickets for completing work and for appropriate classroom behavior. While overall improvement was seen in his classroom behavior, Brian was still having difficulty completing morning work. The teacher suggested to Brian's parents that he see a child psychologist for diagnosis of a possible disorder. Upon consultation with another teacher and consideration of the circumstances, Brian's teacher tried the following modifications. First, the teacher examined the worksheets that she was assigning and tried to ensure that all of the assignments were meaningful. For example, worksheets that required copying letters were replaced by journals for creative writing. Second, the teacher was asked to engage the student in self-monitoring. Brian was given a checklist for monitoring his work. On the checklist, he had to indicate whether he did his best work, completed all of his work, and checked his work for accuracy. After these strategies were implemented, there was a marked improvement in Brian's work completion.

George was also having difficulty completing independent work. Instead of working and staying on task, George had frequent chats with other students, made noises that were distracting to the class, and left his work area quite often. After completing a functional assessment, the teacher learned that the work being assigned to George was difficult and overwhelming. She assigned George a peer buddy who he read to and who listened to him read. After reading a story, George and his buddy were allowed to choose from one of three activities: illustrate their favorite part, act out a skit for their classmates, or use the classroom computer to write a summary.

In an inclusive ninth-grade language arts classroom, Carlos, a student identified as behaviorally and emotionally disordered, was participating in literature circles. After a couple of weeks, it was noted that not only was Carlos coming to class unprepared for the literature circles, but he also was causing a disturbance during the literature circles by making inappropriate comments, being inattentive, and failing to fulfill his assigned literature circle role. After examining all of the factors, the general and special education teachers found a way to adjust Carlos's schedule to allow him time during school to prepare for the literature circles. Coming prepared was all that was needed to improve Carlos's behavior.

One teacher in a first-grade classroom maintained an expectation that students would work quietly during learning center activities. A child with a disability who was included in this classroom made many involuntary noises during learning center time that were quite bothersome to the teacher and appeared to make this student stand out in the classroom. A suggestion was made that the acceptable noise level for the classroom be raised. By doing so, the sounds of this student were not heard above the quiet rumble of the other children engaged in learning center activities and were no longer viewed as a problem.

In these examples, supports included not only teaching students new skills, but also providing help, changing expectations, changing schedules and so forth. These types of support shift the focus from fixing a child to ensuring all students are accomodated by the classroom community.

FUNDAMENTAL ASPECTS OF POSITIVE BEHAVIORAL SUPPORT

There are four fundamentals to be considered in the development of positive behavioral support plans. First, positive support is geared toward preventing the behavior from happening, as opposed to aversives or punishments for the behavior when it occurs. The term "positive behavioral support" connotes that the support plan will use positive approaches to support students.

Second, positive support centers around helping students learn. The primary mission of the support plan is to facilitate learning. Plans that include removing a student or group of students from the learning environment, lowering academic standards, or ignoring academic goals can be counterproductive. For example, if a student is excused from a reading group due to his or her behavior, other plans must be made to ensure that the student is engaged in meaningful reading instruction and not just sent to an isolated area to complete reading worksheets. Supports such as making modifications within the reading group, using peer tutoring, or using a parent volunteer may provide support for the students' behavioral issues, as well as maintaining a learning orientation.

Third, positive support plans include input from the student, as well as peers and parents as appropriate. The community that is charged with supporting the student or group of students will often have the best ideas for support. For example, in a third-grade class, the teacher was worried about including a student with Down syndrome because he was known to flee the room occasionally. When the other third graders were asked for solutions, they came up with several effective plans, including "Let David know that he is our friend," "Go and get him and bring him back," and "Play with him more so that he will want to stay with us."

Fourth, positive behavioral support is a collaborative process. When students receive special education services, are referred for services, or are in need of interventions prior to referral for special education services, positive behavioral support teams can meet to collaborate on the development of support plans. The classroom teacher is a very important member of this team and is crucial to the success of positive behavioral support implementation and evaluation. The Individuals with Disabilities Education Act (IDEA) states, "The classroom teacher must, to the extent appropriate, participate in the development, review, and revision of the child's Individualized Educational Plan (IEP), including assisting in the determination of (1) appropriate positive behavioral interventions and strategies for the child; and (2) supplementary aids and services, program modifications, or supports for school personnel that will be provided for the child, consistent with 300.347(a)(3)." (Individuals with Disabilities Education Improvement Act of 2004, 20 U.S.C. § 1400 et seq. (2004)).

While a classroom teacher can independently implement support for individuals or groups within his classroom, he can also call on a positive behavioral support team and engage in a formal process for dealing with the persistent behavioral issues of individuals or groups of students.

INDIVIDUAL POSITIVE BEHAVIORAL SUPPORT

For individuals with persistent behavioral issues, having the support of teachers, peers, and the school community can make a world of difference. The behavioral support process requires a number of steps—from functional assessment to implementation and evaluation of supportive strategies. Supports can include a variety of strategies—from making modifications in the curriculum to the use of peer buddies. The level of support and the necessary accommodations and modifications depend on the student and the nature of his or her behavior.

Functional Assessment

The first step in developing a positive behavioral support plan is to conduct a functional assessment. The functional assessment is a very practical assessment that identifies relationships between behaviors and the circumstances that may trigger behaviors and inhibit a student's ability to learn. Functional assessment is required by IDEA as a necessary step for addressing the problematic behaviors of students with disabilities. According to IDEA,

> The team should explore the need for strategies and support systems to address any behavior that may impede the learning of the child with the disability or the learning of his or her peers. In response to disciplinary actions by school personnel, the IEP team should, within 10 days, meet to formulate a functional behavioral assessment plan to collect data for developing a behavior intervention plan. If a behavior intervention plan already exists, the team must review and revise it (as necessary) to ensure that it addresses the behavior upon which disciplinary action is predicated.

While functional assessment is required for students with disabilities, it is a useful tool for school teams dealing with problematic behaviors before children are referred for special education, as well as teachers facing behaviors that are disruptive to the learning environment.

The idea of a functional assessment is to collect as much information as possible from as many sources as possible. The following example may help to illustrate why a functional assessment may be important:

> David, a 16-year-old who has a learning disability in math, feels embarrassed to be seen with an assignment different from his peers, hides his assignment in his desk, and uses inappropriate language to inform the teacher that he is not completing his work today.
>
> Rico, an 8-year-old who is a voracious reader, finds his reading assignments boring and, therefore, shoves his book and workbook onto the floor when the teacher comments on his lack of progress.
>
> Alex, a 10-year-old who finds multiplication of fractions difficult, becomes frustrated and crumples his paper when asked to complete worksheets requiring him to multiply fractions.
>
> Bailey, an 8-year-old with an attention deficit disorder finds an assigned word search overwhelming and decides to see what kind of paper airplane it would make.

While in each scenario the problem is similar (failure to complete an assignment), the cause and function of the behaviors are very different and call for different strategies for supporting the student. Functional assessment requires several steps:

Describe the Challenging Behavior(s)
The behavior should be described in terms that are observable and easily visualized and understood by others involved with the student. For example, avoid descriptions like "Haley has a poor attitude about school." Instead, use descriptions like "Haley uses inappropriate language to complain about assignments."

Identify the Circumstances Under Which the
Behavior Is Both Likely and Unlikely to Occur
For example, is there a time of day, a particular setting, or a particular assignment that is more likely to coincide with the behavior? Identifying a pattern to the behavior will assist the teacher in determining the purpose of the behavior. However, please note that many challenging behaviors do not follow predictable patterns. They can be triggered by unknown or unobservable variables, such as allergy flare-ups, disturbed sleep, missed medication, and so forth—hence the need to collect as much information from as many sources as possible.

Collect Information
Traditional functional assessment requires direct observation of the behavior. In addition to observations, the constructivist teacher looks for other sources of information in identifying the goal of the behavior, as well as determining possible supports. From a constructivist perspective, behavior is based on the child's perception of what is true, which may be very different from the perceptions of the adults in his or her life. The following tactics are useful in determining the purpose of a behavior, as well as the perspectives of others:

- **ABC analysis.** Observe the behavior and note (A) antecedents (what happens immediately before the behavior), (B) the behavior, and (C) consequences (what happens immediately after the behavior).
- **Interviews.** Interview the student, parents, peers, and other teachers. Open-ended interviews to gain many perspectives on the challenging behavior, including that of the student, are useful in determining the purpose of a behavior, others' perceptions of the problem, and possible supports.
- **Examination of the context.** Look for other factors, settings, events, and circumstances that may contribute to the behavior. The checklist in Figure 12.2 may be helpful in identifying contextual factors.

Perform a Culturally Sensitive Functional Assessment
Cultural perspectives on behavioral issues are often neglected in functional assessments and the resulting plans for positive behavioral support. Salend and Taylor (2002) suggest that gaining the perspectives of those who are familiar with the student's cultural and linguistic experiences and avoiding professional jargon or negative descriptions of the behavior are helpful in making the support process culturally sensitive.

Gaining multiple perspectives allows the teacher to learn about the student's cultural perspectives and experiences. This information can assist the teacher or team in determining whether the behavior of concern is culturally based. These perspectives can be obtained through interviews with or surveys of the student, other teachers, family, and community members. Salend and Taylor relay an example of a student, Matthew, who often spent time examining the assignment, gathering and checking materials,

Figure 12.2   Contextural factors checklist

CONTEXTUAL FACTORS

THAT MAY CONTRIBUTE TO BEHAVIORAL PROBLEMS

CHILD FACTORS

_____Sickness: Has the student had a recent illness?

_____Allergies: Does the student have allergies that cause discomfort?

_____Medication: Is the child on medication that may have side effects?

_____Fatigue: Has the student had disruptions in sleep or suffered from other factors that may cause fatigue?

_____Hunger/thirst/diet

_____Arousal: Has anything out of the ordinary occurred, such as a fight, to bring emotions to a high level?

CLASSROOM ENVIRONMENT

_____Too high a noise level

_____Uncomfortable temperature

_____Activities presented too easy or too difficult for student

_____Poor seating arrangement

_____Frequent disruptions or distractions in the classroom

_____Traffic patterns that may cause distraction

_____Allergens such as mold or mildew present in the room

CURRICULUM

_____Too few opportunities to make choices

_____Schedule is unpredictable

_____Inadequate assistance available in the classroom

_____Directions for activities are unclear or inaccessible

_____Too few opportunities to talk with classmates

_____Too few opportunities to communicate with teacher

_____Activity too difficult/easy

_____Activity too long

_____Activity disliked by student

_____Activity perceived as irrelevant or useless

_____No assistance or support for activity

preparing the work area, asking the teacher to restate the directions, and talking to his peers. His teachers perceived these behaviors as signs of a lack of attention, interest, preparedness, and motivation. However, further interpretation revealed that Matthew's behavior may have been a culturally based way of getting ready to work on an assignment.

Issues with problematic behavior should be relayed to the family and student in culturally sensitive language. Professional terms should be defined in a language that family members and all educators involved can understand. Some families may perceive definitions of behavior that are presented in negative terms as accusatory. Therefore, culturally sensitive teachers will define the behavior in positive terms. For example, the team involved in Mathew's functional assessment grouped behaviors into the category of "off-task" behavior and avoided the negative connotations of some of the teacher's descriptions (Salend & Taylor, 2002).

Determine the Potential Purpose of the Behavior

Challenging behaviors often help an individual satisfy a need or obtain a goal. In developing a positive behavioral support plan, it is useful to determine the purpose of the behavior. Both behaviorist and constructivist theories lend insight into the potential purposes of behavior.

From a behaviorist perspective, the primary intent of misbehavior is either to avoid an aversive or to gain something, such as a tangible item, attention, or sensory stimulation (DuPaul & Ervin, 1996; Maag & Kemp, 2003). For example, DuPaul and Ervin suggest that the most likely function of inappropriate behavior for students with attention deficit hyperactivity disorder (ADHD) is to avoid an overwhelming task such as independent seat work. A second function is to obtain the attention of peers or teachers in the room. Often, tactics that a teacher perceives as helping a student to see the error in his or her ways, such as a trip to the principal's office, a long lecture from the teacher, or loss of recess, may actually help the student achieve his or her goal of avoiding work or gaining attention. A third function may be for the student to gain access to an activity that appears more satisfying than the activity that the student is expected to complete. For example, the student may be much more interested in playing with math manipulatives than the worksheet at her desk. Finally, children who see the work in the classroom as boring, irrelevant, or merely tedious may misbehave with the goal of gaining stimulation by daydreaming, staring out the window, or doodling on the desk.

Behavioral theorists also recognize that human behavior doesn't always lend itself to such simple classification as avoidance or acquisition with regard to the goals of behavior. Maag and Kemp (2003) postulate that the intent of misbehavior may include the goals of power or affiliation. Students may misbehave in order to obtain personal power by arguing with the teacher about when to start an assignment, ignoring a teacher's directions, influencing peers to skip a class, and so forth. The intent of the behavior is to control, instead of being controlled by others. With regard to affiliation, the function of the behavior may be to identify with a clique or with other individuals in the school with similar backgrounds. Behavior that is unacceptable in the classroom, such as aggressiveness, may be intended to assist the student with being accepted by a particular group.

From a constructivist perspective, the goals of power and affiliation are similar to the goals of misbehavior postulated by Dreikurs. According to Dreikurs(1968), behavior is aimed at social goals instead of the goals of possession or avoidance. Children are social beings with a need to belong and be significant, and the function of misbehavior in the classroom is to satisfy those needs. Dreikurs also maintained that the clues to the goal of a behavior often lie in the way that it makes the teacher feel. There are four mistaken goals of behavior:

- Attention—The student feels that he belongs only when he has the attention of his teacher and/or peers.
- Power—The student feels that he belongs when he is in control and/or has gotten his way.
- Revenge—The student's negative feelings regarding alienation result in a desire to get back at someone or get even.
- Assumed inadequacy—The student feels that it is impossible to belong and gives up.

According to the Circle of Courage, misbehavior may be aimed not only at belonging, but also at a need for autonomy, a sense of competence, and or/generosity. For example, a student who feels incompetent in reading may gain a sense of satisfaction in being good at disturbing the class. A child who has no voice in the classroom may be seeking a sense of autonomy. A student with no purpose in the classroom may be seeking a way to be significant. Searching for the purpose of the behavior will assist the teacher in developing appropriate supports. Table 12.1 synthesizes various perspectives of behavior with regard to the goals, intent, and function of misbehavior in the classroom, as well as possible sources of support.

Evaluation of Information

Use all of the information collected to develop a hypothesis or "best guess" statement. Developing a hypothesis can lead the teacher or positive behavioral support team to appropriate strategies for supporting the student. The following are examples:

> Bill runs from the classroom to escape math work that is too difficult for him.
>> Derek disrupts lessons with inappropriate comments to gain the attention of his peers. John is sluggish in completing his assignments in the morning because he does not eat breakfast.

Possible Strategies and Sources of Support

Professional research and literature provide valuable sources of tested strategies for addressing numerous behavioral issues. These strategies often involve changing the classroom setting, changing academic demands, changing instructional variables, increasing predictability, and soliciting peer support.

Change the Setting
Often, changing a setting that triggers difficult behavior may be warranted. For example, a student may benefit from moving her desk closer to the teacher's desk. A teacher may say, "I'm afraid that sitting near Sally isn't helping you learn. Perhaps moving closer to my desk would better help you learn." In another example, a stand-up desk can

Table 12.1   Behavioral Perspectives and Sources of Support

THE STUDENT'S GOAL	THE STUDENT MAY BE TRYING TO COMMUNICATE	POSSIBLE BEHAVIORS	THE ADULT MAY FEEL	OTHER CLUES	POSSIBLE SUPPORT
Avoid feeling incompetent	The work is to difficult or too overwhelming for me. If I try it, I will probably be a failure	Destroys work. Disruptive behavior which results in removal from the lesson. Does not complete work or loses assignments. Displays disregard for work,	Frustration, despair	Misbehavior typically occurs when the student is engaged in work with which he is generally unsuccessful or significantly behind his peers.	Assure that assignments are at an appropriate level for the student. Peer tutoring
Gain competence	I may not be good at school work, but I am good at...making others laugh, bossing other students, etc.	Class clown, class bully, graffiti artist	"If he would just put the same energy into his school work"	Behavior is not a problem in classes where the student is successful. The student is good at the behavior of concern.	Engage student in projects that utilize her talents.
Assumed inadequacy	I've given up, I won't ever be successful.	Withdrawing from class or lesson, refusing to complete work, resisting teacher assistance, student does not complete homework	Despair, pity	Student makes comments about lack of ability "I'm just stupid"	Assign work or projects in small doses in which the student can experience immediate success.
Gain stimulation	I'm bored, this work is too easy, this work is easy for me or too tedious. This work means nothing to me.	Seeks to engage in activity other than assigned work, reads a book when other work is assigned, focuses attention in area of the room rather than assigned lesson	Frustration, impatience	Misbehavior typically occurs when assignments are tedious, or unchallenging, or uninteresting	Allow student opportunity for movement in the classroom, use hands-on activities that tap into student's interests.

(Continued)

Table 12.1   (*Continued*)

THE STUDENT'S GOAL	THE STUDENT MAY BE TRYING TO COMMUNICATE	POSSIBLE BEHAVIORS	THE ADULT MAY FEEL	OTHER CLUES	POSSIBLE SUPPORT
Gain autonomy	I would like to have a say in what happens to me.	Engages in power struggles with the teachers, refusal to follow commands of teacher, noncompliant	Provoked threatened challenged, powerless	Overly rigid classroom rules, no choices in the curriculum, no responsibility, mismatch of student needs and curriculum	Provide opportunities for choices within the classroom. Engage student in developing of classroom rules, and finding solutions.
Revenge	I feel hurt so I want to hurt you back.	Defacing property, cheating, foul language aimed at the teacher	Angry, hurt	Student has experienced punishment or embarrassment in front of peers.	Hold private conference with student, jointly identify solutions. Gain child's perception of classroom issues.
Gain immediate attention/ from peers and or adults	I need your attention in order to feel significant or important.	Distractions that arouse a response from classmates and or the teacher	Irritated, annoyed	Child works well in one-to-one situations.	Give student attention when behaving appropriately, schedule time for child to have individual attention.
Gain connection/ Sense of belonging	I don't really belong here or fit in here. No one cares about me anyway. I have nothing to contribute.	Talking out, lack of motivation, poor attitude toward academic work and school	Disengagement, feeling of hopelessness for the student.	Student is an outcast.	Engage student in community building activities, use peer buddies, give student opportunity to serve the community.

be an appropriate accommodation for children with ADHD who find staying seated to be a challenge (Reid, 1999). This type of desk is raised to about chest height, allowing for physical movement during independent work.

Ruef (1998) suggests that room arrangements and traffic patterns be considered in a support plan. Adequate space between learning centers and classroom activities ensures that activity and noise levels in one center are not disruptive to students in a neighboring center. Too much space can leave room for too much movement, while too little space can invite distractions from students bumping into each other and knocking over materials. While many children may be adaptable to these conditions, attending to these details may support others in maintaining appropriate classroom behavior.

Change the Academic Demands Placed on the Student

When academic instruction and academic tasks match the student's individual needs, students are more likely to remain engaged with the process of learning and complete academic tasks, and are less likely to engage in problem behaviors (Pacchiano, 2000). A functional assessment may lead the teacher in the direction of changing the academic demands placed on a student or changing the method of instruction.

The academic tasks assigned to students after instruction can follow four criteria. Tasks can be (a) appropriately challenging, (b) given in doses appropriate to the student's attention span, (c) interesting and meaningful to students, and (d) appropriately monitored. Gunter and Coutinho (1997) describe how student frustration regarding work that is too difficult, too easy, boring, or overwhelming can contribute to coercive interactions between teachers and students. Inappropriate assignments might cause both students and teachers to engage in negative interactions. If students receive assignments that they find too challenging or too easy, they may be disruptive in order to avoid the work. If the teacher's reaction is to remove the assignment, it is possible that the disruptive behavior will be reinforced by the avoidance of work. On the other hand, if students stop being disruptive when they are allowed to stop the work, the teacher may be more inclined to terminate or limit instruction next time.

Assignments that are appropriately challenging include tasks that are on a level that the student can experience success, yet be challenged. For pencil-and-paper tasks that require accuracy, such as math problems, an appropriate match between a student and an assignment is one that the student can complete with a low level of error (less than 15% when help is readily available and less than 10% when working independently) (McKee & Witt, 1990; Shores, Gunter, & Jack, 1993). For open-ended assignments or cooperative group assignments such as creative writing or group projects, student expectations and grading rubrics should be clearly communicated and a student should expect that, with effort, he or she should be able to complete the assigned task at an acceptable level.

The student's attention span is considered in determining the length of a task. For some students, especially those with ADHD, assignments can be given in small increments, allowing the student to take a break or have an opportunity to move around between steps or parts of an assignment. For yet other students, a functional assessment may indicate the need to give increased time for certain types of tasks, such as handwritten tasks or reading assignments.

Whether too hard or too easy, worksheets can be tedious for many students. Students often are much more eager to complete assignments that include manipulatives, hands-on activities, and so forth. A support plan might include opportunities for a student to work in learning centers, use manipulatives, or play computer or other games that provide the opportunity to practice the same skills that might typically be used in completing a worksheet. For example, Kern, Childs, Dunlap, Clarke, and Falk (1994) report a functional behavioral assessment with a 13-year-old boy with behavioral disorders that resulted in changing task demands. The student had exhibited high rates of off-task behavior when assigned tasks that required extensive handwriting. When the student was permitted to complete lengthy written assignments using a computer, tape recorder, or language master, productivity and attention to task increased.

Zentall, Moon, Hall, and Grskovic (2001) indicate that because children with ADHD have greater difficulty starting tasks and organizing their work, teachers might be tempted to give them assignments that are rote work or more repetitive in nature and that would provide few opportunities for expressing creativity or for developing self-direction or organization. However, their research indicated that teaching ADHD students to simplify, break down, or categorize assignments, projects, materials, and ideas, and then providing checkpoints along the way can be more effective in keeping students engaged.

In addition to varying the types of tasks, giving students choices about their assignments and relating assignments to student interests, as well as to their lives, can generate more student enthusiasm for the task and reduce problematic behavior (Gunter, Denny, & Venn, 2000). Students who communicate a need for greater autonomy may benefit from being offered more choices. Several studies have indicated that offering choices can positively influence behavior (Cosden, Gannon, & Haring, 1995; Jolivette, Stichter-Peck, & McCormick, 2002; Jolivette, Wehby, Canale, & Massey, 2001; Powell & Nelson, 1997). For example, Dunlap et al. (1994) found that giving students choices in assignments resulted in increased time on task and decreased disruptive behavior. Examples of choices with regard to assignments can include where in the room to complete the assignment; whether to work alone or in pairs; a choice of one of three similar assignments; a choice of writing, typing, or dictating an assignment, and so forth. In addition to choices, including student interests in assignments has been found to be effective in reducing problematic behavior (Clarke et al., 1995). Including student interests may involve finding reading materials that are specific to student interests; using themes for bulletin boards, skill worksheets, and manipulatives that are related to students' interests, and so forth.

Many students perform at their best when given consistent feedback. Some students may become frustrated when too little assistance is offered when completing projects or assignments. Many students need more feedback for assurance and cues to stay on task. Closer monitoring of independent work may be a support offered to a student with difficulty completing classroom assignments and attending to tasks. This type of support can be offered in several ways. First, a peer buddy may provide frequent feedback to a student (see peer-mediated interventions on p. 231). Second, students may be provided with a signal, such as flags at their desks, to indicate that they need assistance. A student can be taught to move on to the next question, problem, or task until assistance is provided.

Another strategy is for the teacher or assistant to schedule a trip to the student's work area every 5 or 10 minutes, depending on the needs of the student, to provide positive feedback with regard to academic work and behavior. Appropriate feedback involves a high rate of praise, as opposed to disapproval. While the use of contingent praise has been consistently shown to have a positive effect on classroom behavior, especially for students with behavioral problems and attention deficit disorders, teachers tend to provide more indications of disapproval than approval, and tend to use praise to acknowledge academic work, as opposed to appropriate behavior (Beaman & Wheldall, 2000; Sutherland, 2000; Sutherland, Wehby, & Copeland, 2000). A support plan may include conscious use of praise on the part of the teacher to let the student know that he is competent and that his appropriate behavior is recognized. As a reminder to provide feedback, coins or paper clips can be placed in one pocket and transferred to another pocket each time the teacher monitors the student and provides feedback, thus making the teacher conscious of how often she is providing praise (Pfiffner & Barkley, 1998).

Change the Instruction to Match Student Needs

According to a review of research by Scott, Nelson, and Liaupsin (2001), there is a strong connection between low achievement and problem behavior and, likewise, between academic instruction and social behavior. When instruction is designed to maximize the likelihood of success and minimize failure in learning new skills, students are more likely to enjoy the activity and are less likely to disrupt the class or act in ways that would cause their removal from the lesson. In fact, success tends to generate more appropriate social behaviors, while failure to facilitate success can lead to classroom instruction being perceived as an aversive, avoidance of academic tasks, and increasing academic deficits. For a student whose behavior communicates a lack of a sense of competence, a support plan that addresses modifications in instruction is in order. Modifications in instruction involve strategies such as modifying the manner in which instructions are given, providing instruction in prerequisite skills or vocabulary, and using direct instruction.

Some students, especially those with ADHD, often have problems completing assignments due to difficulty with attending to and following through with directions. Hence, a support plan might include giving directions in a format accessible to students with short attention spans. Salend, Elhoweris, and Van Garderen (2003) suggest the following guidelines for supporting students with difficulty attending to directions:

- Focus student's attention on directions by using cues such as a flick of the lights, a finger in the air, or a consistent phrase like "This is important" to prompt students to pay attention.
- Describe the assignment, including the reasons for working on it and the motivating aspects.
- Present directions both orally and visually.
- Check for understanding by asking the student to explain the directions, or assess comprehension of the directions by asking questions such as "What are you going to do?" "What steps will you take?" "What materials do you need?" "Who should you ask for help if you need it?" and "How long do you have to finish the assignment?" (p.281).

In addition to difficulties with instructions, some students may lack the necessary background for the content being introduced. Burke, Hagan-Burke, & Sugai (2003) provide a case study in which a third-grade student with a learning disability and English as a second language engaged in disruptive behavior in order to escape tasks requiring reading comprehension. While the student was reading at grade level, a thorough functional assessment revealed that the student had difficulty with reading comprehension and tended to engage in inappropriate behavior when given tasks which required that skill. The support for this student included a change in instruction so that the student was introduced to the vocabulary inherent in the reading comprehension task prior to its assignment. This change resulted in greatly improved behavior.

For some students with behavioral and/or academic difficulties, being presented with opportunities to learn may not be enough to ensure success. Direct instruction is a research-based method that can ensure successful learning experiences for many students. Direct instruction involves the following components: (a) a meaningful rationale, including how the material relates to previously learned material; (b) demonstration or modeling of the content with multiple examples and non-examples of the skill or content to be learned; (c) guided practice with feedback; and (d) independent work. Lessons for individuals or small groups of children requiring this type of instruction can be incorporated within a constructivist classroom while other students are given choices for independent work and projects, as well as opportunities to participate in learning center activities, cooperative learning, and so forth.

Increase Predictability

Knowing what will happen next provides security for many students, while uncertainty can produce anxiety. For some students, increasing predictability as a form of support can alleviate anxiety and frustration (Ruef, 1998). Ruef recommends the following strategies for increasing predictability in the classroom:

> Direct student attention to a classroom schedule. For elementary school students with attentional difficulties, a simple schedule on their desk, on which they can cross off events as they occur, can be helpful. For middle and high school students, a weekly planner can be useful. Teachers can prompt students to check schedules and preview what will be happening during the day. Students with ADHD may benefit from knowing when they can leave their seats for some activity (e.g., taking care of the classroom pet, collecting materials, taking the attendance sheet to the office).
>
> Prepare students for changes in the daily routine. Unexpected changes in the daily routine, such as assemblies, guest speakers, and so forth, are upsetting to some students. When these types of changes are anticipated, preparing students about how those changes will affect them reduces anxiety. For example, a student who receives special education on a regular basis may benefit from knowing when the special education teacher is ill and who will provide services in the interim.
>
> Alert students before transitions. For some students, being aware of transitions from one activity to another ahead of time can increase the likelihood of appropriate behavior. A signal can be given to provide students the opportunity to finish what they are doing before having to put it away. A variety of signals can be used, such as music, a flick of the lights, hand signals, and so forth. Some children have difficulty maintaining the

appropriate behavior if too much time is spent waiting. For these children, it is helpful to have an activity to do if they are finished before their peers or if they are between lessons. When students are engaged with people or materials, they are less likely to exhibit challenging behaviors.

Solicit Peer Support

In the constructive classroom, peers can be a powerful source of support, offering not only a positive influence for students having behavioral and/or learning difficulties, but also by freeing the time typically taken by teachers and assistants for direct adult support. Peer support programs have been shown to offer both academic and social benefits (Christensen, Young, & Marchant, 2004; Cushing & Kennedy, 1997; Utley & Mortweet, 1997). For example, in an urban high school, peers support students with disabilities in a variety of ways, to facilitate inclusion such as assisting with the completion of lab projects, introducing students at lunch, accompanying them at pep rallies and assemblies, and so forth (Copeland et al., 2002). Peers have been used to provide support to other students in a number of ways. These strategies include (a) peer proximity, (b) peer prompting and reinforcement, and (c) peer monitoring.

In proximity interventions, students who need behavioral support are simply placed with socially competent peers. These interventions are based on the idea that children who need support will benefit from opportunities for direct interaction with competent peers. While this strategy has been effective in some cases, especially with regard to increasing the social interactions of children and youth with behavioral disorders (Sarup & Rutherford, 1991), simply placing a student next to a competent peer may not provide enough support to effect the desired outcomes without incorporating other strategies (Utley & Mortweet, 1997).

Another intervention involves teaching peers to monitor and reinforce their peers. Peers can be successfully trained to provide feedback to each other and subsequently to improve behavior and academic performance. In these strategies, peers are taught to give feedback to supported students about the quality of their work and/or behavior through checklists, verbal praise, or point systems. In one study, fifth graders who were identified as low achievers were taught to monitor the behavior of students with high rates of off-task behavior in a fifth-grade classroom. This intervention increased appropriate behavior for both the monitors and those being observed. Of course, an additional benefit included the fact that the monitors were able to experience a leadership role in the classroom (Kohler, Schwartz, Cross, & Fowler, 1989).

In peer tutoring, peers are placed together in one-to-one situations to enhance academic engagement. Guidelines for implementing peer tutoring are presented in Chapter 8. As a strategy for positive behavioral support, peer tutoring has the potential to increase on-task behavior (DuPaul & Ervin, 1998; DuPaul, Henningson, & North, 1993), social behavior, and academic achievement (Maheady, 2001). For students in need of behavioral support, peer tutoring offers the advantages of providing students with immediate feedback, increased opportunities for positive peer attention, frequent prompting to attend to task and less time spent waiting (Reid, 1999).

In addition to receiving assistance from a peer tutor, a support plan can include putting the student who exhibits challenging behavior in the role of the tutor. Otherwise known as reverse-role tutoring (Brown, 1993), this strategy has the benefit of allowing the student to use an area of strength to help another student, affording opportunities for responsibility, competence, and contributions to the community. Tournaki and Criscitiello (2003) describe a project that they had conducted in a New York City public school. Five African American males with emotional and behavioral disorders were given the opportunity to tutor their nondisabled peers who were functioning below grade level in a first-grade general education classroom. The authors hoped to reduce or eliminate such behaviors as hitting, cursing, pushing, screaming, and interrupting others. The opportunity to be a peer tutor resulted in a dramatic reduction of those behaviors.

Evaluation of Positive Behavioral Support

Evaluation is a crucial step in the positive behavioral support process. Once a positive behavioral support plan has been put in place, the teacher can monitor the behavior of the student to determine if the supports provided have had the desired effect. Many support plans will need some adjustment in the initial stages. Direct observation of the student, as well as interviews with the student and/or parents, can provide helpful insight into whether the student is benefiting from the support and whether modifications are needed. As a member of a collaborative team, developing and implementing positive behavioral support, the classroom teacher will provide valuable input regarding the plan's effectiveness.

GROUP POSITIVE BEHAVIORAL SUPPORT

A group of children may have developed inappropriate patterns of behavior as they moved from grade to grade in a small school. Another small group of students may present difficult behavior in the cafeteria or on the playground. When this occurs despite engaging the students in community development and opportunities for problem solving as discussed in Chapter 5, the constructivist teacher can assess the situation by asking pertinent questions and developing a plan for group support. Turnbull et al. (2002) suggest that the teacher ask questions such as

> When does the group seem to have the most and the least problems?
> Why do I send students to the office more often after lunch?
> Why does a particular group of students cause more difficulty at recess than others?

After analyzing the available information, a group support plan can be developed. Various strategies can be incorporated, including reteaching group expectations, providing active adult supervision, and providing precorrections. Reteaching group expectations involves engaging students in lessons and discussion regarding examples of the expected behavior and examples of behavior that is not acceptable (Turnbull et al., 2002). Active supervision involves providing a group of students with positive adult interaction and frequent scanning, praise, and corrections (Lewis, Colvin, & Sugai, 2000). Precorrection entails reminders of rules and expectations with regard to problem behavior before the behavior occurs (Lewis & Sugai, 1999).

SUMMARY

All members of a community need help at some time or other. In the classroom community, some students have behavioral difficulties that require the help and support of the community. Students and small groups of students who have behavioral problems can benefit from positive behavioral support, a useful process developed to address persistent problematic behaviors. Though it is grounded in the behavior tradition, positive behavior support can be used from multiple perspectives to understand behavior and aid teachers in finding means to support all students in the classroom community.

REFERENCES

Beaman. R., & Wheldall, K. (2000). Teachers' use of approval and disapproval in the classroom *Educational Psychology, 20*(4), 431–447.

Brown, J. A. S. (1993). Reverse-role tutoring: An alternative intervention for learning disabled students. *B.C. Journal of Special Education, 17*(3), 238–243.

Burke, M. D., Hagan-Burke, S., & Sugai, G. (2003). The efficacy of function-based interventions for students with learning disabilities who exhibit escape-maintained problem behaviors: Preliminary results from a single-case experiment. *Learning Disability Quarterly, 26*(1), 15–26.

Christensen, L., Young, R. K., & Marchant, M. (2004). The effects of a peer-mediated positive behavior support program on socially appropriate classroom behavior. *Education and Treatment of Children, 27*(3), 199–135.

Clarke, S., Dunlap, G., Foster-Johnson, L., Childs, K., Wilson, D., White, R., et al. (1995). Improving the conduct of students with behavioral disorders by incorporating student interests into curricular activities. *Behavioral Disorders, 20*(4), 221–237.

Copeland, S. R., McCall, J., Williams, C.R., Guth, C., Cater, E. W., Fowler, S. E., et al. (2002). High school peer buddies: A win–win situation. *Teaching Exceptional Children, 35*(19), 16–21.

Cosden, M., Gannon, C., & Haring, M. (1995). Teacher control versus student control over choice of task and reinforcement for students with severe behavioral problems. *Journal of Behavioral Education, 5*(1), 11–27.

Cushing, L. S., & Kennedy, C. H. (1997). Academic effects of providing peer support in general education classrooms on students without disabilities. *Journal of Applied Behavior Analysis, 30*(1), 139–152.

Dreikurs, R. (1968). *Psychology in the classroom* (2nd ed.). New York: Harper & Row.

Dunlap, G., DePerczel, M., Clarke, S., Wilson, K. E., White, R., & Falk, G. D. (1994). Choice making to promote adaptive behavior for students with emotional and behavioral challenges. *Journal of Applied Behavioral Analysis, 27*(3), 505–518.

DuPaul, G. J., & Ervin, R. A. (1996). Functional assessment of behaviors related to attention-deficit/hyperactivity disorder: Linking assessment to intervention design. *Behavior Therapy, 27*(4), 601–622.

DuPaul, G. J., & Ervin, R. A. (1998). Peer tutoring for children with attention deficit hyperactivity disorder: Effects on classroom behavior. *Journal of Applied Behavior Analysis, 31*(4), 579–593.

DuPaul, G. J., & Henningson, P., and North (1993). Peer tutoring effects on the classroom performance of children with attention deficit disorders. *School Psychology Review, 22*(1), 134–144.

Gunter, P. L., & Coutinho, M. J. (1997). Negative reinforcement in classrooms: What we're beginning to learn. *Teacher Education and Special Education, 20*(3), 249–264.

Gunter, P. L., Denny, R. K., & Venn, M. L. (2000). Modifications of instructional materials and procedures for curricular success of students with emotional and behavioral disorders. *Preventing School Failure, 44*(3), 116–122.

Jolivette, K., Stichter-Peck, J., & McCormick, K. M. (2002). Making choices—Improving behavior—Engaging in learning. *Teaching Exceptional Children, 34*(3), 24–30.

Jolivette, K., Wehby, J. H., Canale, J., & Massey, N. G. (2001). Effects of choice-making opportunities on the behavior of students with emotional and behavioral disorders. *Behavioral Disorders, 26*(2), 131–145.

Kern, L., Childs, K., Dunlap, G., Clarke, S., & Falk, G. (1994). Using assessment-based curricular intervention to improve the classroom behavior of a student with emotional and behavioral challenges. *Journal of Applied Behavior Analysis, 27*, 7–19.

Kohler, F. W., Schwartz, I. S., Cross, J. A., & Fowler, S. A. (1989). The effects of two alternating peer invention roles on independent work skills. *Education and Treatment of Children, 12*(3), 205–218.

Lewis, T. J., Colvin, G., & Sugai, G. (2000). The effects of pre-correction and active supervision on the recess behavior of elementary students. *Education and Treatment of Children, 23*(2), 109–122.

Lewis, T. J., & Sugai, G. (1999). Effective behavior support: A systems approach to proactive school-wide management. *Focus on Exceptional Children, 31*(6), 1–24.

Lombardo, L. (1997). Functional assessment: Putting research on methods of behavior management to practical use in the classroom. *Counterpoint, 18, 2.*

Maag, J., & Kemp, S. E. (2003). Behavioral intent of power and affiliation. *Remedial and Special Education, 24*(1), 57–65.

Maheady, L. (2001). Peer-mediated instruction and interventions and students with mild disabilities. *Remedial and Special Education, 22*(1), 4–15.

McKee, W., & Witt, J. C. (1990). Effective teaching: A review of instructional and environment variables in T. B. Gutkin and C. R. Reynolds, Eds., *Handbook of School Psychology.* New York: Wiley.

Pacchiano, M. (2000). A review of instructional variables related to student problem behavior. *Preventing School Failure, 44*(4), 174–179.

Powell, S., & Nelson, B. (1997). Effects of choosing academic assignments on a student with attention deficit hyperactivity disorder. *Journal of Applied Behavior Analysis, 30*(1), 181–183.

Pfiffner, L. J., & Barkley, R. A. (1998). Treatment of ADHD in school settings. In R. A. Barkley (Ed.), *Attention deficit hyperactivity disorder: A handbook for diagnosis and treatment* (2nd ed., pp. 458–490). New York: Guilford.

Pfiffner, L. J., O'Leary, S. G., Rosen, L. A., & Sanderson, W. C. (1985). A comparison of the effects of continuous and intermittent response cost and reprimands in the classroom. *Journal of Clinical Child Psychology, 14*(4), 348–353.

Reid, R. (1999). Attention deficit hyperactivity disorder: Effective methods for the classroom. *Focus on Exceptional Children, 32*(4), 1–20.

Rogers, F. (2003) *The world according to Mister Rogers: Important things to remember*. New York: Hyperion

Ruef, M. B. (1998). Positive behavioral support: Strategies for teachers. *Intervention in School and Clinic, 34*(1), 12–21.

Salend, S. J., Elhoweris, H., & Van Garderen, D. (2003). Educational interventions for students with ADD. *Intervention in School and Clinic, 38*(5), 280–289.

Salend, S. J., & Taylor, L. S. (2002). Cultural perspectives: Missing pieces in the functional assessment process. *Intervention in School and Clinic, 38*(2), 104–113.

Sarup, M. R., & Rutherford, R. B. (1991). Peer-mediated interventions promoting the social skills of children and youth with behavioral disorders. *Education and Treatment of Children, 14*(3), 227–243.

Scott, T. M., Nelson, M., & Liaupsin, C., (2001). Effective instruction: The forgotten component in preventing school violence. *Education and Treatment of Children, 24*(3), 309–322.

Shores, R. E., Gunter, P. L., & Jack, S. L. (1993). Classroom management strategies: Are they setting events for coercion? *Behavioral Disorders, 18*(2), 92–102.

Sutherland, S. (2000). Promoting positive interactions between teachers and students with emotional/behavioral disorders. *Preventing School Failure, 44*(3), 110–116.

Sutherland, S. R S., Wehby, J. H., & Copeland, S. R. (2000). The effects of varying rates of behavior-specific praise on student with EBD. *Journal of Emotional and Behavioral Disorders, 8*(1), 2–9.

Tournaki & Criscitiello (2003). Using peer tutoring as a successful part of behavior management. *Teaching Exceptional Children, 36*(2), 22–29.

Turnbull, A., Edmonson, H., Griggs, P., Wickman, D., Sailor, W., Freeman, R., et al. (2002). A blueprint for schoolwide positive behavior support: Implementation of three components. *Exceptional Children, 68*(3), 377–403.

Utley, C. A., & Mortweet, S. L. (1997). Peer-mediated instruction and interventions. *Focus on Exceptional Children, 29*(5), 1–23.

Zentall, S. M., Moon, S., Hall, A. M., & Grskovic, J. A. (2001). Learning and motivational characteristics of boys with ADHD and/or giftedness. *Exceptional Children, 67*(4), 499–519.

GOALS AND OUTCOMES

IV

Goals, Outcomes, And Assessments

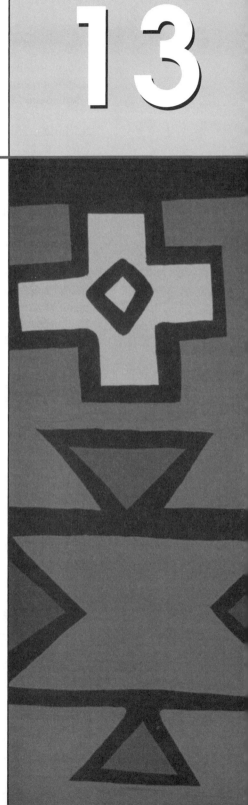

13

As the world becomes more interconnected, organizations that will truly excel in the future will be [those] . . . that discover how to tap people's commitment and capacity to learn.
Peter Senge (Senge, 1990, p. 4)

A shared vision is not an idea . . . it is rather, a force in people's hearts . . . at its simplest level, a shared vision is the answer to the question "What do we want to create?"
Peter Senge (Senge, 1990, p. 206)

Teachers, as well as their students, are learners in the classroom. Effective and responsive classroom management involves being intentional in setting goals and outcomes for the classroom and individual learners; being reflective and using data to learn about classroom practices, their effects on classroom climate, classroom relationships, and student learning; and making adjustments where appropriate. This intentionality also involves thinking about the role of the teacher, developing a mission or vision with regard to how the teacher and students want their classroom to be, examining beliefs about learners, considering multiple perspectives, articulating teacher values and a mission or vision for the classroom, and ultimately setting goals for the class and the learners within the class. Evaluation or assessment involves collecting and examining data from multiple sources and multiple perspectives. Based on assessment data, teachers can make wise decisions about classroom practices. Through this type of assessment loop, the teacher is the learner.

The concept of teacher as learner in the classroom assumes, as Cochran-Smith (2001) posits, that there are no universal solutions or prepackaged programs that address classroom management issues in all classrooms. Context is important; each classroom and student–teacher dynamic is different, and as a learner, each teacher must determine what is appropriate and most conducive to learning for their circumstances. Classroom assessment and action research can help in this journey.

As with learners, Bandura's conception of self-efficacy plays a role with teachers and teaching practices as well. Teachers' sense of efficacy is "their belief in their ability to have a positive effect on student learning" (Ashton, 1985, p. 142). Teachers with high self-efficacy believe that they can reach and make a difference with all learners. High teacher efficacy has a positive effect on motivation, teacher attitude, and student achievement (Ashton & Webb, 1986; Hoy & Woolflok, 1993; Ross & Gray, 2006). With regard to classroom management, teachers with high efficacy show a preference for more positive classroom management strategies (Ashton & Webb, 1986; Emmer & Hickman, 1991) and use practices that promote learning orientations, as opposed to performance orientations (Deemer, 2004). Teachers with high self-efficacy are willing to try innovative approaches and search for new strategies for dealing with classroom predicaments (Ross, 1998; Ross & Gray, 2006). Teacher self-assessment can raise teacher efficacy by helping teachers recognize mastery experiences or experiences of success with their teaching and management strategies, as well as identifying opportunities for improvement (Ross, 2007). Action research provides a framework for teachers to identify classroom management issues and try new strategies for addressing those issues. Action research is a process in which teachers become researchers by framing questions, taking action, and reflecting on their action.

BENEFITS OF GOALS AND ASSESSMENT PRACTICES

The benefits of setting goals and outcomes for the classroom and individual learners, and of making classroom assessment, are many. These practices help the teacher avoid a "blame the victim" mentality; keep centered on the outcomes and goals, as opposed to classroom control; and determine whether certain strategies or practices are effective or need modification.

Avoiding to Blame the Victim Mentality

When things do not go well in the classroom, it is easy to find fault in the learners. Teachers can lament that their learners are irresponsible, disrespectful, immature, and so forth. Classroom assessment practices help the teacher avoid blaming the student for misbehaving, not learning, or not responding as the teacher had hoped. Through classroom assessment, teachers can examine, frame, and solve the dilemmas of classroom practice by attending to classroom and instructional climate and management practices instead of blaming learners. They can become aware of and question values and assumptions brought to teaching and attend to institutional and cultural contexts and multiple perspectives.

Keeping a Goal Focus

Many new teachers focus their efforts on classroom control instead of academic learning. While most administrators, as well as parents, would prefer classrooms where children are under control, careful consideration of the type of control exerted in the classroom is wise. If a teacher's primary mission is one of control, the focus in the classroom becomes that of work completion and obedience over learning and responsibility. Setting learning and responsibility as intentional goals can focus teacher efforts in different ways. Through classroom assessment practices, teachers can determine whether classroom rules serve classroom goals related to learning or student control. Three examples follow.

Consider the contrast in the case of two teachers observed in a middle school. One of the teachers requires each student to bring a pencil to class and enforces the rule by having forgetful students sit in class without a pencil. Unable to complete their assignments, they are required to complete them for homework or during their free time. Another teacher considers learning to be the most important goal in the classroom. Instead of having time in the classroom with students not engaged in learning, this teacher has a ready supply of pencils available. In this example, the first teacher's goal appears to have been to strictly enforce rules through consequences; in the second classroom, the teacher's goal appears to have been to maintain a focus on learning.

In another example, consider the following two elementary school teachers. One teacher sends children to the principal's office when they accumulate six infractions with regard to classroom rules. While the infractions are often minor classroom offenses such as chewing gum, an accumulation of six infractions requires a trip to the principal's office, interrupting the learning process. Another teacher observes gum chewing in her classroom and directs the offender to put the gum in the trash can. The child disposes of the gum and gets back to learning. While gum chewing was not tolerated in either classroom, the disruption to learning is minimal in the second classroom.

In another school, in one classroom, a teacher is struggling with how to get her students to complete a vocabulary workbook that was purchased for each student at the beginning of the year. Students complain about the assignments from the workbook and engage in many disruptive behaviors during the time allotted for the workbook assignment. The teacher considers offering a reward for completing the assignment and a consequence for noncompletion. In another classroom, when students complain about a workbook assignment, the teacher asks herself about the goal she has in mind for the assignment and decides whether the goal is for students to learn vocabulary. She rethinks her approach to having students learn vocabulary. With her new activities, students are eager to participate and learn. In the first classroom, the goal appeared to have been for students to complete a workbook, while in the second classroom, the goal was more clearly a learning goal.

Finding What Works

Finally, many practices are used over and over again without evidence of their effectiveness or thought to their outcomes. For example, some teachers rely on strategies such as having students walk laps at recess or attend silent lunch as a consequence for rule breaking. Often, careful examination of these practices can reveal that the same children are receiving the consequences with no effect or positive change in their behavior. Setting and assessing goals can assist teachers in evaluating classroom practices and making modifications in order to reach desired outcomes.

CLASSROOM MISSION AND GOALS

A teacher's vision or mission for his classroom is influenced by the vision or mission of the school, as well as the teacher's own personal philosophy of teaching. Both are important in considering how a teacher wants their classroom to be. The climate of the classroom and the ways in which students learn will be influenced by the teacher's vision for the classroom. A vision or mission then leads to clearly articulated classroom goals. Although academic goals may be the primary concern of teachers, classroom management goals involve the social and emotional climate of the classroom, and behavioral and social outcomes for students.

Table 13.1 includes questions worth considering in developing a classroom mission and goals, and examples of classroom missions and goals.

ASSESSMENT

The concept of the teacher as a learner in the classroom involves assessment of progress toward classroom management goals. With assessment practices, teachers can be critically reflective with regard to their classroom management practices and determine whether their classroom goals are being met. Classroom assessment may also be cumulative in nature, occurring at the end of the year to gain an idea of whether classroom goals have been met. However, formative assessment is perhaps more useful for class-

Table 13.1

Questions to Consider
What is my mission as a teacher?
What is my role in the classsoom?
What is the student's role in the classroom?
What do I value with regard to an ideal classroom?
What do I assume about learners?
What kind of classroom do I want to create?
What do I want most for the learners in my classroom?
Examples of Goals and Missions
Every learner will have a sense of belonging.
Every learner will have a strong sense of self-efficacy.
Every learner will develop a positive disposition for learning.
Every learner will be actively engaged in learning most of the school day.

Classroom Management Considerations

room management purposes. Formative assessment practices involve an ongoing assessment of progress toward goals. Assessment practices need not be time or labor intensive and are well worth the small investment of time. Useful classroom assessment practices include reflective journals, observations by colleagues, and classroom surveys.

Reflective Journals

Many teachers find writing in journals to be useful in classroom reflection and assessment. In fact, teachers seeking to obtain National Board Certification from the National Board for Professional Teaching Standards are required to conduct rigorous and repeated reflections of their daily classroom activities by videotaping their classroom teaching and by submitting reflective entries in a professional journal. Teachers can write their thoughts and observations about student–teacher relationships, classroom practices, learner characteristics, progress toward classroom goals, classroom predicaments, and so forth. Journal writing can be an independent activity such as a diary or a collaborative activity in which teachers write to and for each other, and/or in a group (Farrell, 2001).

A reflective journal can serve several purposes in evaluating and refining classroom practices. First, it can give teachers the opportunity to recapture an experience, think about it, mull it over, and evaluate it from a fresh perspective at a conscious level. Unconscious processes do not allow us to make active and conscious decisions about teaching and learning. Bringing ideas to a conscious level allows teachers an opportunity for reflection and evaluation, and to begin to make choices about what they will and will not do. Research supports journal writing as a tool that promotes and documents reflective thinking (Hubbs & Hubbs, 2005; Pipe & Richards, 1992). The following excerpt from a teacher's journal shows how journals can provide a venue for exploration of teaching missions, values, and practices:

> Despite all I attempt to do with my students, I still have goals to push myself further in this area. I know there are some students that seem "unreachable" to me at times, perhaps their interests are different, or they do not seem to enjoy additional time with me. I think that I would like to find better ways to ensure that these children do have a positive relationship with an adult in the school, even if it is not me. This requires my taking a step back and pulling my ego out of the process, to determine the type of person that may make a stronger connection than I am able to at this time. (Marie Case, 2006)

A second purpose of a reflective journal is as a tool for articulating and solving problems that occur inside and outside the classroom (Chitpin, 2006). Journals can serve as a data collection tool (Ghaye & Lillyman, 1997), a record of anecdotal events from which patterns or themes may emerge. For example, a teacher may notice that things "fall apart" each day at a certain time. This type of information can lead teachers to finding solutions to day-to-day classroom predicaments.

> I am forever trying to make my teaching and learning experience better for me and my class, but always felt a presence of tension. Because I have the opportunity to tutor all my students, I know there is intimacy between us. But I now realize that probably the control and rules I kept stressing in class were the reason for the tension. Nowadays, I

find that I have very little reason to refer to rules. I think our relationship has improved as I reduce my obsession with rules! I think I had been creating this tension for us in class. The important thing in my class, I believe, is the way we treat each other. I realize now that my class has been a success despite my holding onto control and rules. We believe in good manners and treating each other with the greatest of respect. Expectations had been accomplishing what I thought was due to my control. Now I feel more like a coach and not a police officer seeing to it that rules are followed! On to a more stress-free existence! (Priscilla Ho, 2006)

Finally, keeping a journal can assist teachers in venting their feelings and clarifying their beliefs on teaching and their students' learning, as well as examining bias and attitudes toward learners, other colleagues, and parents. Journals can provide a record of what a teacher learns about his or her teaching skills, classroom climate, and relationships with students:

I know, on reflection, and I think I knew then, that I was dealing with more than the obvious problem of the children's specific learning challenges. I was facing the distance between our two cultures in a new way. Somewhere along the way, I came to the realization that I could never fully understand their culture and their families until I understood my own. I could not embrace who they were until I was willing to embrace myself. That meant only one thing: I was going to have *to talk about it*. The journal was the place I talked about it, at first safely and later more painfully. (Hankins, 1998, p. 85)

Hatton and Smith (1995) caution that reflection does not occur automatically. If journal writing is a collaborative activity, journal writers may conform their writing to reflect preconceived notions of the expectations of the reader or write only superficial accounts of events in the classroom, especially if the writers believe they will be evaluated based on their entries. A pending evaluation may deter a teacher's desire to write for reflection and growth. Thoughtful reflection requires a willingness to be honest and critical. For collaborative journal writing to be effective, journals should be used for constructive dialogue and collaboration, not for evaluation of teaching.

The following are excerpts from a collaborative reflective journal kept by teachers participating in a graduate course in classroom management:

How am I going to flag myself or cue myself to continually view the student's perspective without getting wrapped up in the academic daily obligations? For example: Those days that you don't know where the time went. I wonder if there had been something going on with a student that day that I missed because of it?

I know what you mean as far as having so many academic obligations and then you turn around and a student of yours need to talk or needed someone to listen and you had no idea. I work with high school students and on a weekly basis, I feel like I have to deal with a student's personal problems. I don't mind, but I feel bad when I know the student has no one else to talk to and they put their trust in you and you have other obligations. I honestly think that students need that person to talk to and listen to them. I do not know what grade you teach, but I know that with my students, they have a daily journal they write in and I have told them that if they have a problem and/or need to talk to someone, but want to not let anyone know about it, I tell them to write it in their journal or write me a note saying that they have to talk to me. I keep their journals very confidential and the students know this. Maybe trying something like this would help you not to feel guilty about not getting to talk to the students like you would like.

Journal writing provides opportunities for critical reflection. Whether as a solo or a collaborative activity, it allows teachers to bring to a conscious level their assumptions and beliefs about learners and teaching. It allows teachers to mull over their classroom practices and classroom predicaments, and to note changes and improvements, as well as setbacks and obstacles.

Observations by Colleagues

Observations by a colleague or other professional are another tool that teachers can use to assess classroom management practices. Observations by colleagues can seem daunting to many teachers. When the process is collegial instead of evaluative or judgmental, it can lead teachers to insights that help them improve their practice (Cosh, 1999). Coaching is a process used by many schools to facilitate observations of teachers by fellow teachers.

Benefits
Observations can be advantageous to both the teacher being observed and the one doing the observing. Peer observations can provide useful feedback regarding student–teacher relationships and classroom climate, and can facilitate change, provide information regarding management practices, encourage collaborative reflection, and alleviate isolation.

Providing Feedback.   Feedback is important for teacher growth and development, and to help teachers understand various dynamics in the classroom (Guskey, 2002). While test scores can provide feedback with regard to individual student performance, observations of classroom teaching allow access to actual instructional experiences where knowledge and skills are put into practice. For example, in their study of a first-grade classroom, Fottland and Matre (2005) illustrate how observation can be used to provide feedback regarding student–teacher relationships. These authors identified aspects of student–teacher relationships, such as how the teacher sees and connects with students, and how she inspires curiosity, that can be assessed through observation, but cannot be easily assessed through other methods.

Revealing Unintentional Interactions.   Observation can reveal unintentional interactions in the classroom that can affect classroom climate, learning, and behavior. For example, Eder (1981) observed a first-grade classroom for a year to determine the effect of ability grouping in the area of reading. The author found that in low-ability groups, students who needed instruction and attention the most were distracted more frequently. The social context of learning in low-ability groups was dramatically different than that in high-ability groups. Higher rates of disruption, management, and turn-order disruptions in their reading lessons occurred in the low-ability groups, calling into question the practice of homogenous grouping.

Reflection and Change.   Peer observations can facilitate changes in classroom practices (Bushman, 2006; Slater & Simmons, 2001; Swafford, 1998). Observations can provide a different perspective through which teachers can view their classrooms. Bushman (2006) describes the application of peer observations where teachers in a high school "walked through" each other's classrooms, followed by an after-school meeting with members of their department to talk about what they had seen. This created a process by which observation became a "deeply reflective learning process" (p. 60). For example, one teacher who had observed a colleague noted that "It was beneficial for me to see students of mine in other classes. I was able to compare how they acted in these classes with their behavior in my class. Sometimes they seemed much more engaged, which makes me ask myself, How can I create the same engagement?" (p. 60).

Alleviating Isolation.   Peer observation can alleviate the isolation often experienced by teachers (O'Connor & Korr, 1996; Slater & Simmons, 2001; Swafford, 1998) by providing technical, emotional, and reflective support. Peer observations can support a climate of collaboration and professionalism among teachers.

Peer Coaching

Peer coaching is one model used by many schools to facilitate classroom observations. In this model, teachers observe each others' classrooms, followed by structured feedback and discussion (O'Connor & Korr, 1996). Collegiality, confidentiality, and learning are emphasized, as opposed to evaluation and/or criticism. Research and professional literature provide guidelines for successful peer coaching.

Non-evaluative.   Peer coaching should not be used for evaluation (Slater & Simmons, 2001). Peer coaching models that incorporate evaluation may not be successful. Instead, peer coaching should be done in a spirit of collegiality, with respect and reciprocity, where teachers can learn from each other. Trust among participants is an important aspect of successful peer coaching (Slater & Simmons, 2001).

Flexible.   Peer coaching programs should be flexible. Slater and Simmons (2001) note that observations may be specific (e.g., a colleague is asked to look for specific aspects of classroom practices) or non-specific (e.g., a colleague observes the classroom in general terms). Observations can be geared to the specific needs of each teacher.

Voluntary.   Peer coaching should be voluntary (O'Connor & Korr, 1996). Teachers voluntarily engaging in peer coaching are more likely to learn and grow from the experience.

Opportunity for Dialogue.   Conferences or opportunities to hold dialogues about peer observations are essential. Swafford (1998) indicates that conferences between the observed and the observer should occur soon after the observation.

Timing. There should be early and frequent observations. Swafford (1998) recommends that observations begin early in the year and that they occur frequently (twice a month).

Checklist and Surveys

A teacher-generated or published checklist or survey, such as My Classroom Inventory, can be used either as a teacher self-check, a peer coaching tool, or a tool to gain the student perspective of class climate. Self-reports completed by teachers and students can provide a vehicle for understanding the discordant experiences of the teacher and students within the same classroom. Several examples of classroom assessment instruments follow.

The My Class Inventory—Short Form (MCI_SF; Sink & Spencer, 2005) is a self-report classroom climate scale that measures five dimensions: (a) cohesiveness—the degree to which students understand, collaborate, and are friendly with one another; (b) friction—the extent of tension and conflict among students; (c) difficulty–the level of difficulty that students have with the classroom work; (d) satisfaction—the extent to which students feel satisfied with or like their class; and (e) competition–the perceived amount of classroom competition. With this instrument, students are asked to rate each item as "yes" or "no," which indicates agreement or disagreement. Sample items include "Everybody is my friend," "Most students want their work to be better than their friends'," "Some students feel bad when they don't do as well as others," and "Students in my class fight a lot."

The Learning Environment Inventory (Fraser, Anderson, & Walberg, 1982) is a widely used survey that provides information about the classroom environment of middle school or high school classrooms. According to Walberg and Greenberg (1997), while students need structure and direction, they learn more when they find their classes satisfying, challenging, and friendly, and when they can participate in decision making. This inventory measures nine positive features of classroom groups, such as challenge, cohesiveness, and democracy, and six features that might have negative effects, such as apathy and cliquishness. Students respond to items on a 5-point scale, from strongly agree to stongly disagree. Sample items include "Students know one another very well," "Every student enjoys the same privileges," and "Class decisions are made by all students."

The Classroom Environment Scale (Moos and Tricket, 1995), which is easy to administer and score, assesses learning environments from the student's perspective and is particularly appropriate for junior and high school students. It contains 90 items that tap into student perceptions on aspects of the classroom such as relationships, goal orientations, and classroom systems. Sample comments to be rated by the student include "Students put a lot of energy into what they do here" and "Students in the class get to know each other very well."

The School as a Caring Community Profile II (Lickona and Davidson, 2003) is a 42-question survey developed by the Center for the 4th and 5th Rs (Respect and Responsibility) to assist schools in assessing the perceptions of students, families, and professionals with regard to the school as a caring community. This instrument can be used with both elementary and high school students, although the authors recommend asking fewer questions to elementary school students. Items are presented in a 5-point Likert format. Sample questions include "Students refrain from put-downs," "Students are disrespectful toward their teachers," and "Students are involved in helping to solve school problems."

Students Perceptions' of Classroom Quality For high school students and My Class Activities for grades 3 through 8 (Gentry & Springer, 2002) are surveys designed to assess the students' level of perceived interest and challenge. These surveys ask students about their enjoyment of school, their level of interest in their studies, the amount of choice they feel they have in their academic life, and how frequently they feel challenged by their studies. Sample items include "I find my class assignments a challenge to complete," "I am given lots of choice in my class," and "I find the contents of my class interesting."

The Classroom Climate Quality Analytic Assessment Instrument and the School Climate Quality Analytic Assessment Instrument developed by the Western Alliance for the Study of School Climate (WASSC, 2004) are for schools and teachers to use to assess school and classroom climate. These instruments are based on the assumptions that the school and the classrooms change from within and that given a transparent and concrete assessment system, teachers can make meaningful improvements in school practices. These assessment instruments are analytical in that they provide students and teachers with rubrics for identify the current status of several dimensions of the school climate. In a study of the efficacy of the WASSC system, Shindler, Taylor, Cadenas, and Jones (2003) demonstrate the validity, reliability, efficiency, and benefits of these scales.

The classroom instrument obtains the perspectives of students and has items related to student interactions, a disciplinary environment, learning/assessment, attitude, and culture. The school instrument is intended for a group of faculty to complete collaboratively and includes the subcategories of appearance and physical plant, faculty relations, student interactions, leadership/decision making, disciplinary environment, learning environment, attitude and culture, and school–community relations. Respondents are asked to rate each item in terms of three performance levels, as well as three sub-levels (high, middle, and low). Sample items include "Students feel a sense of community"; "The classroom is defined by a positive feeling among class members"; and "Most students feel listened to, represented, and believe they have a voice."

What is Happening in This Classroom (Fraser, 1998) is a questionnaire that measures high school students' perceptions of their classroom environment. It includes items that measure constructivism and other aspects of contemporary classrooms (Rickards, den Brok, Bull, & Fisher, 2003). There are seven dimensions: Student Cohesiveness, Teacher Support, Involvement, Investigation, Task Orientation, Cooperation, and Equity. These dimensions are represented by 56 items that are answered on a 5-point Likert scale. Sample items include "The teacher helps me when I have trouble with the work"; "I give my opinion during class discussions"; "I find out answers to questions by doing investigations"; "I am treated the same as other students in my class", and "When I work in groups in this class, there is team work."

Figure 13.1   Teacher-Generated Scales for Assessing Students'
               Dispositions Toward Learning

Peer Observation Form

Rate the degree to which you observe each of the following on a scale of 1 to 5, with 1 being the lowest and 5 the highest.

Children are eager to begin work.	1 2 3 4 5
Children talk about what they are learning.	1 2 3 4 5
Most of the peer interaction in the classroom is relevant to the topic that they are learning.	1 2 3 4 5
Students are challenged.	1 2 3 4 5
Learning distractions are minimal.	1 2 3 4 5
Students ask questions.	1 2 3 4 5
Students are engaged in the learning task most of the time.	1 2 3 4 5

Student Survey

In this class, I am excited about the work we do:	never sometimes most of the time
In this class, I talk about lessons with my friends:	never sometimes most of the time
In this class, my friends and I talk about what we are doing in the classroom and what we are learning:	never sometimes most of the time
In this class, I feel challenged:	never sometimes most of the time
I ask questions in this class:	never sometimes most of the time
I spend time learning in this class:	never sometimes most of the time

---

Stewart and Evans (1997) provide a self-assessment checklist for teachers. This list includes items such as "Matches instructional needs to curricula"; "Implements a variety of instructional arrangements"; "Uses relevant, purposeful, and motivating teaching methods, activities, resources, and technology"; and "Monitors progress and provides corrective feedback."

Teachers looking for answers to specific classroom questions or evidence of specific goals can create their own checklist or survey. Figure 13.1 shows a survey generated by a teacher interested in her students' dispositions for learning while in her classroom. She created one survey for a peer observing her class and one for her students to complete.

Interviews

Interviews with students to gain their perspective of their experiences in school, the classroom environment, and disciplinary procedures can provide helpful insights into classroom management practices. Interviews with students can help teachers understand behavioral problems in the classroom (Gable, Hester, Hester, Hendrickson, & Sze, 2005). They can trigger reflection and assist teachers in confirming or challenging their assumptions about learners (Hoban, 2000). For example, in Hoban's study, a high school science teacher discovered through interviews with students that his idea of what constituted a "fun" science lab differed from those of his students. The teacher had been very prescriptive with regard to experiments conducted in the classroom. He provided step-by-step directions, allowing little room for error. The interviews led him to allow science labs to be slightly more open ended, allowing students to take more ownership and allowing for learning from mistakes.

In another example, Black (2006) reports on a fifth-grade teacher who was having difficulty motivating children to follow classroom rules and do homework. He had a token system in place in which kids earned trinkets. He had little success with his system of token rewards—small prizes he handed out to motivate students to obey classroom rules and hand in homework. He asked students for help in researching this problem. The students developed a survey and interview questions. The students concluded that they would behave better if they were working in cooperative groups, could listen to music, and could get a jump start on their homework. The teacher noted great improvement in student behavior and motivation, and noted in his journal, "The basket of tokens magically disappeared and the kids never noticed—and never missed it. I learned to trust my 10-year-old researchers—they're the real experts on motivation" (Black, 2006, p. 35).

Sociometric Scales

Sociometric scales can give the teachers information regarding the social dynamics, sense of community, and social climate in the classroom. They can help assess the social climate in the classroom by determining the pattern of friendships, popularity, and peer rejection (Sherman, 2002). Sociometric techniques allow teachers to easily identify the children who have few friends and are likely candidates for disenfranchisement from school (Davis, Howell, & Cooke, 2002). They have been used to measure peer rejection and the unpopularity of children with disabilities in general education settings (Bender, Shubert, & McLaughlin, 2001; Carlson, Lahey, Frame, Walker, & Hynd, 1987), and can help teachers and counselors identify potential bullies (Cole, Cornell, & Sheras, 2006).

Teachers can create a sociometric scale, developing statements and asking students to rate and/or identify, according to specific criteria, their peers on a class roster on one or more statements. Depending on the purpose of the sociometric scale, students can be asked to answer one or more questions about their peers, which can be ranked on a Likert-type scale. Items might include comments like the following:

- I would like to work with this person on a project.
- I would like to sit with this person at lunch.

The scale can also be made so that students fill in the names of their peers:

- I would most like to sit beside _____.
- I would most like to work on a project with _____.
- _____ is likely to be a bully.

Sociometric scales are scored by tabulating and averaging all responses. A sociogram can also be generated to visually depict the social relationships in a classroom. Figure 13.2 includes directions for a sociogram.

Figure 13.2   Creating a Sociogram

Two types of diagrams can be generated:

1. To create a sociogram, create concentric circles like a target. Include as many circles as the individual with the most peer nominations or high ratings. Put the names of the students in the circles according to the number of nominations they have.

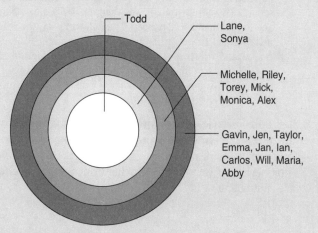

2. Draw a circle for each student. Draw an arrow from each circle to the circle of the individual who the student nominated. Arrows could be color coded for each question. (See text, p. 248.) The resulting figure can help determine which relationships are mutual, which children are friendless, and so forth.

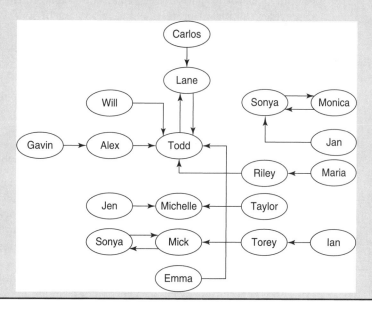

The following excerpt from a reflective journal illustrates the usefulness of sociograms in providing evidence that classroom practices are effective.

> The sociogram was enlightening to her and myself as well. It not only revealed a student in need of social intervention; it also showed the success of an earlier intervention. My wife dealt with her (cartooning) student who was bullying a gifted student earlier in the year. The student was informed of the inability of some to communicate their desire to be friends appropriately and how things outside of class can influence behaviors in school. The gifted student was then challenged to reach out, instead of pushing away, and to see what would happen. The following day, the young student asked the aggressor if he wanted to be in his group during reading time. Since then, the aggression has ceased and the two are now friends. The sociogram showed her that it had indeed worked. The two made mutual choices when asked about seating, class project, and play partners. This made my wife's day; we discussed the student identified as neglected and possible interventions. *Timothy Fagan*

Both interviews with students and sociograms provide vehicles involving students in the assessment of classroom management practices. The benefits of gaining student perspective are described in Chapter 4. With regard to classroom assessment practices, interviews and sociograms provide evidence of the effects of classroom practices from the vantage point of the consumers.

Action Research

For educators, action research is continual disciplined inquiry conducted to inform and improve practice (Calhoun, 2002). Action research allows teachers to examine classroom practices with regard to both classroom management and academic instruction, and provides significant professional development (Russ & Meyers, 2006). As a tool in looking at classroom management practices, action research allows teachers to focus on a particular classroom goal or school/classroom predicament such as the effect of socioeconomic disparities in the school and classroom (Alana, 2006). Action research is a unique form of research that differs from strict scientific research. Unlike strict scientific research, the characteristics of action research allow it to be easily incorporated into the life of the classroom.

Characteristics of Action Research

According to Kember (2000) action research includes the following characteristics:

> *Action research is concerned with social practice.* Classrooms are complex social systems that do not always lend themselves to strict scientific inquiry where a hypothesis is generated and strict controls are in place in order to determine the effects of a given variable. Action research allows for the examination of authentic problems within the context of the unique circumstances presented by a school or classroom.
>
> *Action research is done with the intention of improving practice.* The purpose of action research goes beyond description of classroom variables. The pri-

mary purpose of action research in the classroom is to inform classroom practice and foster continued professional development of teachers. With action research, teachers identify the area that is of particular interest or concern on which to focus action and reflection.

Action research is participatory in that one or more teachers are engaged in producing research. Unlike linear models of research where research is presented to teachers who are then asked to apply the practices in the classroom, in action research, teachers are the researchers. Action research can involve one teacher in one classroom, small groups of teachers, or the entire school. When teachers collaborate on action research, collaboration offers the advantages of the opportunity for the discussion of unconscious assumptions and perceptions, and brainstorming of possible solutions to problems.

Action research is systematic and cyclical. Action research allows for continued learning in the classroom as teachers engage in planning, action, observing, and reflection, which leads to further planning, action, observation, and reflection.

Implementing Action Research

The following steps for conducting an action research project related to classroom management practices are discussed on p. 252–253. Figure 13.3 illustrates the action research cycle.

Figure 13.3   The Action Research Cycle

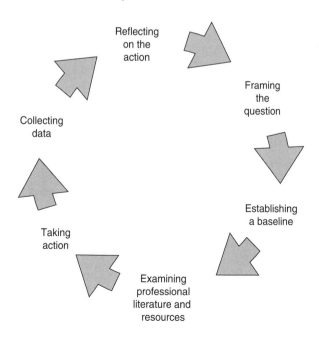

Framing the Question

Teachers can look at classroom goals, classroom predicaments, problems, or potential areas for improvement with regard to the classroom community, a small group of students, or a specific child to frame a question for the action research project. For example, teachers may ask, How can I develop a sense of community in my classroom? How can I help students make easier transitions between classes? How can I help learners solve peer-to-peer conflicts? and How can I help a student with ADD develop attending skills.

Establishing a Baseline

Teachers can look at current classroom practices and the target of the action research project by collecting data through observation, anecdotal records, sociograms, and so forth. Data collected before an action provides a basis for comparison after an action is taken and can also assist the teacher in understanding the current classroom circumstances.

Examining Professional Literature and Resources

Teachers can look at professional literature and research for ideas and to compare what they are currently doing with current research.

Taking Action

Teachers modify their current practice and/or implement a new approach geared to help reach their goal or solve a classroom dilemma.

Collecting Data

Data can be taken through the various methods described in this chapter. Multiple sources of data are recommended. Teachers may choose to do a sociogram, as well as observe target students to see if positive interactions between learners are increasing.

Reflecting on the Action

Teachers can examine data and reflect on the effects of their action. If the action is working well, triangulation of data can help document the positive changes in the classroom. Triangulation involves comparing data from several sources to corroborate results. For example, both observations by colleagues and interviews with students, as well as anecdotal records in a reflective journal, can verify an improvement in classroom climate and provide a solid basis for supporting the action. On the other hand, if data indicate that the action was unsuccessful, reflection can help a teacher determine whether another direction or approach is needed. The following is an excerpt from a reflective journal entry of a teacher using action research.

> I am just delighted with how my intervention—action research project—is working for my student. Moreover, the student, her teacher, and her assistant are also delighted with the outcome. The student began using her "Heart Chart" last week. Today, she

stated, "It's good, it helps. Look at a piece of paper, stop, and clean up." She states that it is a good reminder for her. Without looking at her chart, today, she could verbally give me each step from memory. Her teacher reports that it is a great success for the student's morning routine. The student has handled it very "maturely" and really latched onto the idea of her chart. Yea! I can now see more clearly how self-monitoring, especially for a child with ADHD symptoms, can help them maintain focus. It also builds their autonomy and sense of accomplishment. I definitely see that happening for this student. She was given total involvement with designing and creating the chart, and she loved that as well. *Eve Walker*

Action research affords teachers the opportunity to be intentional with regard to goals and outcomes for their classroom management practices and interventions designed to help individual students. Figure 13.4 presents an action research project "in the classroom."

Figure 13.4 In the Classroom

Anguiano (2001) describes the experience with action research of a first-year teacher in a third-grade classroom. In her reflective journal, the teacher describes her concern about students arguing, roaming the room at inappropriate times, being disrespectful, and not following directions. Her action research included the following steps:

Framing the Question: What strategies are effective for reducing inappropriate behavior during recess, instruction, and transitions?

Establishing the Baseline: Conducted pre-assessment observation of student behavior and pre-survey of students.

Examining Professional Literature and Resources: Review journal articles, websites, and books to see what others have tried, what's been successful, and what other professionals advise.

Taking Action: Implemented the following strategies:

Withitness

Eye contact

Physical proximity

Overlapping

Collecting Data: Post-survey of students, reflective journal, observation of student behavior.

Reflecting on the Action:

The following is an excerpt from the teacher's reflective journal:

This classroom inquiry project affected my students' misbehavior, as well as my own behaviors. As the project progressed, many of the misbehaviors I targeted were

(Continued)

Figure 13.4 (*Continued*)

reduced because of my ability to manage my classroom better, thus giving the students less opportunity to misbehave. My students gained respect for me as a teacher . . . (p. 52)

Action research in middle school

Carpenter describes an action research project in a middle school resource room. He describes the predicament in this classroom as one of students expecting rewards for academic work and appropriate behavior: "The students were in a mind set in which they had an expectation of an immediate reward for most educational aspects, including, but not limited to, meeting appropriate classroom behavior expectations, task completion, task mastery, and appropriate peer relationships . . . If the students thought that I wasn't paying attention (before class officially started), then there would be quite a bit of 'name-calling.' If the students thought that I was paying attention, then they would act appropriately. It became apparent that the students were either seeking praise as a reward or trying to avoid punishment. This became an immediate concern. Any sense of community that was established in the classroom felt very artificial."

Framing the question: If the classroom were designed as a place where students can identify that they belong, are capable of meeting the academic challenges set forth, and can establish a sense of autonomy, will intrinsic motivation increase?

Baseline: The Supportive Classroom Student Survey (Williams et al, 2001), http://tfox.blog.uvm.edu/supportiveclass/: This survey focused on the issues of belonging, trust, respect, and caring.

Literature and Resources: Literature on self-determination theory and enhancing community were reviewed.

Actions: Applied self-determination theory through the use of choices and classroom meetings. Classroom meetings, student-generated solutions to classroom issues, phase-out of rewards, choices of assignments, differentiated assignments.

Collecting Data: Teacher observation, student journals, post-survey of students, teacher-made checklist. The method that was chosen was to have the students respond to journal prompts related to belonging, appropriate academic challenges, and autonomy.

Reflecting on the Action:

After an administrative review, an assistant principal remarked, "It is obvious that the kids really enjoy being in your class and that says a lot considering how these kids traditionally feel about school." The other evidence that this project was a success was that for the last four weeks that the project was being implemented, there were zero behavior problems in the classroom. . . .

Overall, it does appear that the use of the self-determination theory in this classroom has increased the intrinsic motivation of the students. The key findings that point to this are the students' willingness to pick more challenging work even though no reward is being offered for doing so, an increase in the students' time-on-task, and the steady increase in the number of checks on the student checklists.

USING GOALS, OUTCOMES, AND ASSESSMENTS TO ENHANCE BELONGING, MASTERY, INDEPENDENCE, AND GENEROSITY

From the perspective of the Circle of Courage, teachers can set goals for belonging, mastery, independence, and generosity, and intentionally choose classroom practices that will achieve those goals. Goals related to the Circle of Courage might include the following:

Develop a sense of community in the classroom.
Develop a sense of belonging for all learners.
Develop a sense of autonomy and responsibility in learners.
Develop and maintain a learning orientation in the classroom.
Develop high self-efficacy in learners.
Develop generosity in each learner.

If a teacher articulates those goals, then practices supportive of those goals can be implemented and evaluated. Figure 13.5 includes possible classroom goals related to the

Figure 13.5 Goals, Outcomes, and Assessments

	GOAL	POSSIBLE PRACTICES	POSSIBLE ASSESSMENT
Belonging	Develop a sense of community in the classroom.	Engage learners in developing classroom mission and norms/covenants or rules. Hold classroom meetings. Use cooperative learning and peer tutoring.	Sociogram Classroom climate survey
Independence	Assist students in developing autonomy and responsibility.	Engage learners in developing a process for mediation and solution generating for problems that arise in the classroom. Provide choices. Seek and use input from learners in classroom decisions. Engage learners in self-evaluation and self-monitoring.	Student interviews Peer observations

(Continued)

Figure 13.5   *(Continued)*

	GOAL	POSSIBLE PRACTICES	POSSIBLE ASSESSMENT
Mastery	Develop a strong sense of self-efficacy in each learner. Develop and maintain a learning orientation in the classroom.	Avoid competitions and grading systems that allow learners to compare themselves with their peers. Establish individual learning goals and hold learning conferences. Assign work at the appropriate level of challenge for each student.	Student interviews Peer observations
Generosity	Provide each learner with an opportunity to contribute to peers, classroom, school, and community.	Institute peer tutoring and cooperative learning. Conduct service learning project for the school or community. Recognize instances of caring in the classroom.	Classroom climate survey Student interviews

Circle of Courage, possible practices that can achieve those goals, and possible classroom assessment activities.

SUMMARY

Establishing goals and outcomes for the classroom and evaluating progress toward those goals and outcomes can ensure that the teacher is creating the kind of classroom that he or she wants, as well as effecting desired outcomes for his or her learners. Classroom assessment practices can include reflective journals, observations, checklists and surveys, sociograms, and interviews with students. Assessment practices such as peer coaching can also engage teachers in professional collaboration and development. Action research provides a structure to engage teachers in classroom reasearch. It utilizes classroom assessment practices to provide solution to classroom predicaments, and information on issues and areas of interest to the teacher. By engaging in action research, teachers, as well as students, become the learners in the classroom.

REFERENCES

Alana, J. E. (2006). A study of participatory action research as professional development for educators in areas of educational disadvantage. *Educational Research, 14*(4), 525–533.

Anguiano, P. (2001). A first-year teacher's plan to reduce misbehavior in the classroom. *Teaching Exceptional Children, 33*(3), 52–56.

Ashton, P. T. (1985). Motivation and the teacher's sense of efficacy. In C. Ames & R. Ames (Eds.), *Research on motivation in education: Vol. 2. The classroom milieu* (pp. 141–174). Orlando, FL: Academic Press.

Ashton, P. T., & Webb, R. B. (1986). *Making a difference: Teachers' sense of efficacy and student achievement.* New York: Longman.

Bender, W. N., Shubert, T. H., & McLaughlin, P. J. (2001). Invisible kids: Preventing school violence by identifying kids in trouble. *Intervention in School and Clinic, 37*(2), 105–112.

Black, S. (2006). Students as researchers. *American School Board Journal, 193*(7), 34–36.

Bushman, J. (2006). Teachers as walk-through partners. *Educational Leadership, 63*(6), 58–61.

Calhoun, E. (2002). Action research for school. *Educational Leadership, 59*(6), 18–24

Carlson, C., Lahey, B., Frame, C. Walker, J., & Hynd, G. W. (1987). Sociometric status of clinic-referred children with attention deficit disorders with and without hyperactivity. *Journal of Abnormal Psychology, 15*(4), 537–547.

Chitpin, S. (2006). The use of reflective journal keeping in a teacher education program: A Popperian analysis. *Reflective Practice, 7*(1), 73–86.

Cochran-Smith, M. (2001). Reforming teacher education: Competing agendas. *Journal of Teacher Education, 52*(4), 263–265.

Cole, J. C. M., Cornell, C. G., & Sheras, P. (2006). Identification of school bullies by survey methods. *Professional School Counseling, 9*(4), 305–313.

Cosh, J. (1999). Peer observation: A reflective model. *English Language Teachers Journal, 3*(1), 22–28.

Davis, S., Howell, P., & Cooke, F. (2002). Sociodynamic relationships between children who stutter and their nonstuttering classmates. *Journal of Child Psychology and Psychiatry and Allied Disciplines, 43*(7), 939–947.

Deemer, S. A. (2004). Classroom goal orientation in high school classrooms: Revealing links between teacher beliefs and classroom environments. *Educational Research, 46*(1), 73–90.

Eder, D. (1981). Ability grouping as a self-fullfilling prophecy: A micro-analysis of teacher–student interaction. *Sociology of Education, 54*(3), 151–162.

Emmer, E. T., & Hickman, J. (1991). Teacher efficacy in classroom management and discipline. *Educational & Psychological Measurement, 51*(3), 755–766.

Farrell, T. S. C. (2001). Tailoring reflection to individual needs: A TESOL case study. *Journal of Education for Teaching, 27*(1), 23–28.

Fottland, H., & Matre, S. (2005). Assessment from a sociocultural perspective: Narratives from a first-grade classroom. *Scandinavian Journal of Educational Research, 49*(5), 503–521.

Fraser, B. J. (1998). Classroom environment instruments: Development, validity, and applications. *Learning Environments Research, 1*(2), 7–33.

Fraser, B. J., Anderson, G. J., & Walberg, H. J. (1982). *Assessment of learning environments: Manual for Learning Environment Inventory and My Class Inventory* (3rd ed.). Perth: Western Australian Institute of Technology.

Gable, R. A., Hester, P. P., Hester, L. R., Hendrickson, J. M., & Sze, S. (2005). Cognitive, affective, and relational dimensions of middle school students. *Clearing House, 79*(1), 40–44.

Gentry, M., & Springer, P. (2002). Secondary student perceptions of their class activities regarding meaningfulness, challenge, choice, and appeal: An initial validation study. *Journal of Secondary Gifted Education, 13*(4), 192–205.

Ghaye, T., & Lillyman, S. (1997). *Learning journals and critical incidents: Reflective practice for health care professionals*. Wiltshire, U.K.: Dinton, Wiltshire Quay Books.

Guskey, T. R. (2002). Professional development and teacher change. *Teachers and Teaching, 8*(3/4), 381–391.

Hankins, K. H. (1998). Cacophony to symphony: Memoirs in teacher research. *Harvard Educational Review, 68*(1), 80–96.

Hatton, N., & Smith, D. (1995). Reflection in teacher education: Towards definition and implementation. *Teaching and Teacher Education, 11*(1), 33–49.

Hoban, G. (2000). Making practice problematic: Listening to student interviews as a catalyst for teacher reflection. *Asia-Pacific Journal of Teacher Education, 28*(2), 133–147.

Hoy, W. K., & Woolflok, A. E. (1993). Teachers' sense of efficacy and the organizational health of schools. *Elementary School Journal, 93*(4), 335–372.

Hubbs, D. L., & Hubbs, D. L. (2005). The paper mirror: Understanding reflective journaling. *Journal of Experiential Education, 28*(1), 60–71.

Kember, D. (2000). *Action learning and action research: Improving the quality of teaching and learning*. Sterling, VA: Kogan.

Lickona, T., & Davidson, M. L. (2003). School as a caring community profile—II (SCCP II). Retrieved March 1, 2008, from http://www.cortland.edu/character/sccpii.htm

O'Connor, R., & Korr, W. S. (1996). A model for school social work facilitation of teacher self-efficacy and empowerment. *Social Work in Education, 18*(1), 45–51

Ochoa, S. H., & Olivarez, A. (1995). A meta-analysis of peer-rating sociometric studies of pupils with learning disabilities. *Journal of Special Education, 29*(1), 1–19.

Pipe, J. P., & Richards, J. C. (1992). Reflective thinking and growth in novices' teaching abilities. *Journal of Educational Research, 86*(1), 52–57.

Rickards, T., den Brok, P., Bull, E., & Fisher, D. (2003). Predicting student views of the classroom: A Californian perspective. *Proceedings Western Australian Institute for Educational Research Forum 2003*. Retrieved November 13, 2006, from http://www.waier.org.au/forums/2003/rickards-1.html

Ross, J. A. (1998). The antecedents and consequences of teacher efficacy. In J. Brophy (Ed.), *Research on Teaching: Vol. 7* (pp. 49–74). Greenwich, CT: JAI Press.

Ross, J. A., & Gray, P. (2006). Transformational leadership and teacher commitment to organizational values: The mediating effects of collective teacher efficacy. *School Effectiveness and School Improvement, 17*(2), 179–199.

Ross, J. R. (2007). Teacher self-assessment: A mechanism for facilitating professional growth. *Teaching and Teacher Education, 23*(2), 146–159.

Russ, F., & Meyers, E. (2006). The bright side: Teacher research in the context of educational reform and policy making. *Teachers and Teaching, 12*(1), 69–86.

Senge, P. M. (1990). The fifth discipline: The art and practice of the learning organization. New York: Doubleday/Currency.

Sherman, L. W. (2002). *Sociometry in the classroom: How to do it*. Retrieved October 28, 2006, from http://www.users.muohio.edu/shermalw/sociometryfiles/socio_are.htmlx

Sherman, L. W. (2002). Sociometry in the classroom. Retreived from http://www.users.muohio.edu/shermalw/sociometryfiles/SOCIO_variation.htmlx, March 20, 2007.

Shindler, Taylor, C., Cadenas, H., & Jones. (2003). Sharing the data along with the responsibility: Examining an analytic scale-based model for assessing school climate. Paper presented at the annual meeting of the American Educational Research Association, Chicago, April, 2003. http://www.calstatela.edu/centers/schoolclimate/research/aera2003.html Retrieved on, May 18, 2007.

Sink, C. A., & Spencer, L. R. (2005). My Class Inventory—Short Form as an accountability tool for elementary school counselors to measure classroom climate. *Professional School Counseling, 9*(1), 37–48.

Slater, C., & Simmons, D. L. (2001). The design and implementation of a peer coaching program. *American Secondary Education, 29*(3), 67–76.

Stewart, S. C., & Evans, H. (1997). Setting the stage for success: Assessing the instructional environment. *Preventing School Failure, 41*(2), 53–57.

Swafford, J. (1998). Teachers supporting teachers through peer coaching. *Support for Learning, 13*(2), 54–58.

Tricket, E. J. and Moos, R. H. (1995), Classroom Environment Scale Manual. 3rd Edition. Consulting Psychologists Press, Palo Alto, CA.

Walberg, H., & Greenberg, R. C. (1997). Using the learning environment inventory. *Educational Leadership, 54*(8), 45–47.

Western Alliance for the Study of School Climate. (2004). Classroom climate quality analytic assessment instrument. Retrieved from Western Alliance or the Study of School Climate, www.calstatela.edu/schoolclimate http://www.calstatela.edu/centers/schoolclimate/classroom_survey.html, November 19, 2007.

Williams, W. Fox, T. Fow, W. Roche, K. Prue, J. Farr, L. and Dillenbeck, A. (2001). The Supportive classroom. Retrieved on May 16, 2008 from http://tfox.blog.uvm.edu/supportiveclass/

Name Index

SUBJECT INDEX

Academic demands, changing, 226–228
Achievement, mastery and, 26–27
Action research, 85, 250–254
    characteristics of, 250–251
    in classroom, 253–254
    collecting data, 252
    cycle, 251
    defined, 250
    establishing a baseline, 252, 253, 254
    framing the question, 252, 253, 254
    implementing, 251–254
    in middle school, 254
    as participatory, 251
    in practice improvement, 250–251
    professional literature and resources,
        252, 253, 254
    reflecting on action, 252–253
    social practice and, 250
    as systematic and cyclical, 251
    taking action, 252
Active learning, 147–148
Adhocracy, 82
    bureaucracy comparison, 83
    emergence, 82
    structures, 83
Advisory boards, 70–71
African American students, 114
    discipline and, 116
    perceived behavior, 117
Aggression. *See also* Bullying
    early warning signs, 205–206
    effective programs, 208–212
    imminent signs, 205–207
    precursors, 205–207
Anger management, 203
Antecedents, 47
Appreciation systems, 85
Assertive Discipline, 9–10
    criticism, 9–10
    defined, 9
Assessment, 240–254
    action research, 250–254
    benefits, 238–240
    checklist and surveys, 245–247
    Circle of Courage and, 255–256

classroom, 238
    elements of, 237
    formative, 240–241
    functional, 219–223
    interviews, 247–248
    loop, 237
    observations by colleagues, 243–245
    practices, 241
    reflective journals, 241–243
    sociometric scales, 248–250
Assignments
    appropriately challenging, 226
    choices, 176
    open-ended, 146
Attachment
    belonging and, 24
    insecure, 25
    place, 56
    school, 25
Attention, 44–46
    span, 226
    teacher, 44–46
Attention deficit disorder (ADD), 137
Attention deficit hyperactivity disorder
    (ADHD), 222
Attitudes
    family involvement, 95
    learning, 13
Attribution theory, 178, 180
Authoritative leadership, 135–136
Autonomy
    in engagement and motivation,
        187–188
    in student-teacher relationship, 158,
        168–170

Background knowledge, 186
Baseline, establishing, 252, 253, 254
Behavior
    appropriate, encouragement, 172
    challenging, describing, 220
    choices and, 227
    circumstance of occurrence, 220
    consequences, 203–204
    context, 215

cultural perspectives, 114–115
    disruptive, 172
    expectations, 122
    management, family involvement in,
        102–103
    mastery and, 26–27
    on-task, 172
    potential purpose, determining,
        222–223
    prevention, 217–218
    styles, accommodating, 123
Behavioral problems
    delayed action, 199
    minor disruption, 199–201
    precursors, 199
Behavioral theory, 11, 41–50
    application in the classroom, 48–49
    classical conditioning, 42–44
    classroom implication, 178
    constructivist theory versus, 49–50
    defined, 178, 180
    information classroom teachers, 232
    operant conditioning, 44–47
    peers in, 50
    self-instruction, 48
    self-monitoring, 47
    use of, 42
Beliefs, changing, 190
Belonging, 22, 23–26. *See also* Circle of
    Courage
    attachment and, 24
    communicating, 34
    as culturally responsive practice, 124
    fostering, 25–26
    importance, 24
    practice, 22
    school, 24–25
    student perspective, 57–61, 67–68
    teacher response, 67–68
Blame the victim mentality, 238
Bullying, 13, 205
    approaches to, 13
    early warning signs, 205–206
    effective programs, 208–212
    effects, 207